D1593231

Secret Wings of WWII

Nazi Technology and the Allied Arms Race

Lance Cole

Illustrations by the Author

Pen & Sword
AVIATION

First published in Great Britain in 2015 by
Pen & Sword Aviation
an imprint of
Pen & Sword Books Ltd
47 Church Street
Barnsley
South Yorkshire
S70 2AS

ISBN 978 1 47382 344 0

A CIP catalogue record for this book is available from the British Library

Typeset in Ehrhardt by
Mac Style Ltd, Bridlington, East Yorkshire
Printed and bound in the UK by CPI Group (UK) Ltd,
Croydon, CRO 4YY

Pen & Sword Books Ltd incorporates the imprints of Pen & Sword
Archaeology, Atlas, Aviation, Battleground, Discovery, Family History,
History, Maritime, Military, Naval, Politics, Railways, Select, Transport,
True Crime, and Fiction, Frontline Books, Leo Cooper, Praetorian Press,
Seaforth Publishing and Wharncliffe.

For a complete list of Pen & Sword titles please contact
PEN & SWORD BOOKS LIMITED
47 Church Street, Barnsley, South Yorkshire, S70 2AS, England
E-mail: enquiries@pen-and-sword.co.uk
Website: www.pen-and-sword.co.uk

Dedication

For B.S. Shenstone and A.M. Lippisch – men of future vision. And with thought to a man I once talked with, Air Marshal Sir Peter Horsley, and those sounds from another room.

With thanks to my grandfather Tom, and my father Francis, both for imbuing me with a love of flight.

Also for my uncle, the late Paul Minet, for encouraging a love of old and rare books. And to Anna – the soulmate without whom I would never have flown again.

Contents

Acknowledgements

T his book is the product of more than twenty-five years of research and enthusiasm (maybe even obsession), with the all-wing or nurflügel, gliding and design. There are many people who have helped me, tutored me and guided me along the way. I would like to offer thanks to all of them, sadly some have passed on. The following people are owed my specific thanks and admiration:

H. Geissler, who taught me so much and showed me such kindness. Fly well old pelican.

T.R. Godden; H.C.N. Goodhart; B.P.H. Shenstone; B.S. Shenstone; C. Wills; B. Trubshaw.

All of them taught me something about aerodynamics, all-wing flight, or the German and British aviation industries.

I am indebted to the *Flight* archive and to the RAeS and the National Aerospace Library at Farnborough where many rare items were consulted. I have to thank numerous authors and figures, as reference sources, including: Derek Wood and his *Project Cancelled*; David Myhra for his defining work on the Horten brothers; Clarence G. Lasby's 1971 tome, *Project Paperclip*; Chris Wills at the Vintage Glider Club for tutelage and documents. Thanks also to friends at the Wasserkuppe, the British Gliding Association, the Vintage Glider Club (VGC) in the UK and the VGC in Australia, all brought new information to my attention. Acknowledgements also to *Flightglobal*, its archives and the help of friends on that esteemed publication. Special thanks to TWITT – The Wing is the Thing (www.twitt.org) group – a small band of all-wing devotees and aerospace members whose resources have been of support; also to D. Bullard's nurflügel web resource.

Thanks to the Shenstone family for archive documents. Thanks also to John Kirk, hang-glider and inspirational bird man; also to Bavarian relatives and my thoughts to a man of the von Reitzenstein, for the clues from beyond the barrier.

Introduction

'Some day the flying wing will emerge as the accepted form of a passenger airliner.'

Flight 9 January 1947

This book is not about unidentified flying objects (UFOs) and does not deal in delusions or fashionable conspiracies, yet neither does it support the establishment version of aerospace history – one created by a narrative of victory and its own prejudice. This text is about the referenced German science and technology that are the foundations of a modern aerospace era and a future not yet delivered.

Inherent within the events of this story lies the secrets and the stolen science of Germany and its seized 'war-prize' designs that were themselves subsequently part of a 1950s mass 'psy-ops' UFO campaign to obscure their origins, their development testing, and the men who had originally invented them.

The UFO story is a paradox, for we are told by rational learned men that UFOs do not exist and believers in them are conspiracy theorists or liars – yet this part of the UFO phenomenon itself was actually deliberately designed and delivered as a 'lie' by those same learned men in order to shield the stolen German science they were developing. It is a supreme irony that amongst learned societies and academics, any mention of the UFO subject allows them to characterise the author's work as eccentric, lightweight, or based in conspiracy or delusion, yet the biggest paradox is that the UFO 'lie' was delivered to cover up something else – the work of those learned men on their seized science. The feint of creating a story about little green men in spaceships is a bizarre and long-lasting contradiction. The UFO story is, we are told, a falsehood about something that does not exist, but then we are also asked to believe a government created myth about the very science the UFO story was shaped to cover up in the first place. Confused? You were meant to be.

So the great UFO story was just part of various governments' games that shielded stolen German and Nazi-funded future technology – science that is now manifest in the air, in space, and even in our homes. Yet the reality is that the much of the UFO story post-1945 is a deliberate construction; designed as a ruse to confuse the perceptions of the masses from the truth of what secret science was up to. In terms of behavioural psychology, the UFO 'story' contains internal inconsistencies – which an able analyst could easily expose. It remains no accident that the great UFO era began soon after the Second World War amid the seizing of Germany's entire mother lode of science and technology – a uniquely advanced global resource that was by common consent, years ahead of Allied know-how.

Indeed, the 'psy-ops' programme to frame seized aviation science as so-called UFOs in post-1945 America, as the nation developed its new German technology, was, by the early 1950s, led by a man who had been a senior figure within Operation Paperclip – itself the very mechanism by which German science was seized and transported back to the United States. So the 'double feint' was an intriguing mechanism.

The man in question was Dr Howard Robertson, a Princeton physicist. Robertson was not the only Princeton academic and physicist involved, because another Princeton luminary was high up in the intelligence field and also leading a Canadian National Research Council team investigating aeronautical technology. His name was Allen G. Shenstone and he happened to be a decorated wartime intelligence officer and the uncle of Beverley Shenstone – the Junkers, and Lippisch-trained aerodynamicist who had shaped the Supermarine Spitfire's modified twin-axis ellipsoid wing design. By 1946, Beverley Shenstone also just happened to be in Toronto leading the Avro design function, shortly after leaving a senior post within the Canadian Government, that following a period working at the top US experimental research facility of Wright Field (Wright-Patterson AFB) – the home of America's seized secrets and the precursor to what begat 'Area 51'. Also on the scene, via Vienna, Paris, London and Wright Field, was Beverley Shenstone's old friend and mentor Alexander Lippisch – 'Mr Delta' – the man who had brought the swept, delta-wing, all-wing planform to reality. But Lippisch was (like Shenstone) also an expert in aerofoil design, the boundary layer, Coanda-effects, disc-shaped wings, and vertical take-off and landing (VTOL) technology – as well as hydrofoils and 'lifting body' work.

Throw in the OSS/CIA setting up a research unit at the same time in Canada and it all begins to look somewhat obvious for the 'theorist'. Such circumstances may explain why so many books about German or Nazi wartime technology are hung off the 'UFO' hook. But calmer analysis simply reveals mankind up to his usual tricks of manipulation, deceit, and advancement. These behaviours were not solely manifested in Operation Paperclip by Americans – the British, the Soviets, and, often forgotten, the French were up to it too. It is just that America threw more money at the subject.

For UFO conspiracy theorists, the circumstantial evidence would provide great evidence for their cause, but we can simply and rationally observe the synergies of alignments of clever and powerful people that were created by the establishment.

We can only suggest that this was done in order to develop and shield its new German-sourced secret technology; that is why this book is not about the UFO, but about man-made science and the seizing and the use of it. Of course, not every UFO was a German-derived test airframe, but, conversely, not every UFO was a 'real' UFO.

Both sides of the 'Nazi-UFO' landscape – for and against – have made errors of claim. In books, articles and in the web realm, the breathless UFO-ologists, randomly cite Nazi-built (and flown) disc and delta devices that may be more a reality of repeat suggestion than of verified flight science. On the other hand, the anti-UFO brigade seem to have an agenda in denying any real aerodynamic or technological achievements that stemmed directly from Nazi or German technology – other than the now undeniable basis of the NASA space programme. At first the Americans denied even that but have eventually had to admit the Nazi origins of von Braun's achievements for NASA. But wait, having admitted that the USA's space story had Nazi science inherent, the subsequent version of history to be presented is that the aerodynamics science of the Nazis existed in a separate dimension and that there were (a) no links between von Braun's rocketeers and the aerodynamics men of Germany and (b) that American (and British) advances in aerodynamics had little to do with German research – even if it is admitted that rocket science did.

So the current narrative is that, although America can admit to NASA's Nazis, it cannot and will not admit that post-war aerodynamics and recent all-wing work, were similarly influenced. All the German experts and their wind tunnels and research institutes, were, we are invited to believe, entirely separate from each other's functions, which is untrue.

So the establishment's current 'patriotic' line is that today's swept-wings, jet engines, all-wings, delta-wings and the new blended-wings have little or nothing to do with German aerodynamics and 'wing' science. Perhaps in another fifty years, the Americans and the British will admit to the German roots of such science – just as they have finally had to do over von Braun and his men's help in getting America to the moon. The internal inconsistencies in the establishment's story are all too obvious, yet rarely challenged. And then of course, there were the Russians…

The corporate or establishment narrative now suggests that the rocketeers of von Braun, Oberth, et al, existed in isolation, and is evidentially most definitely not the case. The critics of the UFO-ologists also claim no delta-winged craft (let alone disc-craft) were developed by the Nazis or were ever actually flown, and it was American genius that turned Lippisch's apparent early forays of delta-design into actual delta-winged airframe success. An American agenda is obvious – notably within today's web-based forums and patriotic publications.

Such an agenda peddles its own falsehoods, for Lippisch flew a powered, true delta-wing aircraft at Berlin Tempelhof in 1931 – long before Hitler took power. Lippisch, Messerschmitt, Heinkel, Focke-Wulf, and the Hortens all developed deltoid and highly swept airframes (including composite construction and 60 degree sweepback) before and during the war – with jet, athodyd, and rocket power, with viable flight and combat-use status.

The two extreme viewpoints of the story are both locked into their own de facto theology and are unlikely to admit that their certainties are flawed. People who peddle certainties are notorious for denigrating the views of those who do not agree with their version of certainty. If you start with certainty, the road ahead is always blocked in advance. In between these positions lies the more balanced, evidenced, referenced facts of the thousands of tons of German research paperwork and prototypes that were vitally seized and shipped to America, Britain and Russia from 1945 onwards and which formed the future of aerodynamics and airframe design, as well as underpinning wider science.

Let us not forget that the first high-speed (Mach 4+) wind tunnel in the USA was the unique tunnel that had been 'stolen' from Germany post-1945 and shipped straight to the US Navy's base in Maryland for study. And what of Sir Roy Fedden and his attempts to get the British Government to continue the development of German aerodynamics research in Germany in 1945? Why would he pursue such a course if the science was not unique, and vitally advanced?

The story of the Allied seizure of German technology is not without its funnier moments. In late 1943, Winston Churchill asked Josef Stalin for help in finding out more about von Braun's Peenemünde rockets. So, when a Peenemünde test rocket went off course and crashed in Russian held territory, Stalin ordered assistance in securing the remains and transporting them to Moscow and then onwards to London. The only trouble was that when the vital crates were opened in England, they contained not rocket motors and flight guidance technology, but old car parts. The Soviets had kept the rocket parts for their own use and, as we know, they did not waste the opportunity.

The sheer desperation of the Allies to secure the German science can be framed by further incidents that demonstrate how far ahead Germany was.

When a von Braun A-4/V-2 crashed into a Polish river during a test flight, the Polish resistance (with British aid) sank the device at the bottom of the river bed and left it there until Germans had given up searching for it. Only then did an RAF DC-3 fly a dangerous mission into enemy airspace, land by night in a field in Poland to load the retrieved rocket, and then fly onwards to London.

Seizing war-prize materials was all in the Allies 'national interest' – which as so often before and since has been an excuse for concealment. Seizing German science justified any means – *during* the war and after it had been won. Denying its advance and its provenance continues to this day.

Of course, the evils of Nazism and its war, gave the Allies every right to recompense and the death toll might be held up as a reason to make the most of the defeated Germany's works. The sheer scale of the looting of Germany's science and technology and the benefits-in-kind accrued, are one thing, but what of the benefits of the dubious ethos and practices that produced that science, and their absorption into American and British science and society? Those issues are something else entirely. It is also a great hypocrisy from those who claimed the moral high ground. Yet it is also the behaviour of man and, the cost of doing business.

Clearly, German science left a legacy.

Of the men who invented that science, little is known, other than the much quoted name of von Braun and his rockets, or passing reference to Lippisch and his delta-wing works. Some of these men were Nazis, some were not; some were victims of the Nazis. Indeed, Hitler, in 1933, took hold of the previous German scientific discoveries (some of which had German-Jewish origins) and re-branded them all as the outcome of his political movement and personal efficacy. German citizens, like many others, did what they were told to by the men who led their nation at war.

From 1933 (before the Americans, the British and the Russians stole the lot in 1945), Hitler used pre-existing, non-Nazi, German science to wage his war and his beliefs under a 'Nazi' hallmark. As he lost the war it was easy to 'copy and paste' the entire Nazi and pre-Nazi German scientific genius directly into the annals of Allied brilliance, and thence to frame the Cold War and today's technology from a repackaged basis amid the 'white-heat' of western technology in the so-called 'golden era' of British and American aviation.

Now, we have the 'flying-wing' and the new-speak metaphor of 'Blended-Wing-Body', the BWB, which we are led to believe, is a new invention, a new iteration of man's brilliance. In 2007, when NASA and Boeing framed their new all-wing BWB design future, *TIME* Magazine gave the idea an award for being a new invention! This must be just another ruse in the story of the flying-wing, or the more accurately termed all-wing. We could have had such aircraft decades ago, but a deliberate delay was factored into history and design development by powerful and so-called learned men. Such is the veneer of aeronautical history as presented not just to the layman, but also to the engineering students of today. It is, of course, a created consensus that smothers alternative evidence and blinds its observers to any other perspective. False trails have been laid. Any reader, who scoffs at such suggestions, ought to forensically consider the evidence.

It seems strange that the all-wing (be it tailless or not), with its probable minimum of 20–25 per cent less drag than a normal fuselage and tail-equipped airframe, should have been ignored by all except a few, until now it has suddenly become a new discovery. A really well-designed all-wing is a pure lifting body with no part of its form not creating a function – lift. The all-wing is all-lift and has much less drag of several types than a conventional machine. The best all-wings might be 40 per cent more aerodynamically efficient than a 'normal' fuselage device. What aerodynamic advance, what fuel saving, what speed, what range, have all been denied by orthodox practice and its refusals.

The likes of Penaud, Dunne and Junkers hinted at all this as long ago as 1890–1910, yet they were denied, as were the Hortens. How ironic that now the all-wing type is all the rage with designers, engineers and aeroplane makers, or 'airframers' as new-speak terms them.

I wrote this book after decades of fascination with the all-wing aeroplane; that is an aeroplane that has no fuselage, nor tailplane, no actual body, and which contains itself within its entirely lift-giving shape and form. The incredible aerodynamics and the unique sense that flying an all-wing delivers, is utterly different from the normal act of flight. The all-wing is the thing – to paraphrase from an American all-wing enthusiasts group of the same name.

Many years ago, strapped to an all-wing, I jumped off Walbury Hill, near my home, in a hang-glider and then graduated to sailplanes and the amazing works of Reimar and Walter Horten. I was lucky enough to know a world record holding glider pilot, a man named Nicholas Goodhart, but I called him 'Admiral', because he was. Goodhart taught me about all-wing gliders and he built his own almost all-wing, man-powered airframe. He was a British inventor and designer of excellence, with the life-saving aircraft carrier 'mirror' landing deck system for the Royal Navy to his credit. Behind the Admiral's front, was a man who encouraged young people and young designers – people like me. Without decrying his own country or its achievements, Goodhart, like many in gliding, knew that German aerodynamic findings had been key to the future, post-1945. Goodhart had also designed a glider with an advanced wing, and he did it with a team that included a recurring name in the story of wing technology – that of Beverley Shenstone. Other sailplane pilots such as Christopher Wills and Beverley Shenstone, all knew about the Horten brothers, Lippisch, Multhopp, and many more.

My record-breaking glider pilot friend, Hilmer Geissler, lectured me long into the Australian nights on the secret science of aviation and where it came from, his once native Germany. Brian Trubshaw, the world's leading delta-wing test pilot (Concorde), also tutored me in the Lippisch legacy and on how he flew such a device. I knew Douglas Bader as a teenage boy, he was not loved by all, but he really was a goldmine when it came to flight and handling an aeroplane, and he knew all about the Spitfire's amazing abilities and where they came from. At that time, few believed anything other than the myths of history as written by the victors.

I know I have been lucky in the people I have known and learned from – people without whom this book would never have been researched, written and referenced. I name-drop because I can and because I admired these men so very much. I just wish I had met the Hortens, Lippisch, and Dunne.

Having noted Penaud's all-wing from pre-1900 and Junker's actual all-wing patent of 1910, this provided me with inspiration from an early age and proof that a secret knowledge had been denied. It struck me that, perhaps in the same way that when the churches were built with astro-alignments upon the sites of previous stone circles that were similarly aligned, the work of the churches was presented as perceived factual state-of-the-art wisdom by learned men, yet the old knowledge (upon which, and using such sites, the churches were built) was decried and denied by the new creed. How odd that a stone circle can be dismissed as 'pagan', or nonsense, by men who proceeded to worship their own proclaimed wisdom in buildings built upon the same sites, the same places of power, with exactly the same alignments to the compass points and the stars and the sun. What a paradox. Throw in a medieval example such as William Tyndale and his attempts to challenge an existing perceived Bible wisdom, and all that happened to him during a life on the run, and the dangers of learned men and their assumptions of the now, become obvious. These examples correlate to the years 1899–1912, when a biplane-based 'religion' became a received wisdom against previous evidence of another system of belief – all-wing monoplane shapes.

It seems to me that a feint of perception occurred *circa* 1910 with the biplane, when its perceived wisdom, which was little more than a fashion promoted by learned men, usurped the advance of the monoplane and the all-wing; only for learned men to announce twenty years later (around 1930), that the monoplane had now been 'discovered' as the stepping stone to the future. Again, in 1946, a great swept-wing, all-wing movement 'arrived' for the learned men – no doubt spurred on by the discovery and seizure of Germany's all-wing researches. Yet suddenly it was all effectively killed off by a new narrative – a new 'religion', and a claim that the all-wing could not work. By 1950, the all-wing future proclaimed by the journal, *Flight*, on 9 January 1947, was over. How odd, that just as with the story in 1910, 1950 should see a repeat exercise in denial. Yet the all-wing, and specifically, a delta-wing iteration, would suddenly reappear for the 1950s and 1960s – designed in Britain and America, of course. Concorde's wing came from Germany, but they kept quiet about that and it became British and French instead.

Little did we know that behind the scenes, composite, radar-reducing, jet-powered, swept-back all-wing airframes, with advanced controls and aerodynamics, were being tested and held back from public consciousness for fifty years – only now to be 'revealed' as the latest step into the future in the form of the all-wing fighters, bombers, and BWB airliner prototypes which are, surprise, surprise, the new future creed for aerodynamics and aerospace. It all smacks of a game of smoke and mirrors and denied provenance. The Allies, from Moscow to Washington D.C., have had their fingers in the pie of stolen German science for decades and it got them to the moon. Maybe it is, without decrying all the great things achieved by these nations, time to reveal just what really went on and try to credit the forgotten and ignored men of German science – after all, they cannot all be rabid Nazi war criminals, can they…

One look at a Horten all-wing – especially one with up to 60° plus wing sweep, advanced airflow patterns, superb controls and handling, anti-radar composites and a cranked or blended leading edge, will reveal that, even though Northrop's entire fleet of 'flying-wing' bombers for the United States Air Force were binned – deliberately destroyed in the 1950s – behind the scenes, seized German science in America was solving the all-wing aerodynamics, just as German science solved the problem of getting into orbit and on to the surface of the moon. German science also impacted every aspect of scientific inventions and processes across a wide spectrum after it had all been scooped-up in 1945–1946 in a retrieval campaign that cost millions, yet delivered treasures beyond measure in terms of knowledge and money in the bank, and continues to do so.

Any reader with a sensitivity to a book framing, and in a context, praising German science from a period of horror in the history of man, really ought to examine their own nation's record before getting upset about a story that is solely focused on the incredible science that is now in use on a daily basis all over the world – science that stems in great degree from the dark days of the Second World War and the horrors that went with it. A quick check of 1930s, familial, commercial investment, and banking partner relationships between the Allies and the Germans – and the Nazis (Germans and Nazis being two *differing* entities) – will also reveal how any howls of anguish about praising such science are nothing but utter and very rank hypocrisy framed within a politically correct mirage.

So from this author's personal standpoint, it must be stated that an apparent fascination with, or admiration for, German and Weimar Republic pre-war science, or the study of separate, *later* Nazi-funded science, does not imply nor constitute admiration for the Nazi Party or any such politics. No far-right empathy is suggested herein. Extremism of any type is not this author's remit. Flight and the study of it, remains the writer's fascination. I have no shame in trying to credit the inventors and designers of German aerodynamics, the historical record should be corrected. Those offended by the content of this book have the opportunity to turn the off button, and to go away and consider the record of their own nations and citizens in the story of what happened in, and to, Germany in its various incarnations, before, during, and after the madness of the Austrian – Adolf Hitler.

Today's experts seem keen on claiming to have 'discovered' things that their education has denied them knowledge of. Have they been conditioned into a conceit of the 'now'? This is surely a good reason to examine history and not be trapped by the current cliché of 'moving forwards' thinking, with all the denial of knowledge and experience that a refusal to examine past events creates. Aviation has tainted secrets, and the Allies very cleverly swept those secrets under the carpet of public perception. This book is intended to lift that veil – focusing on aerodynamics and all-wing flight.

And yes, of course there were many talented men in post-war American and British aerodynamics and engineering who developed new ideas and new designs. It would be unfair to deny them due credit, especially the 1970s and 1980s 'gurus' of aerospace engineering. Yet it is also unfair that German science and its experts remain denied by many in the American and British academic and aerospace establishment. The roots of today's aerodynamics are, in many ways, derived from a sometimes murky and usually denied past. What really went on is a fascinating story. Realising just how many American and British scientists, engineers and designers rushed to Germany in 1945–1946 to scour the advanced design bureaus and academic institutions, is still a shocking discovery for those previously ignorant of those events. As early as April and May 1945, leading American and British aviation companies had representatives rushing through Germany in aircraft, cars and motorbikes, hunting down advanced aerospace science. Men from Avro, Bristol, de Havilland, Handley Page, Short Brothers and Vickers, grabbed drawings, blueprints, models, prototypes, anything they could lay their hands on. How revealing that the Bell Aircraft Corporation's chief designer, Robert Woods, just happened to find himself standing in Oberammergau, Bavaria, in early 1946, staring at the stunning (but overweight) swept form of the Me.P1101. Even Charles Lindbergh toured Germany and General Electric had an expert sifting through research materials; aerodynamicist Theodore von Kármán, from California, was interviewing German experts in London before the war in Europe had ended. There was much that was known and unknown, once certain minds were rudely disturbed by advanced German science.

True thinkers, philosophers of design, do not normally begin or end with certainty – for that way lie the blinkers of assumption and bigotry. The swept-wing and all-wing designers threw off perceived realities and acquired new knowledge at a pace that was unique. They knew that know-how was a certainty, but that science as it was assumed to be, was *uncertain* – just a collection of fashionable ideas of information waiting to be challenged by those who dared think beyond the rules of the learned men and their self-perpetuating societies and egos. The all-wing men challenged the acceptance of science that those who had fallen into the trap had assumed to be definitive, which it was not. Somehow, there was something anarchic in the process of the all-wing story, maybe something even Marxist in context – for whilst the philosophers of the biplane and the fuselage configuration pontificated upon the perceptions of the now, the all-wing men tried to change thinking and tried to change the world: 100 years on, they have achieved it.

The likes of Alphonse Penaud, John Dunne, Geoffrey Hill, Ernst Heinkel, Reimar, Walter and Wolfram Horten, Hugo Junkers, Alexander Lippisch, Hans Multhopp, August Kupper, Heinrich Hertel, Jack Northrop, Beverley Shenstone, and others, must surely be watching with some degree of 'I told you so'.

Lance Cole
Walbury Hill, Inkpen, Berkshire.

Chapter One

Germany – Stolen Science and Denied Provenance

Bavaria, April 1945

The 26 April 1945 was an auspicious day in the history of military and civil aviation and the science behind it. On that day, jet engine development and wing design for both transonic and supersonic flight were taken to a new place by the discovery of treasure. This was the day that a team of American experts in aircraft design, who were racing to seize wartime German science, fell upon Lechfeld airbase in Bavaria, Germany.

The day dawned misty and overcast, yet soon, light fell upon the wet tarmac and war-weary patina of the place. Here, a future was about to be illuminated.

Gathered at Lechfeld was the entire retinue of swept-winged and jet-powered Messerschmitt 262 flight test airframes, their pilots, and all the design and operating manuals to go with the hoard. Here, the JG7 fighter squadron, which towards the last months of aerial combat operated from Brandenburg in northern Germany, had now gathered as the Reich collapsed. Also present were a few pilots from the non-operational KG54 Me 262 training wing. In January-March 1945, the Me 262 fleet had shot down thirty Allied aircraft – the last just over three weeks earlier. These Me 262 pilots had been trained to kill, as all fighter pilots are, and their revolutionary machines had swept the lumbering prop-powered Allied marauders from the German sky when a few, brief encounters had taken place. But it was all too late; the crazed-mind of Hitler had delayed the Me 262s development and its use as had been intended – as a fighter. Instead, he had demanded it be deployed as a bomber.

Like many things of the Reich, it was madness and no amount of science could outweigh the course of fate.

Also secured from Lechfeld was another advanced machine – the Arado 234 – which had unusually podded engines and host of new design features, including a very interesting crescent-wing design that was unique. An all-wing Me163 rocket plane is also said to have been found.

The Americans, from a special team based out at Wright Field (now Wright-Patterson AFB), are reputed to have arrived at Lechfeld in a high-speed cloud of noise, revving engines, shouts, and drawn weapons. The men who poured into Lechfeld on that damp morning were headed by Colonel Harold E. Watson, USAAF (Air Tech/Intel), as leader of the team from the secret research facility at Wright Field, who, with his men, descended upon the treasure like vultures in a feeding frenzy. Within days, long convoys of trucks had taken everything they could across Germany to France and an airfield south of Paris, and then onwards to Cherbourg. There, a fleet of large vessels, including the HMS *Reaper* (previously an American vessel), waited to steal the booty of the future away to its new resting place at Wright Field and at the US Navy flight test centre at Patuxent River.[1]

Of the twelve flying examples of the Me 262 – machines that could only be flown by trained, German Luftwaffe pilots of officer and flight sergeant ranks, who were immediately hired to fly the Me 262s to safety – there was much to study. These machines represented a treasure trove only exceeded by that of the Me 163's swept-wings of Lippisch and others, and the rockets, nozzles, vanes, and gyro-stability kit of von Braun et al. From Lechfeld and all the other German advanced research facilities, over 1,500 tons of documents were recovered – with 50 tons of paperwork on jet engine design alone. In total, nearly a million separate documented items were recorded, with over half a million of those referring to aerospace technology. By 1948, two million individually indexed documents had been recorded by the teams of several hundred researchers of the Office of Technical Services at Wright Field – with the help of many hundreds of the German experts who had invented such science in the first place. The Lechfeld hoard and other treasures of technology were collected under a 'Luftwaffe Special Technology' project entitled Operation Lusty: this alone collected over 16,000 items, weighing 6,200 tons, which yielded nearly 3,000 items of specific interest for study. Large teams of analysts and translators worked for over two years to assess and understand the scientific treasure trove.[2]

Of great significance, the world's only wind tunnel capable of Mach 4.4 (modified in January 1945 to Mach 5.18), 40ft wide and built as part of the Nazi rocket research, was dismantled, driven across Germany and shipped to the US Navy's Ordnance Laboratory in White Oak, Maryland. There, it began to provide advanced flow analysis, but also became part of the tribal war between competing research arms of the three American services in a vivid illustration of the constraints of egos.

Another high-speed wind tunnel was seized by the British and taken to the Royal Aircraft Establishment (RAE) at Farnborough. Thanks to having monitored German technology during the war, and surveyed crashed German aircraft that had contained new science and new ideas, the British and the US Army Air Force Technical Intelligence Service (Air Tech/Intel) had some idea of the advanced materials that would be there for the grabbing when tactical or strategic intelligence became something else. By the summer of 1944, just a few weeks after D-Day, intelligence men at Wright Field had begun to create and then deploy a science and technology-gathering mechanism.

Science and Society

Of adjunct importance to the aerospace secrets that were stolen in 1945, 300,000 German documents *not* associated with aerospace, covering everything from nuclear science, electronics, medicine, transplants, cryogenics, agriculture, synthetic foods and preservatives, refrigeration, advanced textiles and plastics – in fact a massive mother lode of industrial and social science advances – were also seized by major American manufacturing concerns. Micro-electrics; Magnetic tape recordings; Synthetic Mica; Cold Extrusion; Advanced chemical processes and dyes; Food preservation (pasteurisation of food or liquids, such as milk or fruit juices) by ultraviolet light; Composite plastics; Pesticides; Metallurgy. All were taken.

The first contact lenses were invented in Germany. Daimler and Benz invented the modern combustion engine and 'car' in Germany, Diesel did likewise with his engine's combustion cycle. From X-rays to quantum physics, to the invention of 'Aspirin', German science dominated academia and research from the mid-1800s onwards. All of it was German science that was to be absorbed and re-branded into all-American output after the Second World War ('Aspirin' had actually been seized in 1918 after the First World War). The 'Magnetophon' recording technology was, of course, taken by America from its German inventors in 1945. And a plastics-based recording tape had been a 1935 German invention.

Unique advances across all scientific disciplines were involved in this mass raid on German science, but the creators of such, were denied, ignored, and whitewashed out of history under the convenient cover of the 'ex-Nazi' headline. Their only footnotes are the thousands of pages of Combined Intelligence Objectives Sub-Committee (CIOS), Field Intelligence Agencies/Technical (FIAT) and other reports that today lie in the dusty archives of the Library of Congress, the National Archives and Records Service Washington D.C., the Public Records Office London, the Royal Aeronautical Society, the German archives, and other repositories.

Similarly, the Technical Industrial Intelligence Branch (TIIB), latterly the Technical Industrial Intelligence Committee (TTIC), was set up as an agency of the Joint Chiefs of Staff, but transferred to the Department of Commerce in January in 1946. The TIIB sent more than 400 investigators into Germany, its task was to look into every aspect of German industrial research and obtain any technology that might benefit USA PLC.

So it was not just aerodynamicists and rocketeers that the Allies 'lifted' out of Germany from 1945 onwards; physicists, electronics experts, chemists, geophysicists, optical experts, nuclear experts, food scientists, agrarian scientists, transplant surgeons, doctors, and a vast cadre of high-IQ inventors and thinkers were transferred to the USA, and not just in 1945–1946. As late as 1959 America was still securing German expertise and exporting such men back to American academia and military and industrial institutions. Often ignored were the German experts who were sent to Fort Monmouth, New Jersey. These men ranged from physicists to electronics inventors[3] and only very recently have the realities of advanced German nuclear research been revealed with declassification and freedom of information releases largely stemming from the 1990s onwards.

The benefit to the USA and its society in terms of transferred intellectual property as technology, patents processes and spin-offs, can be rated in the many hundreds of billions of dollars – far in advance of any fiscally rational war reparations due. Indeed, in terms of supersonics and spaceflight, the benefit-in-kind could be said to be incalculable.

Prior to 1933, the majority of Nobel Prizes had been won by Germans. German science, and German qualifications were the leading academic mechanism and left many legacies upon the post-Weimar Republic that became the Germany that the Nationalsozialistiche Deutsche Arbeiterpartei (NSDAP) – or 'Nazis' – ruled; German scientific history was laced with achievement long before the madman Hitler intervened.

Of significance, modern chemical petroleum engineering is in large part reflective of the discoveries of Baron Karl von Reichenbach (1788–1869). It was von Reichenbach of Stuttgart who owned iron and chemical factories and discovered processes that gave us paraffin, kerosene, phenol derivatives and paraben refinements. He would go on to research medicine, psychology and 'new age' subjects – a move that allowed scientists to categorise him as eccentric and consign him to a forgotten corner of science's annals. But it was from his chemical engineering that industry took many themes, earning von Reichenbach a fortune in patent and licence payments from big business. Synthetic paraben fuel processes were created in Germany (the country had few oil resources) and it had to rely on synthetic fuel derived from Silesia's rich seams of high quality, low sulphur coal reserves. The synthesising process, called the 'Fischer-Tropsch Process', used water, gas, hydrogen and carbon monoxide, derived from hydrogenation of coal and coke over catalysts at altered high pressures and temperatures, to generate straight-chain hydrocarbons and resultant blends or 'cuts' that could be further processed to yield fuels and lubricating oils. The process of 'PVC' or Polyvinyl Chloride was also taken from Germany in 1945 as a war-prize.

From Volt to Diesel; from Einstein to Planck; from Koch to Ehlrich; from Daimler and Benz to Junkers and beyond, Germans of *varying* genetic extractions utterly dominated global science, invention, and technology prior to 1933. In America, Dwight D. Eisenhower was of direct German descent. In 1945, America's leading financiers were also of close and recent German extraction and even after the Second World War had close connections to German money: I.G. Farben, makers of glues and fatal gases, had had an office in Chicago even when the Nazi's had been shareholders.

The Germans were everywhere and so was their science.

Even something as mundane as train travel was touched by seized German science. When America and Britain were producing coal-fired steam trains in the 1930s, German railways were speeding ahead with 100mph capable diesel-powered, streamlined and swept-nosed expresses that had no locomotives, but 'power-cars' that were an integral part of the train. Today, train manufacturers the world over, mimic such 1930s futurism. Yet, from 1939, it would take the British another twenty-five years after the Second World War to throw off their steam locomotives. Ironically, the British, inventors of the railway and locomotives, replaced their steam-powered monsters with German devices. New British diesel-electric and diesel-hydraulic engines, which were direct copies of German designs that had been honed and proven on German rail networks, and in German war service, soon dominated British railways.

Strangely, in light of the stolen 1940s German science that the British had deployed, notably in aerospace, the British Government of the 1950s decided that direct purchase of German railway locomotives for British Rail would be too sensitive an act for the British public and national pride to accept within ten years of the war's end. Therefore, these new advanced German diesel-hydraulic locomotive engines with their greater efficiencies would have to be built under-licence in Great Britain, under the 'cover' of a British manufacturing name. German science had to be re-branded for a British audience – by official government policy.

British Rail's famous 'Great Western' region would be run with direct transfer of Germany's advanced diesel-hydraulic engines and their roots in the Second World War military applications. As early as 1956, the Krauss-Meffei company sent their design drawings for their diesel hydraulic V200 and V300 (2000/3000 bhp) locomotive designs to British Rail as the basis for the 'Warship' and 'Western' classes. From the German designs came the new licence-built 'British' locomotives with their advanced stressed-skin monocoque bodies housing Maybach-MAN engines, Mekydro, and Voith transmissions – all recreated as British engineering marvels for an unsuspecting public. In the 1960s, even aircraft manufacturer

Bristol-Siddeley got in on the act by licence building another German–Maybach engined locomotive known in Britain as the 'Hymek' – but being substantially a German device. Little did the steam train and Great Western Railway aficionados realise that their beloved railway had gone German – using Nazi-era technology.

Even the English Electric 'Deltic' class locomotives had 1930s German–Junkers engine design roots of aviation and U-boat engine origins. Another English Electric product – the P.1 'Lightning' supersonic fighter was a direct derivative of seized German science too. Today, after a recent £200 million refit, Britain's HST high speed trains motor along at 125mph powered by a second generation of advanced, low pollutant, German engines of Maybach heritage. Again, strangely, when it came to the Avro Vulcan, Handley Page Victor, or Vickers Valiant nuclear V-bomber force, and other airframes (even Concorde), no such concerns about offending British public opinion about using German science were raised, despite the fact that these aircraft were packed with such technologies. It was all an odd paradox, a game of what today we might term 'smoke and mirrors'.

May 1945 – Germans in Kensington and Mayfair

A fact little known in Britain today is that in May 1945, just days after Hitler's suicide, yet before the end of the Third Reich and the war in Europe, an expensive housing block in London's Kensington Palace Gardens area of the very exclusive West End, became home for some very interesting Germans. Just the other side of Hyde Park, in Mayfair, was also to be found number 32 Bryanston Square, W.1., this was the home of the British Intelligence Objectives Sub-Committee (BIOS) and the location of a number of the 'retrieved' German scientists, who were interrogated there.

These two buildings were the officially sanctioned, UK Government-funded, homes to a collection of Nazis, Germans, and notables of German wartime technology, that only weeks earlier had been deployed against London and the Allies. Ironically, much of Kensington Palace Gardens was owned by the Crown Estate – the British Royal family's property arm. The buildings in Kensington Palace Gardens and Bryanston Square were operated by the British and American Intelligence services under the Combined Intelligence Objectives Sub-Committee (CIOS), a British Intelligence Objectives Sub-Committee (BIOS)/British Interrogation of German Scientists (BIGS) programme. These apartments (and other locations), were home to those men – some of whom would surely have been lynched by baying mobs on the streets if the local citizens had known of their presence.

The facts are that in the sunset hours of the war in Europe, Germans, including some ardent Nazis, and of note, the lead cast of men who had designed the weapons of mass destruction arrayed against the Allies for the Third Reich, were hosted in the heart of London.

Protected by armed guards, the 'safe houses' contained leading names that included Willi Messerschmitt and members of his design team. Also present were Ernst Heinkel; Alexander Lippisch; Richard Vogt, the Horten brothers; Kurt Tank of Focke-Wulf and some of his top designers – including Hans Multhopp. These men and others – notably the top ten of Germany's uranium research nuclear fusion group and further experts – were held at this and other British addresses.

The British Intelligence services knew about many German advanced processes. As an example, the British had rushed to Germany to find and interview it's top expert in the 'Fischer-Tropsch' fuel process – a Dr Otto Roelen of Ruhrchemie AG (Ruhr Chemicals Company). Seized by British Field Intelligence Teams – from a farm deep in the Russian zone of Germany in October 1945 – a remarkable feat in itself, Dr Roelen was then transported to London on 5 November 1945 and housed at a Mayfair address.

The interrogations in London's West End – at special locations – were vital examples of how far the Allies would go to gain technological advantage from seized German science.[4, 5, 6]

Also present in the Hyde Park interrogation zone was von Braun and the 'other' V-2 rocket man, Peenemünde's General Dornberger – who passed through en route to the Island Farm Prisoner of War Camp – known as 198/Special Camp: X-1, at Bridgend, South Wales. This was where Dornberger remained for many months as a suspected war criminal. Dornberger's involvement in the A series, or 'V' for *Vergeltungswaffen* (revenge weapons) V-2 bombings, reputedly made him a candidate for trial over alleged war crimes, yet he was released to a new life at Fort Bliss in the USA, building NASA space rockets and missiles with von Braun. Dornberger's and von Braun's rockets had killed over 5,000 Londoners, and yet in 1945, before VE day, Dornberger was living in London just weeks after their last V-2 landed and exploded in the city. Other experts, academics and Luftwaffe officers were also present – as were high ranking German officers from other services, some of who were held at Trent Park in north London and Wimbledon in south London.

The American authorities were involved in the holding and interrogation of many of these men and their eventual release to American custody. Of interest in terms of the CIOS/BIOS arrangements, the fact that noted émigré aerodynamicist, Theodore von Kármán, from California (Caltech), just happened to drop in on the west London apartments for chats with the designers (including the Hortens), at the invitation (and transportation) of the USAAF, was no fluke. Well-fed and watered, living in a smart area for several months, such men were resident while top British and American experts interviewed them to learn what they could of

Germany's secrets. The 'internees' were even taken on exercise walks in Hyde Park and in other parts of London, and to the areas devastated by V-1 and V-2 rocket technology. They were also placed at RAE Farnborough and ordered to tell their secrets, only then to be barred and, dispensed with. How incredible it seems today that the British citizens and taxpayers should host and protect leading exponents of the weapons of war that had just been waged upon them for five long years. Yet in May 1945, this was just the cost of doing business.

Many more advanced designs and processes that are today's normality, came directly from seized German science and technology. America, Britain, and Russia, secured significant technological advances for their science and their products as a direct knowledge transfer from the vaults of the Third Reich. From trains to dyed clothes, plastics, and synthetics; from wall paint, anti-malarial pills, biological warfare, to fruit juice; from machined and extruded alloys and beyond into radio and electronic advances, German science was years ahead.

The societal benefits for the plunderers of this intellectual property were, at the time, infinite, and soon took man beyond his own planet; such was the measure of the stolen science. It is a known fact that so concerned were the Americans about the legality of their seizing of science as war-prize booty, that, on the request of the Secretary of State for Occupied Areas under the US Military Government of Germany, the USA had to take expert legal advice and redraft the Second World War peace treaty to specifically sidestep any potential legal claims against the USA from German scientists and inventors whose intellectual property had been stolen.[7] All these years later, we cannot ignore the reality, that under the guise of revenge against the evil Nazis, German (not just Nazi) scientific research and expertise was seized and stolen by America, Britain and to some lesser degree, Russia, on a scale and manner not seen before or since. No other nation has ever been the subject or victim of such actions. It is an incredible, yet inconvenient true story, which the taint of its Nazi connections has allowed modern society to forget.

No less astounding than German and Nazi designers living in exclusive Kensington in May 1945 – yet considerably more finessed and framed for public consumption – were the close links between German and British institutions before the Second World War, not least through the British flagged, but German blooded, 'Windsor' royal family, living across Green Park at Buckingham Palace. This was the bizarre situation when the British continued to deify their post-1914 rebranded, 'House of Windsor' – in reality the utterly Hanoverian, Saxe-Coburg and Gotha-Altenberg, Mecklenburg-Strellitz, Wettin, Welf, Brunswick-Wolfenbüttel, Luneburg, Hesse, German Hanoverian noble lineage royal family that was immersed in Germanic bloodlines. Perhaps, by 1945, maybe the British public *had* forgotten the fact that, upon the outbreak of the First World War in 1914, the British king's own cousin had fled from Buckingham Palace and returned to his German roots to fight with his relatives against the very nation that housed his own royal relatives and where he had so recently been happily resident!

The British had had an extraordinarily close relationship with the German peoples and the Catholic branch of its noble lineage prior to the First World War, but selective amnesia was, it seems, the order of the day and remains so.

In a further paradox, soon after 1945, the average American man and wife and their homes, their very lives and society itself, were not just touched by German and Nazi science, but advanced by it, into the new so-called 'All-American' or 'British' technological marvels of the 1950s and 1960s. The origins and morals of how such science was developed and at what cost, have rarely been discussed outside the von Braun space flight story. It was von Braun who was carried as a hero through the streets of 'Rocket City', Huntsville, Alabama, in August 1969, after man had landed on the moon. The fact that von Braun had been a major in the SS and his work had rained slave-labour built rockets on to the streets of London was ignored. In the 1950s and 1960s homes of America, the German and Nazi origins of many of the products used in such households were never considered by the consumers of such science. From being kept under guard on arrival in America, to being lauded in the streets, was but a short journey for von Braun.

The details of Operation Paperclip and its predecessors were – as the means to scoop up science and scientists – deniable, classified affairs for decades. Prior to this, a series of 'operations' of varying names had presaged Allied interest in seizing science under the presidential edict of the 1946 Operation Paperclip project.

Not even a Nazi party sponsored car in the form of the Volkswagen Beetle, sitting on the front of so many millions of American and British driveways across the 1960s and 1970s, caused any self-analysis or doubts as to its tainted origins. American youth of the 1960s was mobilised by Hitler's car, and the origins of the derivative of the Beetle – the VW camper van – similarly failed to register upon the consciousness of millions of its buyers. These same people fought wars flying German-derived aircraft and also flew on American and British branded airliners that were directly derived from German and Nazi science. They were also people who watched Apollo rockets reach out into space upon the science of their Nazi origins as weapons of mass destruction against the Allies just a few years earlier.

It is claimed that the US Department of War forbade any use of proven Nazi Party members, political activists or sympathisers under Operation Overcast – which became Operation Paperclip. But that caveat was soon discarded when it was realised that nearly every expert had been made to become a Nazi Party member. The Joint Intelligence Objectives Agency (JIOA) sidestepped the problem of 'previous history' by allegedly creating and laying down false trails, and where necessary, reinventing records in an act of 'cleansing'. A 'top secret' classified status was stamped on the affair as German experts poured into America from the summer of 1945 onwards; only recently have the facts of what occurred been released.

In its own way, this bizarre phenomena of German-based science being rebranded as new and all-American or British, was a social science phenomenon in that this grand hypocrisy was reframed as being acceptable. This was how the victors of the Second World War claimed the rights to recompense – by grabbing the spoils of war, whatever their origins. They then quietly reframed this technology and regurgitated it as their own output – with no mention of the occult practices, war crimes, weapons of mass destruction and torture that were layered within much (though not all) of the seized science. Today, we might argue that such science should have been destroyed or ignored out of respect to the dead that were part of its discovery, but no such politically correct scruples were raised at that time by any of the Allies as they rushed to steal the science of Germany and leave its scientists uncredited and framed. The 'guilty' of Nazism were prosecuted at the Nuremburg Trial, but many were missing, and some, guilty and not guilty, could be found in Allied hands doing something different. Meanwhile, the citizens of the Reich who had created the Holocaust were, it seems, to be cherry-picked as deemed necessary, even if they may have had some involvement in the crime.

War criminal, inventor, designer, producer of weapons of mass destruction, fighter pilot, participant of the Third Reich? Senior SS officer? Attacker of the Allies one day, yet by the next day, employee of the Allies? This was a fact, a post–May 1945 reality – not a conspiracy theory, nor an exaggeration. It can no longer be denied.

A rare note of diplomatic caution was stated by the famed British engine designer and director of the Bristol Company, Sir Roy Fedden, in his report of the Fedden Mission to Germany of June 1945. The mission was a belated British attempt to seize advanced science from the disintegrating bowels of Germany – more than six months after the Americans first started to scour Germany for its secrets and science. Yet, as Sir Roy Fedden wrote in *Flight*: 'Far-reaching decisions face us over the future of the German scientists and research workers. Are we to use their vast accumulated knowledge for peaceful ends, or treat them as outcasts?'[8]

The reader will note the reference to 'peaceful' ends, a strange suggestion given that the seized German knowledge would go on to prop up the Cold War – its corporate profits, employment, political careers, and all its malevolent technology – stolen as it was by America, Britain and Russia from German scientists.

We should not forget that it was General Dwight D. Eisenhower (not then president) who categorically stated in 1945 that the work of the German scientists was twenty-five years ahead of the science of the United States of America: this estimate may be modest – but even twenty-five years was a stunning scientific short cut if it could be leapfrogged. An advance of this magnitude, and the admission of such, is what lay behind the proof of the scale of the seizure of science and the denial of its origins. Initially, the British simply refused to accept it, the Americans – by 1945 less psychologically constrained and less wrapped in a class and academic structured mindset and torpor, did believe it, and they grabbed everything that they could. British arrogance had yet to face the reality of its complacency.

Malignant Ingenuity and Perverted Science

The famous American commentator of the time, Edward R. Murrow, called the advanced science of the Reich a 'malignant ingenuity'.[9] This was a nice piece of 'spin' from the espousers of the moral high ground on the victorious side, but it was a ruse that hid the mad scramble to steal German technology for the Allies' own use, with scant or no regard to its origins, or the claimed 'malignant' morals of its creators. Even Winston Churchill, in his 'Finest Hour' speech, referred to the threat of Germany's 'perverted science', yet within a few short years, such science underpinned American and British science and aviation, from the swept-wing jet age to orbital flight – all in a perversion of the truth of its origins. So much then for Britain's 1950s 'Golden Age' of home-brewed aviation technology.

Not only were over 1,500 German scientists shipped back to America by 1949, but there were more than 3,500 experts who had become American citizens. Moving in the other direction, and little realised even today, was that teams of American experts were reverse-engineered back into Germany – to be placed in the heart of its scientific institutes and the research departments of major industrial companies during 1946–1948. Over one thousand of America's industrial and scientific experts were tasked with scouring Germany for industrial science as part of Joint Intelligence Objectives Agency (JIOA) search teams, under the Office of Strategic Studies (OSS) – the forerunner of the CIA.

The Technical Industrial Intelligence Committee (TIIC) was one of these search groups, composed of 380 civilians representing seventeen American industries – that is with direct links to major American manufacturing concerns. Then came teams of the Washington D.C. based, Office of the Publication Board. Even groups from private industry were allowed access inside Germany. There, 500 operatives, badged under a Field Intelligence Agencies/Technical (FIAT) umbrella, formed teams that were placed directly into the offices of German industry. Germany was mined, its science scoured and plundered for technology that was then used to create not just American aerospace, but the 'golden age' of western technological consumerism and its products and services for the second half of the twentieth century. FIAT's remit was most active between 1945–1948, when its aim was to secure German technology under the guise of 'the advancement and improvement of production and standards of living' under a United Nations remit that cited the 'proper' exploitation of Nazi technology. 'Proper' being fluid in terms it seems.

Russia is estimated to have grabbed over 6,000 German scientists and technicians, as well as achieving the removal of major German scientific research equipment back to Moscow. At one stage in the early 1950s, the east–west Cold War technology tension was framed by questioning which side had got the 'better' German experts. The indisputable fact was that by late 1947 Germany had been stripped of its science, and not just in a fit of Allied revenge and reparation. Such is the amazing tale of how German and Nazi science became the heart of an America-led western society that framed itself as the defender of the world, and the home of moral values, and notably, the centre of technological knowledge and scientific advances in the modern era. Maybe Wernher von Braun and his rocket men of Peenemünde were – when the secret came out years later – a good cover story. Perhaps they were a convenient shield for the wider dissemination and use of Nazi science that permeated American technology and everyday life – and its export to the world.

By 1947, the unique and specific aeronautical treasure trove of German aerospace secrets resided at Wright Field, Dayton, Ohio, and in Washington D.C.'s Library of Congress, and the Department of Commerce. One Washington official framed the hoard as the greatest single source of this type of material in the world, and that seizing the documents and the thousands of tons of actual machinery, aircraft and rockets, represented the first planned and structured exploitation of an entire country's brainpower.[10] All this was planned back in 1944 when the Allied Combined Chiefs of Staff, acting on the advice of their various research groups, created military-civilian teams of a Joint Intelligence Objective to scour Germany for its scientific secrets.

But what of those Me 262s at Lechfeld? The answer to what happened to these airframes and their Luftwaffe and Messerschmitt test pilots in April 1945 was simple. The pilots – who had been test pilots and operational combat pilots flying against the Allies on one day – were immediately absorbed into an officially sanctioned, and stamped, American 'test-flight' section and, incredibly, by the next day, were new employees of the American government. They would fly their Me 262s to an airfield near Paris. There, firstly, to spend two months teaching Americans how to understand, operate and fly the Me 262 and then onwards to deliver them to another airfield near Cherbourg. There, the advanced jet-powered Me 262s would be dismantled and shipped to Wright Field, Dayton, Ohio, USA; Wright Field is the home of publicly unknown secrets today – just as it was in 1945.

The 26 April 1945 was not the only date in April-May 1945 when undreamed of secrets of the science of flight were discovered by the American and British men who scoured Germany for such knowledge. At this time, across Germany, amazing technologies and designs and powerplants were being discovered and looted – stolen as war-prize booty by the victorious Allies as recompense for war. The British Fedden Mission did its best to secure advanced design for Britain, but it was up against a British establishment who refused to believe in the German advances and certainly did not want to supply new lives and research resources for Germans, however clever they might be. Meanwhile, the Americans and Russians were seizing entire factories, research departments and their staff. Indeed, the Russians virtually rebuilt the factories of Junkers of Dessau, and Bosch of Spandau, and Heinkel of Marienehe, back in Russia – staffed by many of their former technical experts.

But the seized war-prizes were not just recompense; they were far more valuable than that, for they were a vital key to a future not yet dreamed of in America or Britain (or the Soviet Union). From those days across Germany in April, May, and June 1945, came technology, modern science, and even our travels in sky and space as we accept them today. The names and the deeds (good and bad) of the men who made such science have long been hidden, deliberately whitewashed in a politically correct clean-up and reframed as the giant leaps of science that the experts of America, and the Allies created in a post-war world of the 'white heat of technology' and the reality of the Cold War and its machines. The science was stolen and the originating scientists deliberately left uncredited as part of a politically designed cover-up; this is fact and not conspiracy theory.

So is written apparent history and, to the victors the spoils.

Thus was framed the American 'overnight' acceptance of German and Nazi science into its society without citing or crediting the scientists who dreamed it all up. It was as simple as that. As for morals; no questions, no soul searching, were allowed. It did not matter if you were a combat pilot killing and shooting down Americans one day, or a scientist launching weapons of mass destruction the next day, you were an employee of the Allies, and (in most cases) the American Government and funded by the American taxpayer. This was fact not speculation. To this day it is a story only known amongst certain parts of science and society.

Soon, those 1,000 plus German scientists (not the dozens reluctantly admitted to in later years), would also depart for Mitchell Field and then onwards to Wright Field, Dayton, Ohio; Fort Bliss, Texas; and White Sands, New Mexico. New homes and new careers would be provided for the scientists. And from von Braun and his colleagues came the foundations of everything, even today's legend of 'Area 51', itself the secrets superstore and modern equivalent of Wright Field (Wright-Patterson) and its legend. It has been all too easy to frame the stolen science as

'Nazi'. Yet much of this advanced knowledge stemmed from pre-Nazi German administrations up to the end of the Weimar period before 1933. The Germans in the 1920s had laid, not just the foundations of global military and civil aviation, but the design and construction systems of an advanced cadre of planes and pilots.

Of the fabled von Braun, Oberth and Stuhlinger of General Dornberger's Peenemünde men – they and their families lived in a new town especially built for them and their research in America. A few Germans scientists would end up in the Royal Aircraft Establishment (RAE) at Farnborough, England, and then go into the heart of the British aviation industry, and 6,000 men of the German teams would reside east of Moscow, but in the main, it was America that accepted and very quickly absorbed the science of the Third Reich. The British went through a period of stunned, humiliated denial, and wasted years of opportunities from such tainted science, and then handed much of what they had discovered to a grateful America. In the Soviet Union, no such attitudes existed, because the Russians, like the Americans, simply stared in awe at the war-prize technology and then got on with the job of exploiting it, whatever the cost to their national exchequer.

The Politicisation of Science

The politicisation of science may have begun in 1930s Germany, but that tactic was soon embraced in Washington D.C., and in Moscow. This was how the second half of the twentieth century was to be framed, formed and fought over.

The British and American taxpayers who funded it all were left to stare at the 1950s and 1960s products of what they were told were *their* national intellects. And of the unknown and uncredited German scientists from who so much was stolen? Little was known or advertised. Even the scientific establishment itself has veneered over such origins of today's technology. Apparently, technology, advanced aerodynamics and the all-wing or blended wing, are *recent* discoveries. This laughable charade is a perceived wisdom amongst many academics and their students, who know little of the true origins of these scientific themes or other aspects of technology.

Such are not the claims of the contrarian, but the facts of reality. Only recently has officialdom begun to admit it all. Even books written before the B-2 all-wing stealth bomber emerged, or the latest blended-wing announcements were revealed, underplayed the impact of German aerospace technology. Now, we can see that Lippisch, Junkers, the Hortens and others, have directly impacted the latest twenty first century technology. It is no longer possible (as it was the absence of then unknown American reinventions of such technology) to opine that no actual direct legacy occurred from seized German science – that claim was a feint, a ruse, to assuage the court of public opinion and academic and military egos. Post-

Apollo, amid the current all-wing revolution, stealth technology and much more, the truths of what the Allies stole and sat upon for seventy years, are now obvious.

Who built the world's first 'stealth' low-radar signature, low drag, swept-wing, all-wing jet aircraft? Was it America in the late 1980s? Of course not! Because it was the Horten brothers in 1944, in the forms of their wood, plastic, reflective surfaced, specially shaped jet fighter of all-wing configuration. The Horten Ho 229 was quickly seized by advancing US forces and shipped back to America and its secrets have emerged decades later in recent US airframes. Recent tests on a rebuilt version of the 1944 Ho 229, showed it to be over forty per cent less radar-visible than any other machine. This test-airframe contained differing, less advantageous construction details and more metal than the Horten's original airframe, so the forty per cent figure may be doing the design no favours, but even that figure proved the point. And of course, the American narrative is that the Horten's may have used such low-radar signature composite construction as a coincidence. Meanwhile, the F-117 and Northrop Grumman B-2, followed by recent fighters and drones, all closely mimic the Horten design in shape and composite detail – and that is clearly not by coincidence.

Before the period 1945, to date, we need to look back to the very origins of aviation and its science. Only there, in the years of the early pioneers, can we understand how the events of that day at Lechfeld in April 1945 happened. Then, the secrets of all-wing and monoplane design and jet power, from Silesia to Paris, to Farnborough and onwards to Dayton, White Sands, and Long Beach, can be known. This truly was a case of the afterwards and the before – or the future – backwards.

In a bizarre paradox, the Germans, (constrained by those very British and the French establishments application of their *Treaty of Versailles* in 1919) after being simplistically blamed for 'starting' the First World War entirely on their own, used such applied constraints to take a massive leap ahead in aviation research and knowledge terms, at the expense of their vanquishers. The irony of this is one that should not be forgotten when we think of the Edwardian British and their own 'empire attitude' and know-it-all conceits of certainty across a social and cultural landscape. Like many people held in the certain grip of their own convictions, the establishment had difficulty accepting the views and opinions of other people who had the temerity to think differing thoughts.

Back to a Future Long Forgotten?

Today, in the technology of the now, aircraft design (and industrial design) is going curved again and a blended, biomorphic, all-wing; tailless school of aircraft design leads the pursuit of low drag. The all-wing revolution is back from the past. The monoplane finally rules, and sleekness – or smoothness criteria – dominates amid a boundary layer research edict. The term 'back to the future' seems very apt indeed, because in the beginning, aircraft were smooth, sleek and monoplaned – and often all-wing. Many were elliptical or curved in a manner denied by the products of the biplane era that manifested soon afterwards – yet to which curved technology has now brought us.

In a strange parallel, in a quest for downforce and stability at the expense of drag, today's Formula 1 cars have become rough edged biplanes in their adornments of drag inducing multiple wings, fences, boards, tabs and triggers, in a horrific rash of speed-sapping, brute force design. Yet earlier such cars had both downforce *and* lower drag – through curved and clean design that required less power to push their 'barn door' shapes through the air. Formula 1 racing car design would seem to be stuck back in a biplane era circa 1910. It is an example of how the knowledge of the 'now' can usurp the knowledge of the 'before' – which by apparent scientifically conceited default, has become second rate.

Back with aviation, if we put aside unproven antecedents ranging from ancient cultures in China, South America, and Egypt, from thousands of years ago, if we put aside Leonardo Da Vinci's drawings and models, then the 'father' of modern, aeronautical thought – that is of the 'aeroplane' as a potential viable aerial device as an entity, is cited by those in charge of perceived history, to be Sir George Cayley (1773–1857).

Is Cayley where aircraft design can, in 1799, *really* be said to have begun? If so, we have to wonder why, by 1913, the monoplane and the all-wing thoughts he and others pioneered were to be discarded in favour of the biplane, only for that to be latterly framed as the 'steeping stone' to the 'discovery' of the monoplane and the all-wing craft of the 1930s. And it would be almost the year 2000 before a bigger all-wing movement in military airframe design secured a wider currency as a portent of the future.

But the obvious very large question is; what happened between 1799 and 1999 to delay and retard aerodynamic development? What made us go from the all-wing and the monoplane, forwards to the biplane era and thence back to a past future in the subsequent monoplane and now, all-wing modern era? Why did the British, the French, and the Americans, throw off the advance, yet the Germans persevered with monoplane and swept-wing all-wing research to great effect? What on earth happened in the minds of the learned men of early aviation?

Britain and France were at the centre of the early rush to fly, and the pioneer French-born, but American-based, Octave Chanute's, early ideas were of Lilienthalesque planform, but Chanute, the man who collated global aviation knowledge at a time when communications were sparse, became a biplane proponent; whereas the early works of Percival Sinclair Pilcher were ellipsoid, all-wing monoplanes (albeit with vestigial tails). Can we cite Chanute as the instigator of a switch to the biplane configuration that would influence wing configuration (but not the control mechanism) of Chanute's compatriots – the much younger men who were the Wright brothers? Is this where 'biplanism' as a movement began, after Chanute, Henson and Stringfellow? Can we imagine the detached design thinking that would have existed in the void between Penaud's Parisian all-wing ideas and those of the compiler of early European and American aviation that was Chanute, across the vast, Atlantic void?

To illustrate the fact of an early all-wing and normal configuration monoplane dominance, let us for now, cite just three examples: the aforementioned Alphonse Penaud's *Amphibian* of 1876, Armand Deperdussin's monoplane, with Ruchonnet and Bechereau having designed and applied the concept as the Monocoque of 1912, and John Dunne's swept-wing all-wing monoplane of 1911 (with of note, a young Richard Fairey assisting Dunne). These three airframes were the pathfinders of an advance that was deliberately stifled – smothered in its birth pangs. These massive advances in design and aerodynamics, with their smooth, monoplane wings and, in two cases, all-wing configurations, were effectively and deliberately denied, 'killed' by a learned-society psychology, in a movement *not* of known-knowns, but of a deliberate, retrograde design choice. This, despite the stunning speed records attained by the Deperdussin machine – far in excess of the 'norms' of 1912 – and despite the fact that a Dunne all-wing flew across the Channel with ease.

The quest for flight stability (and in France and Britain, a reaction against the Wright brothers' success) led to the dumbing down of any idea that might be a risk, or less than utterly stable. And if (like the Horten brothers) you did not go to the correct university to be taught what to think by the so-called thinkers of the now, then you and your unqualified ideas, were of no consequence. And even if you had got the correct academic paperwork, you had better not be a maverick, or think new thoughts. For that way lay the term 'eccentric' and all that stemmed therefrom in the isolation of a career ruined by the risk of independent thought. The grip of certainty ruled supreme in a society of theocracy and hierarchy.

Of Alphonse Penaud, who (with Paul Gauchot) created an amazing all-wing, asymmetric double-elliptical planform machine in the 1870s, we can say, poor Penaud, he really was a true futurist, a fact proven by how close subsequent and more recent designs are to his work. Yet the learned men, the might of conditioned society and thinking, destroyed him and his ideas. Depressed and decried, with establishment funding withdrawn, he cut all links with the learned men, their limited thinking and their societies. He committed suicide and faded away into aerodynamic history for all except those in the know. Penaud ought to be a hero, not a footnote – surely?

And where *did* Jules Verne and Robert Esnault-Pelterie get their strange ideas of all-wing, monoplane, deltoid flight, and of space travel from? For the English, amid their cautious and imperialist constrained thinking, who *were* these eccentric 'Johnny Foreigner Frenchies' and their mad and silly thoughts? Did they not know that there was a way of doing what we know and most certainly *not*, of wanting to know what we might do.

Through such attitudes and personality constructs, through an apparent almost psychopathy, came the great caution, the biplane mindset and the consequent lost years of aerodynamics and of aviation's advance. So was borne the back-step of the biplane era that was eventually allowed via the monoplane and all-wing era, to lead to the shock of the 'new', in the form of the sudden 'discovery' of the mid-1930s sleek monoplane era and the steps to today's designs that stemmed therefrom. Such is the veneer of aeronautical history as presented not just to the layman, but also to the students of today. It is, of course, a created consensus that smothers alternative evidence.

In between then and now, there lay one hundred years and many blind turns and false dawns; there also lay the legacy of French, British, and most prominent of all, German, and then Nazi aeronautical and aerospace design. Parts of the story have been told, but of the all-wing, of Arnoux, Penaud, Dunne, Hill, Prandtl, Lilienthal, Lippisch, Espenlaub, Etrich, the Hortens, Parkin, Hill, Shenstone, Fauvel, and many more names, there is much to be unravelled. The place of fulcrum, the moment-arm in the story of effect and all-wing cause, centres on the lands of Bavaria and Bohemia. Quite why such a region was the centre of focus remains an enigma; it is a riddle in the drag wake of history. Maybe it had something more to do with gliding than with the UFO-borne little green men now so often cited by those 'UFO-ologists' who have prejudged their opinions.

Leaping to 1933, we all know that Hitler had a personality disorder – he was a man driven by delusion and other failings that included a rarely cited disease of the central nervous system. Yet for all the correctly expressed horror at his deeds, the world seems to have suffered a bout of selective amnesia when it comes to aspects of the incredible technology that grew from the Führer's ever more crazed flights of fancy and the advanced designs his boffins dreamed up in response to their dictator's demands. For the uncomfortable truth is that it is from such technology that many of today's aerospace advances have come. Hitler was indeed very strange, yet in the 1930s, it was Hitler who banned smoking in public places, and enacted anti-vivisection and anti-animal testing laws. He even funded a Reichs Research Council – the first collection of research bodies with state funding of this type. These were the strange and bizarre twists amid his acts of later evil.

There should be no excuses and yet, in terms of science, Hitler was a bizarre benefactor of global scientific knowledge – even if he himself stole much of it from a pre-Nazi era of the other Germany – the nation the Americans and the British were so very close to in geopolitical, cultural, religious, royal, and financial terms. Pre-existing German science, prior to 1933, seems to have been tainted by post-1933 Nazi related events – with even Hitler himself encouraging such suggestion to milk the knowledge for all it was worth.

It appears that after the Second World War the redundant 'names' of Nazism were put on trial at Nuremberg, but that the more useful scientists of Nazism were spirited away to new lives working for the victors of war, their records ignored or cleansed, their deeds forgotten. Perhaps this really was, just the cost of doing business.

Germans, Not Nazis: a Distinct Difference

Not all of the German output actually stemmed from Nazi order, much of it had been researched and framed before 1933 and the rise of the Austrian, Hitler. There was little that was 'Nazi' about Germany's top aerodynamicists and scientists prior to the mid-1930s, but Hitler made the most of pre-existing works that have subsequently become tainted by association with later outcomes of knowledge transfer. As an example, Hugo Junkers lost everything, and his life, because he refused to deal with the new Nazi regime of Hitler. Alexander Lippisch was not a Nazi, and neither were many others, although some others did have unclean connections – not that this bothered the Allied establishment post-1945. Indeed, Lippisch and the Horten brothers attempted to leave Germany before 1939, but failed – unlike T. von Kármán who succeeded and never let anyone forget it.

The great designers and scientists who were German nationals – citizens who supported their nation at war – have been labelled as 'Nazis', but this is a simplification designed for a purpose.

Indeed, Alexander Martin Lippisch was fêted as a lecturer in London at the Royal Aeronautical Society as late as December 1938 and it was hoped he might even work for Vickers-Supermarine via his friendship with Spitfire aerodynamicist Beverley Shenstone. (Lippisch did not join Supermarine, but within seven years he was working for the Americans.) Claudius Dornier and his men landed a flying boat at Supermarine's home base on the River Itchen, in Southampton, in order to meet R.J. Mitchell. And despite the cinematographic lie portrayed in the biopic of R.J. Mitchell and his Spitfire, Mitchell never went to Germany to meet Willi Messerschmitt around a dinner table packed with Nazi figures. It was 'spin' of the classic propaganda type.

It is of note that, although Messerschmitt was arrested and charged with being a Nazi supporter in May 1945, he was never prosecuted, and after a brief imprisonment and the payment of fines for working for the evil regime, he was deemed to be de-Nazified and returned to his home after the war to begin car manufacture. Whatever his issues, Messerschmitt knew how far advanced German aerodynamics were and viewed the Allies as hypocrites who would face a Russian aerospace design onslaught in the coming years post 1945. Some would say that this was not an inaccurate opinion.

Mankind, be that of American or Russian genes, got to the moon off the back of Nazi wartime research and we conveniently forgot about the Nazi slave labour and weapons of mass death and destruction that were the genesis of space travel in the form of the Nazi rocket building programme of the Second World War. But that was just the tip of the iceberg in terms of stolen science.

The fact that the post-NACA body that was NASA, offered, in its own words, a 'welcome' to von Braun et al and went into space via his work is, of course, accepted fact. But what of the triangular wings of Concorde, the Vulcan, or a host of American and Russian machines? What of the wing-only F-117 stealth fighter, or the B-2 stealth bomber, what of *Aurora, Demon*, NASA or BAE hypersonics, the latest proposed Boeing blended-wing and more?

Dare we conjecture about the hypersonic atmosphere skimmers and the all-wing airliners that will dominate the world in decades to come? What of the delta-wing, the T-tail, swept-wings, leading edge slats, wing-to-fuselage fillets, elliptical shapes, high altitude medical research, and a host of advanced aerodynamic, propulsive and other advances that gave us the jet age? Incredibly, many such techniques stemmed from the great receptacle of research that poured from Germany circa 1900–1945 and which was then seized as war-prize science and secreted away to be later claimed.

Today's space race, current aviation science, even today's airline travel, has been touched by the science of a period in time and place in central Europe that created the greatest advances in aerodynamics ever seen – the great leap forwards from string and canvas biplanes to supersonics, jet power, delta-wing and all-wing flight. This occurred in a very short time period of less than thirty years and stemmed from a concentrated nuclei of research establishments located in central Europe. Today's composite plastic airliners reflect the research and building of the world's first plastic-built composite aircraft – the plastic prototype Me Bf 109 and the wood/plastic-built, radar-signature reducing Horten Ho 5, Ho 8, Ho 9, and the Ho 229 variant. Anyone in any doubt about the significance of this science needs to recall that in early 1945, as the last days of the Second World War still raged, the Americans, British, and Russians, devoted huge resources to racing through Germany to scour the landscape and 'steal' German 'Nazi' science and scientists and spirit them away, back to new lives as war-prize material.

A Day in October 1957 – *Sputnik*

The 4 October 1957 was another day of infamy for mankind, for it was the day the Russians, using their German war-prize science, launched not just *Sputnik*, but engendered the American response that framed the 1960s and a geopolitical era – everything from the Berlin Wall going up and coming down, from President Kennedy, to Ronald Reagan and Margaret Thatcher toying with Mikhail Gorbachev, to the Northrop B-2 all-wing tailless bomber.

Sputnik was coded as the PS1, it meant *Prostreishy Sputnik* or 'simple satellite'. Just months later, on 31 January 1958, the American's fired their first space vehicle, *Explorer,* using a Jupiter-class rocket that, just like Sputnik's launch vehicle and control systems, stemmed from Peenemünde and Wernher von Braun and his men. They now lived very comfortably in America's 'Rocket City' while Congress and the American military and scientific community sat back, fat and happy in the certain belief that Russia would never get into space before them. The American military up to 1957 was, it seems, at war with itself, jealously guarding which service would achieve spaceflight first. Ego, not science, ruled.

In a delicious irony, one that frames the torpor of egos and certainties amid military and civilian hierarchical structures and their authority gradients to this day, the military and political in-fighting cost America the dream of being the first into space. The 'simple' Russians pulled it off without von Braun and his men, but using his science. The American administration and the bloated American military were stunned into momentary silence. Their response was a classic case of PR upon the masses. Eisenhower's close associate, John Foster Dulles, simply told the American people that *Sputnik* – as the reality of Russians in space – was no big deal and had been achieved by the use of stolen German wartime science that was just a small step of theft and copying. One that should not be exaggerated, which involved no basic discovery and to which fears should be not be attached, he also stated that that America brains could do better. Apparently, it was all the fault of the defeated German scientists the Russians had taken.[11]

John Foster Dulles' message to America was clear – don't panic, and rely on American science, not the Nazi-tainted, dangerous, flawed, stolen stuff that the Russians had used, but had not really come up with on their own anyway. Rely on American invention to win. This was the amazing piece of hypocrisy that conned the American public in a manner that framed psychological manipulation and, of importance, constituted the beginning of the Cold War.[12]

The Truman administration's 'con' was incredible, the hypocrisy even bigger – Dulles never mentioned the reality of the Wernher von Braun, Ernst Stuhlinger and the General Dornberger-led Peenemünde team and thousands of other Germans and ex-Nazi-funded experts, being hard at work deep inside America (also with over a thousand ex-German aviation scientists being at work at Wright Field), *all* being taxpayer funded. The Americans, via von Braun's team, were using the same knowledge the Russians had just demonstrated – and were being blamed for! With the US taxpayer funding American use of it all to the tune of billions of dollars, the 'con' was immense. But John Foster Dulles and his brother Allen were no strangers to 'spin'; they would be an influence upon the Oval Office and head the CIA respectively. Like many American luminaries, the family had an airport named after it – the airport of the nation's capitol – Washington Dulles, in Washington D.C.

The American response to *Sputnik* was not the stuff of a conspiracy theory; it was a rational, predetermined act of manipulation or mass psy-ops. For, faced with the reality of the incredible in *Sputnik* and its orbit, in a bizarre structure of denied rationality of almost theological bent, packed with internal inconsistencies, the impossible was reframed as the probable and was presented to the American people and the world by the American political establishment. *Sputnik* shook America, it shook the president and it shook society, it began a new era – the 'Space Race' and the Cold War respectively. These were the people who also brought us the great UFO era and its success at persuading the mass population that little green men were really responsible for secret American attempts at flight using re-engineered Nazi technology. And what of any potentially 'real' UFOs? The psychosomatic 'psy ops' cover-up absorbed them too – if they ever existed.

Ironically, the Americans were ahead of the Russians in terms of missile and rocket knowledge because they had grabbed the cream of the German aerodynamic and rocket research men. There really was no need for fear, or a Cold War, just because Moscow had got into space first. The Americans had access to the same science, but more of it, and with many more V-2s to experiment with, not to mention the von Braun team. The knee-jerk reaction to Russia getting orbital first, was more to do with politics than with scientific reality. The Americans simply did not want to admit that they were using and copying German science in the rocket programmes, let alone in any other research arenas. Part of the Allied ruse has been that the German rocket men and German aerodynamics and airframe men who were taken to Wright Field in 1945–1946, were somehow kept apart and that their researches were and remained entirely separate. This was not the case.

What of the 1950s and the Avro Canada flying disc experiments? What were they? Feints to distract attention from secret works on disc technology and anti-gravity experiments, or the unlikely origins of the 1950s UFOs and reports of fuselage-less wing-only craft with arrow-shaped forms, or parabolic, scythe-bladed, silhouettes? Was the Roswell incident nothing more complicated than the crash of an American-built, re-engineered example of German war-prize all-wing/disc technology?

There are many myths and legends about the advanced German aeronautical technology of the Second World War, there are also facts and proven events. Yet within the story there lie conspiracy theories, mistaken assumptions and denials that seem to contradict the evidence. On both sides of the east-west divide, German or Nazi science, call it what you will, was about to frame the next seventy years of world history, it's just that the people never knew. In a way, Hitler had his nationalistic result, and the West German 1960s economic miracle was just an offshoot of unintended consequence. That the Cold War was a global manifestation of power and science, and of note, that advanced, incredible, German science was behind it all, was perhaps a chilling irony that has been little commented upon.

The truth about the Nazi origins of America's space programme is now out, but what about the other aspects of science? And what about the all-wing and tailless revolution that is sweeping aerospace today and framing military concepts. The so-called 'flying wing' is today's true inheritor of a somewhat murky past.

'Flying-Wing or All-Wing?'

Some people use the term 'flying wing' to describe the arrow-headed V-shaped wing-only design concept, but of course, every wing (including those attached to fuselages) is a 'flying' wing by definition – because wings 'fly', that is what they do. So, wing-only (a nurflügel), or all-wing (be it tailless or not), seems a far more reliable term to frame the subject of our story. If you prefer 'flying-wing' that is your choice, but from here on, it is the all-wing.

Glider design and the act of sailplaning, or gliding, has a huge role in the story of all-wing design and the design research culture that frames it, yet gliding (once an Olympic sport, yet inexcusably denied such status today) seems to have become marginalised, niched and rarely touched by the designers and pilots of the now. Glider design is where the genesis of today's aerodynamic advance lies. It seems as though a massive tranche of ancient knowledge and its origins, have been forgotten by the current crop of electronic, full digital authority, composite, supercritical aerofoil designers amid the output they claim as innovative and new.

In a report in *Flight International*,[13] a team of designers with university funding claimed to have 'discovered' that the location and shape of control surfaces upon the all-wing planform is a crucial arbiter of their aerodynamic performance. How many millions of dollars did they spend to decide on that little gem? Surely it would have been cheaper to go to an aeronautical library and read the pre-Second World War aerodynamicists notes on the subject from Steiger, Penaud, Adler, Junkers, Prandtl, Horten, Lippisch, Dunne, Hill and others; therein the fundamentals were discovered and explored many decades ago.

A quick look at nature's ultimate flying wing, the Manta Ray, would also have revealed the importance of control surface shape and location *prior* to any three-year funded student thesis. What of Professor Freidrich Ahlborn's study of the *Alsomitra Zanonia Macrocarpa* flying-wing seed that so inspired Dunne and Lilienthal's followers? Was Penaud inspired by the all-wing planform of the butterfly? And what of birds – are they not all-wing and devoid of a vertical tail surface?

It seems that sometimes, both nature and the Nazi-tainted knowledge of the past, as well as non-Nazi study into the subject, have been ignored or dismissed at the altar of a modern reproduction under a new name. As so often in aviation, subsequent events are found to have had precursors that went either un-actioned or ignored, and even denied by design. When was the first all-wing design patented? We might say it was of Alphonse Penaud in 1876, but that was on paper, not in the metal. But does Hugo Junkers' February 1910 patent for a 'Tragflächen' (literally a 'carrying surface') flying-wing, as an almost all-wing planform, really define the first such practical consideration of the all-wing aerial vehicle that led to the tailless revolution? We should also cite John Dunne circa 1910.

The Junkers Patent application of 1910 stated: 'Aeroplane consisting of one wing, which would house all components, engines, crew, passengers, fuel and framework'. Therein lay the deep-bodied cantilever wing structure that was adopted by 'normal' wing planform configuration aircraft. Meanwhile, the biplane-based French and the British learned men did not want to know.

From Conrad Hass to Kazimierz Siemienowicz and beyond, to the amazingly radical 1876 design of Alphonse Penaud and Paul Gauchot, to Dunne, Zuhkouskii, Prandtl and Lippisch, to the Hortens, Kracht, Voigt, Vogt, through Messerschmitt, Heinkel and Junkers, to Shenstone, Hill, Parkin, Chadwick, Northrop, Tupolev, Edwards, and others, the why of the swept-wing, all-wing and tailless shapes that made history is a stunning story.

A very British secret history to the all-wing and delta-wing was framed between 1940–1950. Unbeknown to many, in the depths of war, with all its demands for traditional weapons and normal aircraft, the British still found the time to set up a Tailless Aircraft Advisory Committee in 1942. By 1946 that committee, its members and its recommendations, were examining German wing research and framing the Air Ministry Specification B.35/46 – the roots of the British nuclear bomber airframe and the 'V' force of the later Vulcan, Victor and Valiant. Vehement supporters of that ultimate all-wing (albeit with a tail fin), the 'first' big delta that was the Avro Vulcan, will say that it was designed by Roy Chadwick – undoubtedly it was – but did he *invent* its deltoid wing configuration? No, he did not. And surely R.J. Mitchell and B.S. Shenstone designed the world's first large, four-engined delta-winged military aircraft in the form of the 1936 design of the Supermarine bomber to Air Ministry Specification B12/36? This was the design that George Edwards was stunned by – and said so.

A similar claim of history says that the de Havilland Comet was the world's first commercial jet airliner. Indeed it was (if we dismiss a certain Canadian Avro design) and Britain claimed the plaudits in a féte of national pride. But hidden in the de Havilland records was the proof that the Comet's wing stemmed directly from seized German wing design knowledge and that the DH 108 swept-wing research aircraft had also been an immediate product of this knowledge. It was a precursor to de Havilland's reputation for producing brilliant, high-speed, swept-wing designs. For under CIOS, de Havilland had got an expert into Germany and that expert was soon ensconced in Messerschmitt's aerodynamics research office, gleaning all he could about swept-wings and high speed aerofoils.

From the straight-winged de Havilland Vampire jet designed in 1943–1944, to the swept-winged DH 108 that emerged soon after 1945, there was a huge step in design terms – one fuelled by knowledge taken from Messerschmitt. How else do we explain the straight-winged Vampire being followed by the radical advance of the swept-wing DH 108? And after all, in 1945, who had the advanced supersonic wind tunnels necessary to research such speed?

The answer was, Germany – not Britain or America.

In de Havilland's Comet archives, there are the early drawings for the Comet-type jet airliner. These plans reveal a highly swept, all-wing, tailless machine, with a Comet fuselage mated to an advanced German-derived wing planform of over 35° sweepback that had shades of Lippisch and Horten. Back in Britain, the RAE experts and de Havilland spent months interviewing Lippisch, and the two remaining Horten brothers, mining their knowledge for swept, tailless expertise.

According to the CIOS reports, representatives of British aviation not only interviewed the Hortens in London in May 1945, but it is also reputed the Fairey Company interviewed Reimar Horten and were keen to employ him on advanced all-wing and tailless designs. Several meetings in Germany and London in 1946–1947 are specifically cited, not least by Myhra in his definitive Horten work.[14] Yet the British, via the contentious (and with hindsight, perhaps scandalous) CIOS Wilkinson report, then dismissed the Hortens – but not before they had secured much (but not all) of their knowledge. The Horten work on wing lift distribution patterns was absorbed by the German swept-wing research community and thus directly impacted German or later Allied outcomes from the use of such research. Surely it was no surprise then that, within two years of the end the war, we should see the forms of the DH 108 and the original Comet jet airliner design – which was of a remarkably Horten/Lippisch style. But the advance was sidelined and the production Comet, with its more conventional configuration and planform, went on to become Britain's 1950s device of claimed 'jet age' prestige.

As for its Rolls-Royce jet engines, well they were the product of Whittle – and von Ohain and Coanda had nothing to do with that.

The very British, Bristol Company, purveyors of aircraft, engines and cars, contained an all-wing enthusiast in its director, Sir Roy Fedden, he of the Fedden Mission to Germany in June 1945. As early as 1944 Fedden presented an RAeS lecture on the future of large civil aircraft, and framed it as an all-wing future. Fedden's enthusiasm for the all-wing configuration stemmed in large part from his time listening to a man who lodged in Fedden's own home during a wartime secondment to the Bristol Company. That man's name was Beverley Shenstone – the Spitfire's aerodynamicist. Also ensconced at Bristol was Malcolm Sayer, the aerodynamicist and elliptical enthusiast who would go on to shape Jaguar's iconic aerodynamic cars.

The reader may indeed wonder, given such all-wing expertise at Bristol, how on earth the lumbering Bristol Brabazon subsequently came about. The answer lay in the constraints of the British attitude, and the shock of discovering in 1945 just how far ahead the Germans were – which Fedden had leveraged with his research mission to Germany and which Shenstone, with his fluent technical German and previous relationships with German designers, had helped frame behind the scenes.

The first internationally demonstrated, viable and test flown, swept delta-wing designs of Lippisch, manifested in 1930–1931 and, as Lippisch admitted, they were designs achieved with the help of B.S. Shenstone, who went on to design the Spitfire's unique asymmetric, conjoined ellipsoid wing, with its uniquely modified elliptical lift patterns and swept forwards trailing edge. Shenstone became a Second World War Air Ministry boffin and President of the RAeS, latterly a director of Avro Canada, BEA, BOAC, and a guru of wing design. Where did Shenstone learn about such science? The answer is, in Germany circa 1929–1931, at the hands of Junkers, Lippisch, and Prandtl. The Spitfire's wing stemmed in-part from Heinkel, Junkers and Prandtl research links with Lippisch tutelage[15] and earlier roots: such an idea is underlined by the RAeS Paper by Ackroyd on the subject.[16]

The suggested heresy of a German link to the Spitfire of R.J. Mitchell could never have been revealed in a post-war Britain of 'empire' mindset, of course. Even today, it results in reactions of bile and disgust, but the facts are as referenced.

Some authors, even a leading proponent of the all-wing story, have stated that, while the Americans did use the rocket science of the Germans, the aerodynamics and all-wing expertise were not exploited to any great degree. Such a claim appears to now be contradicted by the evidence. A whole cast of American, British, and Russian military (and civil) aircraft dating from 1945 to date, clearly demonstrate the aerodynamics science of pre-1945 Germany. Perhaps the legends of the Cold War aircraft that America and Britain turned out from their aviation industries under their own branding, have blinkered the perception and recorded history of just where such aircraft drew their advances from – German scientific ideas stolen and seized, carted off by the thousands to Wright Field, Ohio, and the RAE Farnborough. American and British egos are still reluctant to admit what went on beyond the von Braun story. A false trail has been laid and today's science and engineering students have little idea of what went on circa 1945.

Ironically, Russia's Cold War machines that presented such a problem to the West from the 1950s up to recent examples such as the MiG-29 stem directly from the experts at Heinkel – Gunter, Benz, Wocke – who were offered employment post 1945 in Russia, after American and British aviation had decided to ignore their talents. The MiG-15/17 series of the 1950s were also direct copies of Focke-Wulf designs. Meanwhile, over the Atlantic, a whole fleet of German designs appeared in reframed and renamed forms as America's 'X' series prototypes.

Surely society should credit those scientists who created today's science? Not it seems, if they were Germans, and wrongly or rightly, by association, Nazis. For the Americans and the British, it appears it was acceptable to use these scientists and their knowledge, but it was not acceptable to admit it. And it was perfectly acceptable to verbally assault the Russians for using such science and tell people not to worry. After all, it was all stolen Nazi information and America had higher intelligence – its own brilliant designs. The British even refused to accept the knowledge, so admitting it was never going to be a problem until after they had.

War is a dirty business and so are the spoils of war. The 1960s irony of America's ballistic missile defence systems and of NASA's Apollo both being Nazi themed, is fact. So too is that of Hitler's Nazi-sponsored Volkswagen Beetle becoming one of America's best-selling cars of all time. Such facts seem to prove the point for any offended reader who needs reminding of reality. Even the VW Beetle story is wrapped in intrigue because, although a Nazi-sponsored concept, there is evidence that its design was reputedly, partly related to the work of a Jew named Josef Ganz, rather than 'just' F. Porsche. Being Jewish, Ganz's role was airbrushed out of the story by the Nazi PR machine and only recently revealed in a new historical work by Paul Schilperood.[17]

The Science of Silesia

From aerodynamics, rocket research, high-altitude medical knowledge and pressurised airliner cabins, to weaponry, sub-orbital and space travel, electronics, and to human body transplants, and even to anti-malarial drugs, the science of Silesia, the brilliance of Bavarian and Bohemian research, amid what became Germany and German science as a whole, have an amazing, yet for so long, politically incorrect and, denied tale to tell. Throw in the DNA 'strain' of technical people found in the demographics of social science and IQ within northern Europe – France, Italy, Poland, Great Britain and Sweden – in the early aviation era and a swathe of central European technical mindset amid a certain confluence of aeronautical history becomes obvious.

Many people have become addicted to the secrets of the all-wing device and its utterly pure aerodynamics, its supreme act of levitation. We should note the words of the all-wing tailless proponent, B.S. Shenstone, who wrote as early as 1940:

'Ideally, one day there will be no tails at all. The tail, an anachronistic swollen thumb getting in the way and a constant reminder of our present primitive methods of balance, will drop off one day.'[18]

What did *Flight* magazine say in its lead editorial, on 9 January 1947, of the flying wing in the immediate post-Second World War and the effects of seized German science permeating British and American aviation? The words speak volumes and prove the point:

'Someday the flying wing will emerge as the accepted form of a passenger airliner.'[19]

In the forced interregnum that followed such a statement, there was a void, yet now, the age of the all-wing and tailless aerial device is finally upon us – well over one hundred years after it was invented and over seventy years since *Flight* made such a bold statement. Without the research that gave us the swept, all-wing planform, supersonic flight and space flight would not have been developed. In the all-wing's story a secret history is revealed.

Chapter Two

Pioneers

From All-Wing and Monoplane to Biplane – a Curious Reversal of Intelligence

When we look at the Wright brothers' aircraft and also at the corollary that became the biplane devices of the early era circa 1910 and the First World War 1914–1918, it looks as though aviation developed in a series of steps that led to the monoplanes of the early 1930s. The apparent history is that aircraft design slowly evolved from early aviation, through to the biplane era, and then beyond into the 1930s, monoplane advances that in turn, led to today's technology. This accepted, or received, version of the story is an untruth, an academic manipulation. It is in fact a gross error, because monoplane design and its flight happened *first*. Monoplane and all-wing design was actually researched between 1850–1910. As a result, monoplane design, offering a massive advance in speed-record breaking, was achieved in 1912 in France, in the form of the Deperdussin airframe. This was just four years after the British had finally staggered into the air upon the wings of a foreign machine (a Voisin).[1]

The feint of the biplane concept hides how a massive monoplane and all-wing advance that early aviation gave birth to, was discarded in submission to a new fashion – that of the biplane – a fashion that became a 'faith'. It was a 'biplane-ism' whose preachers and prescribers ruled supreme and decried the alternative viewpoint. How familiar such behaviours in history must seem across so many arenas. Were the monoplane and all-wing men, the Tyndales of their day, fighting off a more powerful doctrine? We can only wonder.

Man's Early Flight

In the beginnings of aircraft design, 1800–1890, the monoplane configuration was the dominant design choice. Much design was also curved and more was all-wing – being devoid of fuselages and tail fins. Biplanes were in the main an experimental condition that looked old before they were new. The early pioneer designs of the monoplane were remarkably different from the biplanes that would come to pass and fight the world's first aerial battles in the First World War.

Accepted history has it that by getting rid of biplane wings, struts, wires, and fabric coverings, aviation evolved from the biplanes that contained those elements, to the smoother monoplane. In plain English, this is a lie, because long before the process as perceived occurred, there was a pre-biplane era of monoplanes, flying wings (all-wings) and designs devoid of the struts, wires and rough skin surfaces that framed the biplane era. It is as if history has been reversed and then re-spun.

Before the first so-called 'Great War' of the First World War, in a curious and often unreferenced moment, aviation went straight and level. Lines and angles ruled in a strange paradox of a so-called 'step forwards' into box kite and plank shaped wing planforms – yet actually into a backwards world of drag-inducing biplane features. There came about a fetish for fuselages, wires, bracing, woodwork, thick wings and huge tail fins that literally stuck out like sore thumbs. Adding such drag-inducing features became a very odd fashion in the world of already known and understood smoothed-over and faired-in monoplane and all-wing aerodynamics. A conceit of the biplane consensus overwhelmed the actuality of opposing evidence. It was as if the future was denied. But there was no decline in British aviation as a result of denying the monoplane or all-wing, indeed, British aviation was built upon the myriad of companies that emerged from the Edwardian era and which lasted until government imposed rationalisation in the 1960s.

So theories of a declining or dying aviation industry were wrong (the British motor industry provides no parallels, despite suggestions of such), but the expansion of aviation masked a reality of a reversal in knowledge, a period when the biplane took over in its draught of self-induced turbulence and trailing vortices. So much then for an aerodynamic art supposedly designed to reduce drag and *not* add to it with extra adornments and excrescences as promulgated by the biplane and its proponents.

Surely, no open-minded researcher could deny that British and French aviation worlds of the Edwardian, early 1900s, era, were locked into a torpor of conceit. From such arrogance stemmed the establishment of the biplane age and the denial of advanced aerodynamics for two decades by the powers of a prescribed 'establishment' view. Learned men and learned societies abandoned the radical monoplane and all-wing thoughts of the early aeronautical designers and, for a number of reasons, became the zealots of a box kite, biplane design ethos, that is often cited as having cost aviation over twenty years of learning and design development. Yet, by 1935, the previously discarded monoplane and all-wing and swept-wing design trend was to be hailed as a giant 'new' discovery that opened the doors to the high-speed age. It was, we are told, achieved by a step by step evolutionary process from the biplane era.

This is inaccurate, and can be proven so by analysis of the facts. A great historical 'con' seems to have taken place. Something was definitely missing, and two decades of time for advancement, lost.

Ironically, as the British lay in a sea of assumptions after winning the First World War, it was the 'defeated' Germans who used the applied rules of the *Treaty of Versailles* to create the massive aerodynamic advance of the German sailplane (segelflug) era of the early 1930s. This led to the German superiority in powered airframe, wing and airframe design in the Second World War. The irony should not be ignored, not least as such technology got man to the moon, and beyond the sound barrier. And could the First World War have been ended in half the time if one side had used the monoplane and all-wing technology that existed to build a fleet of fast fighters to win the aerial war? Could the same scenario be applied to the Second World War? Was it only Hitler's deranged decision-making and policy that stopped the Germans deploying such a trick?

This scenario may not sound as unlikely as the reader may think. If minds had been open to what had just been dismissed in aircraft design, the aerial war of 1914–1918 may have been very different. But the attitudes of the day prevailed; biplanes were the thing and, just in case they were not, parachutes were banned in case of any lack of moral fibre (known as 'LMF') that might manifest upon a pilot as he burned, blinded, as his skin was seared from his bones. We should not forget that the idea of the tank was initially resisted because it would affect and change existing infantry practices. Change, it seems, has always been resisted by the forces of perceived wisdom. But with the monoplane-biplane argument, it is not even a case of 'doing what we have always done', as monoplanes came *first*. The biplane was the cuckoo in the pre-existing nest, but few realise it.

During the Second World War, the Allies were in a desperate race to keep up with German advanced technology. It was a close-run thing. Surely then, this proves that had the same argument about one side having superior technology in the Second World War, existed in the First World War, a similar dynamic could have applied? The intended narrative of aviation history is to portray that steps were taken to evolve biplane design (perhaps framed by monoplane racing developments as epitomised by the various types designed for the Schneider Trophy series of the 1920s) into the 1930s monoplane advance. Racing trends might seep into normal design applications – slowly and by honing known-knowns – as prescribed by learned men. Yet this was a ruse, a feint of denied, prior knowledge.

As for privateers and maverick men such as Schneider victor, R.J. Mitchell, he only became a hero when he stunned the world with a design that the establishment could not ignore, or do so at its peril. Then, the maverick was reframed as the darling genius of the establishment. Mitchell was a genius, but he was not 'posh'. If his privately designed Spitfire had not been a revolution, a gateway to the future, and a war-winner, he would have been sidelined by the system and consigned to history as an 'eccentric'. 'Thinking outside the box', to use an apt but clichéd phrase, was, in 1935, only allowed if you proved (against huge odds) that you were correct in your calculations. R.J. Mitchell did indeed think outside the establishment's box and they castigated him for it – they even tried to interfere with his Spitfire and make it more like a monoplaned-biplane derivative. A bigger tail and thicker wings were advised by the learned men who thought they knew everything, but did not. Thankfully, Mitchell and his 'dream team' of designers and engineers including Clifton, Faddy, Fear, Fenner, Smith, Shenstone and Shirvall, were strong, and Supermarine was solvent enough to fight off the attack of established aviation practice and the learned men.[2]

Yet the reality, before all that took place, is that the great biplanes, circa 1910–1920, were that strange step backwards in comparison to the shapes aircraft designers created before this era. There is a large, gaping hole in the history of aerodynamic learning.

In the Beginning – Cayley and a Precursor

Of curious note, in this earlier era of aerial devices and aeronautics, the monoplane ideas of Sir George Cayley's early drawings of the early nineteenth century were to be usurped by his biplane configuration designs. What caused this change we do not know, but Cayley may have adapted his ideas from the semi-monoplane or 'convertiplane' works of the unknown Englishman, Robert Taylor.[3]

Cayley died in 1857 – after years of aerial experimentation and thought. Cayley drew helicopter ideas with elliptical blades and, of great note, sketched aeroplanes of monoplane and almost all-wing, fuselage-less configurations. In 1799, Cayley had designed a podded, triangular tailed, monoplane machine to create a 'fixed-wing' definition of configuration of single-wing design and of mainplane and tailplane layout. He went on to define ideas for heavier-than-air flight using winged devices (as opposed to dirigibles).

Cayley's 1852 fixed-wing glider design had inherent longitudinal and lateral stability and a cruciform tail. Of principal note, the machines had a monoplane of swept, curved, all-wing planform – Cayley had devised aerodynamic pitch control ideas, a tail-fin effect, and flew model gliders as early as 1804. These and other aerodynamic researches by Cayley were published in various articles; of note, Cayley wrote 'On Aerial Navigation' in 1809, published in *Nicholson's Journal*. Yet even the now esteemed Royal Aeronautical Society (RAeS), which began its existence in the 1860s, ignored Cayley's claims and articles. Cayley's first monoplane model glider that actually flew, was in 1804 and his all-wing glider design was featured as a cited 'Governable Parachute' in the 25 September 1852 edition of *Modern Mechanics' Museum, Register, Journal, and Gazette*. Therein, Cayley's device was framed (with discussion by the editor J.C. Robertson) of its trimming and control surface devices, yet it was ignored by the establishment.

Like many pathfinders and polymaths, was Cayley pigeonholed by the arrogance of society and its blinkered perceived wisdoms of certainty?

The French were the other main aeronauts and the fact that Leonardo da Vinci (at the invitation of King François I of France), with his collection of drawings and model 'cars', 'aircraft' and other devices, had resided at the Manoir of the Chateau du Clos-Lucé in Amboise, of the region of the rivers of the Eure et Loir (amid what later became the 'Loire') from 1516, may have benefited the later, early French aeronautical researchers. The act of Cayley's researches being translated into French for an 1850s audience of Parisian inventors cannot have been insignificant either. Da Vinci turned up at Le Clos-Lucé on a donkey, with the 'Mona Lisa' and his designs for machines rolled up in canvas and strapped to the side of the beast. Da Vinci's last years of his life were in the Loire, there he was '*Premier Peinture, Architecte, et Mécanicien du Roi*' – or first painter, architect and engineer to the King (which is why the 'Mona Lisa' is in a French, not Italian, resting place). By the 1800s, it was but a leap of learning that led to the establishment in Paris of the likes of the *École Nationale Supiéure de l'Aéronautique et de Construction Mecanique* – the '*Sup'aéro*' – where advanced design manifested and latterly even gave us the essence of Citroën.

Apart from highlights like actual flight-tested airframes including Deperdussin's *Monocoque* monoplane, Levavasseur's *Monobloc*, even perhaps Esnault-Pelterie's *REP.2*, set alongside the ideas of monoplane themes of Bleriot and Fokker, it seems that a great, square-edged, plank-winged, wire-braced biplane era manifested after a period of monoplane, all-wing and sleek design evolution. This biplane 'movement', with all the resultant increases in aerodynamic drag and decreases in speed, strength, and lifting ability that it created, is the great conundrum of the history of aviation. It is a period and an effect that delayed development and, even today's achievements. Aviation 'lost' twenty years, and not to an untried or untested idea, but to an idea that was tested and flown. Few have ever asked why?

Deperdussin's *Monocoque* – the Future Thrown Away?

Armand Deperdussin's 1912 monoplane – the *Monocoque* – was surely an early signal of the future, for it was the first true self-supporting monocoque fuselage body and one that was smoothly skinned and curved – ellipsoid and parabolic. It was also monoplane amid a sky of biplanes and devoid of the addenda of the fashion of the moment. Here in the Deperdussin, designed by Ruchonnet, with Bechereau as engineer, we saw a device that made the biplanes of wire and paper look like antediluvian dinosaurs from a long lost era. Yet these other biplane craft were designed during the same period, from 1908 to 1912. In late 1912, beside them

Deperdussin's *Monocoque.*

came the utterly revolutionary Deperdussin *Monocoque* – as if it had landed from a future not yet known. Only Penaud's all-wing design had been more shocking.

The Deperdussin *Monocoque* was the first 'designer' style machine to reduce drag and raise speed. The fuselage was made from tulip wood that was steamed, moulded and joined together in a composite, with an outer smooth covering of fine grained fabric. Like many, later, fast machines, the Deperdussin had a small-wing area and a higher wing loading – which did little for its low speed characteristics – but who cared after it taken ten speed records and topped nearly 130 mph. The pilot sat low in the body to reduce external cockpit area, and although wire bracing could not be dispensed with, the rotary engine was faired-in and a large spinner added to the front of the prop as an aerodynamic point of entry. The machine even spawned a float-plane version.

For the French, 1913 became the 'Glorieuse Annee', not least because the Deperdussin, powered by a totally enclosed Gnome rotary engine of 160 bhp output, was a speed-shattering event. With the airframe's smoothness and single-wing, a world-record breaking speed of 126.67mph (201km/h) was achieved at the Reims air race. The Deperdussin set a dozen world speed records and could cruise at 90mph, whereas most aircraft of that year could only manage 50–60mph. The performance of the Deperdussin was unheard of and should have been a launching point for technological advance. Why it and its advance were denied by the forces of the establishment is a salutary lesson in human behaviour.

This aircraft was not all-wing – but it *was* a a broad chord, smoothly skinned, advanced concept of monoplane, monocoque design with excellent wing strength levels and much lower drag – seen amid a world of non-monocoque, torsionally flimsy fuselages covered in doped fabric and paper and held aloft by wings of struts and wire braced biplane design. These ancient aircraft were shaped like flying sheds, or bewinged bath tubs. The Deperdussin was of a completely new sleekness. Was it the Spitfire of its day?

And yet, within three years, the future of smooth, strong, aerodynamic monoplane aircraft design, as framed by the Deperdussin, was thrown away; destroyed and denied in a strange and bizarre takeover of aircraft design by the might of the learned men and their societies and their companies. Although highly successful, the *Monocoque* fell victim to the 'fear' factor created around the monoplane after a series of accidents that were the result of pilot or training error, as opposed to design failure. Biplanes were apparently more stable and, with more wing area, had lower wing loadings, they were slower too – an advantage it seemed.

The biplane came from assumptions that were deductive in their research thinking, the all-wing might be said to be inductive, or disruptively abductive in its thought – something far too much for Edwardian Britain to accept where men of certainties knew what they knew and anything else was heresy.

From 1913–1915, with a couple of exceptions, the monoplane was dead. Even Anthony H.G. Fokker, designer of the 1912 *Spin (*Spider), a swept-wing type monoplane, gave up on monoplanes for years afterwards. The monoplane 'advance' was thrown away as the dinosaur biplane fashion swamped aviation's mindset. Yet by late 1916, the combat biplanes of the First World War were no longer stable, they had been redesigned into short span, 'flickable', highly manoeuvrable devices with clipped and short fuselages. The combination of such design traits made machines that had lethal spin and spin-recovery characteristics. Intriguingly, the Fokker *Eindecker* monoplane of 1915 did deliver an advance, yet its design superiority was masked by its innovative through-the-propeller machine-gun firing ability. This was itself a response to the early French attempt at such a technique that was mounted on a Morane-Saulnier monoplane used by the Royal Flying Corps.

We can prove to ourselves that the denial of the monoplane at this time was wrong, because nearly twenty years later, guess what? The 1930s dawned and the 'advance' of the monoplane was announced. Suddenly the future was here. It was as if the monoplane past and Deperdussin's machine, Fokker's *Eindecker,* or Dunne's all-wings, had never occurred, blanked out by a higher power. Overnight, circa 1935 fashion and the powers that be deemed that the weak-structured, high-drag days of the biplane were over! Science had 'created' the monoplane and the learned men and their societies and their great aviation companies, rushed to create monoplanes.

What then of the wasted two-decades beforehand? Imagine how advanced aircraft design would have been by 1930 if the biplane era had been consigned to the dustbin of design history in 1913, as it should have been. How far further ahead could monoplane inspired designs have been? How much further ahead would aircraft design have been if the monoplane of 1913 had been the starting point, instead of 1935?

Bipolar British Biplanism

We can blame the British mindset, or the British 'conservative' approach to many things, for the backwards era of the biplane and its dominance from 1915–1930. Despite the research papers and the learned societies, the British had not flown a powered craft, nor a craft of their own design. There were howls of protest in the media and upper echelons of society. On 1 December 1908, J. T. Moore-Brabazon made the first powered flight by a British subject, amazingly, given the British 'empire' mindset; he had to do it in a French aircraft, designed and built by Eugene Gabriel Voisin, from Issy les Moulineux, Paris.[4]

It was perhaps this utter national humiliation that led to the race for instantly achievable goals; the stable, the known-knowns or perceived wisdom, the easy-to-glue together biplane and its subsequent dominant era. Yet, even in 1929, two decades later, the British preferred to develop existing designs on a step by step basis. This is proven in the existence of the Gloster Gladiator biplane and its design. Was this not a 'tweaked' 1915 biplane with the rough edges smoothed off by two decades of consideration of how to improve the known, rather than dare to design something new?

Even the Hawker Hurricane monoplane was created with a mindset that took a biplane and simply removed the wings and replaced them with a monoplane wing, yet retained the biplane tail fin, chassis construction and fabric/canvas covering. It would take German design works, and the not unrelated British Spitfire, to revolutionise the monocoque-built, advanced aerodynamic wing and body design to 'launch' the high-speed monoplane era in the late-1930s. From that stemmed the likes of the P-51 Mustang, and a host of high-powered radial and in-line powered monoplane fighters and coupé class aircraft that soon became jet-powered, swept-wing iterations of the same concept.

Why was it then, that in late 1912, after a rash of biplane and monoplane crashes that brought early aviation's death toll to nearly forty pilots killed, and on the basis of a report written by the monoplane exponent Bleriot that discussed the structural safety of *some* examples of the monoplane that a knee-jerk and overnight reaction from the learned men, their societies and the military they advised, saw the monoplane instantly banned? Was this the perfect opportunity for the biplanists to claim ascendancy? So was stopped – dead in its tracks – the aerodynamic and structural development of the British, French, and American monoplane (with a few of exceptions) – until the 1930s. Biplanes, with their double lifting wings and long bodies and stable main and tailplane configurations, offered low wing loading stability, safety and, slowness. Their braced wings were deemed to be stronger than a monoplane's (even a braced one).

All this was more of fashion than fact and the biplane would soon be turned into a smaller, shorter, unstable combat device for the First World War. Remember, when the British were building giant dinosaurs such as the Handley Page HP 42 biplane – a braced, box kit of an airliner – the Germans were building monoplane Junkers of all-metal monocoque construction. The Germans had flown a Junkers all-wing monoplane before 1930 and were also flying the swept-winged all-wing machines of Lippisch. All this, even after the limits of the *Treaty of Versailles* had been forced upon them – in all its paradoxical effect.

The explanation as to why the move to the biplane dominance was a deliberate event of intellectual retardation lies in several tangents of early aviation history.

Crossed Controls

It cannot be denied that early aviation was divided into two subsets – men (designers) who dreamed up flying machines, yet who had never flown, nor would ever 'fly' or control an aircraft, and other men who would design aircraft, but would actually take to the air and learn to become airmen. Some designers built flying models but were never pilots; some flew models and then did pilot full-sized aircraft.

It is argued by learned men that these 'tribes', these differences, accounted for the problems with defining a control system for early aircraft; and this factor itself created the biplane era – because the stability of the biplane and the work of the Wright brothers led to a defining mechanism of control and control surfaces. We are told that the pioneers failed to realise this, hence the decline of their ideas of monoplane and all-wing design. But can this narrative be wholly accurate? If we note Penaud's stable flying model in its main and tailplane configuration (as copied today), why do we dismiss his all-wing design with its de facto elevons and trailing edge dampers that reflect later delta and all-wing control surface technology? It cannot be denied that there were talented men, circa 1880, whose aeronautical ideas were, by even liberal analysis, 'off the wall'. Their machines would never fly, yet among the layers of men and their ideas, can it all come down to dismissing a designer or a design because the designer had not flown?

Wilbur and Orville Wright may have made the first practical 'flights' (but not initially in the latter sense of powered take-off and landing), but can it be said, as it is by some, that they were the world's first to master gliding flight? Had they not been inspired by Lilienthal – whose exploits they were fully aware of?[5] At the altar of their development of control systems, the Wrights and their aircraft type – that of a box kite biplane (yet notably of canard layout) – defined the era 1902–1908.

The Wrights were clever, far more than the bicycle tinkerers so often portrayed, and they learned to fly their non-powered gliding machines – not something all the pioneers did. Thus they understood the issues of actual flight far better than a non-pilot designer. Was this the root of their control system ideas? Reaction to the Wrights' ideas in Europe was a bizarre rejection, a stupor, and then a rush to redefine their designs and stability and control issues.

The twisting of wing surfaces, with resultant aerodynamic effect, became framed by the misnomer of 'warping' of the wing. But this stemmed from early works and Octave Chanute's thoughts. Upon such narratives many arguments about flight have been made. But whatever the nuances, the Wright brothers knew about lift and centres of aerodynamic pressure; this led to their variable wing positioning idea and its resultant directional effects upon the airframe in flight. Clearly, the Wrights' had engineering brains that could not only learn by rote, but also to think laterally and create new solutions devoid of past prejudices. However, paradoxically, the Wrights choice of the biplane can only have come from Chanute (with whom they liaised), but he and Cayley and Stringfellow, had all previously dabbled in monoplane and all-wing layouts before adopting the easier to solve and control, biplane configuration of box kite stability.

For the Wrights, Lilienthal's influence was strong and admitted, yet they ignored his monoplane, all-wing planform layouts, and went with the canard biplane. Like Pilcher, Lilienthal was killed trying to solve the problems of control. Of vital significance was the fact that the Wrights designed stability-biased biplane wings, which were actually unstable in that, unlike a test model, they required a pilot to intervene and command and control the airframe via control surface inputs.

By altering the angle of incidence to each wing respectively, as opposing positive and negative values, the Wrights laid the foundation for roll control and aileron evolution. Early Wright gliders had no horizontal tail surfaces, and used a vertical rudder similar to a boat. By late 1902, the Wrights were tuning, or slaving, their rudder and vertical tail fin designs to their wing-warping mechanisms. So the two aerodynamic surfaces did not fight each other, or offer opposing aerodynamic forces, the Wrights perfected a slaved, turn and bank control application. This was their stepping stone and the basis of their early patents. However, further flight and pilot skills developments saw them disconnect these slaved mechanisms, which allowed great turn and bank control and lessened the risk of an in-turn stall due to the turn being tightened too much.

Interestingly, the Wrights' choice of canard wing, which stalls before the main wing and therefore is protective to the main wing and much safer, did not become a fashion and was abandoned by aviation at this time – only to resurface decades later. How many death stalls would have been prevented if the fashion of the establishment had let the canard design rule? How odd that a safety device was thrown away at a time when safety was cited as the biplane's raison d'etre.

As a result of the American Government's refusal to believe what the Wrights had achieved by 1905, the US administration turned down the brothers' application for the US to adopt their craft for the national good. Disgusted, the Wrights offered their machines to the British, who, despite having one visionary in its ranks (Col. J.E. Capper), spent so long denying and procrastinating that they took years to turn the Wrights down. The French embraced the Wrights, and the brothers enjoyed a residence in Paris in 1908 where they fully explained their ideas.[6]

Were the Wrights the first true powered flight pioneers? We have to accept that they were, but there are other, earlier claims. Until other evidence is defined and accepted, the Wrights and their box kite biplanism, have it.

Prior to 1900, Otto Lilienthal had amassed many more piloted gliding hours than most people; but by 1907, the Wrights had amassed more piloted gliding hours than anyone (over 1,000 hours between them). Perhaps this explained why the French and the English – both with very little actual piloting experience, took so long to grasp the issues of flight controls and controlled powered flight. They wasted years before grasping the idea, yet 1908 would be a defining year in French aviation. The French claimed to have invented aviation and, here were two American brothers wiping French (and other) egos on the floor with their machines. Yet, perversely, it was during their time in France that the Wrights would see their first appreciations of the true monoplane types that littered the scandal of French aerodynamic debate and seemingly wilful inaction.

The Blinkers of Perception

Around 1905, the French and the British were undoubtedly trapped in their respective torpors of conceit. They appear to simply have refused to believe that the Wrights had solved the issues, and for the French (initially) the answer was to copy them, but to adapt ideas. So became established another tangent of the rush to the biplane period and the reverse effect of a retardation in aerodynamic design. Once again, the quest for inherent trimmed stability swept aside anything risky or advanced. Indeed the Wrights' advanced control systems, canard wing, and piloting demands in a less stable airframe, were all eschewed by the French and the British learned men and their relevant societies.

The likes of Ernest Archdeacon and, of singular note, Ferdinand Ferber, modified and adapted their own *and* the Wrights' ideas and configurations, notably dismissing the canard layout and creating a stable, main-wing, tail-wing and finned configuration of biplane stability. So was set, aircraft design for the next twenty years.

Quite why or how the likes of the smooth, advanced prophecy of the Bleriot monoplane *No. VII* of 1907, or the Esnault-Pelterie *REP.2* of the same year and an almost all-wing monoplane, or the Deperdussin *Monocoque* monoplane of 1912, were allowed to be considered and built prior to being dismissed, illustrated the power of fixed minds and perceived wisdom amongst the learned men of Paris. It was all a very strange paradox, for true advanced design had existed in French aviation minds circa 1880. Yet, by 1902, a long delay and a descent into stagnation and dispute had manifested for several years. It would take Santos-Dumont, Hubert Latham, and Henri Farman to eventually stir things up in 1909.

The 'Wright effect' also motivated German scientists in the post-Lilienthal period with, in 1904–1910, Prandtl and Junkers leading the way, notably in wind tunnel research and wing theory analysis. Such finite wing theory work laid the foundations for German research advancement. The French and the British abandoned the Wrights' idea of deliberate instability and complex flight controls, to create a distinct box kite, biplane future. Samuel Cody may have flown a box kite glider type in Britain as early as 1905, but it would be 1908 before a British man took to the air in powered flight in a French machine.

An illustrative paradox of the era comes from the supplier of that machine, Gabriel Voisin, who was a genius of automotive invention; his cars became highly advanced in terms of drivetrain, structure and - significantly – aerodynamics. Yet his aircraft were ungainly box kite devices that contained only mild experimentation. However, across the French border in Germany, the institutes of Göttingen/Darmstadt and Stuttgart were pursuing a different route that would lead to giant airships and then onwards to advanced wing design. One of the few places in Europe where early monoplane powered aircraft were continued with, in development terms, was Germany. The first patent for a researched, viable aerodynamic all-wing type of machine was that of the Junkers Patent Application of 1 February 1910, which stated: 'Aeroplane consisting of one wing, which would house all components, engines, crew, passengers, fuel and framework.' Junker's Patent No. 253 788 KL 77H Gruppe 5 was granted on 14 November 1912.

Despite knowledge such as Deperdussin's *Monocoque* and Dunne's iteration of a swept-wing, all-wing machine and a huge advance in wing and control surface design, it seems that the First World War was deliberately fought upon the wings of consciously created, slow, 'agricultural' biplanes that were easily and quickly built with great economy by major companies who resisted investment in new technology on the grounds of cost, amid a denial of the advantages of the monoplane.

We might ask why one side of the wartime opponents did not simply 'copy' the high-speed Deperdussin and win the aerial war in much quicker time? We might ask why, in the 1920s, the likes of R.J. Mitchell's monoplane designs for the Schneider Trophy series were limited solely to competitive racing craft and not deemed a suitable design basis for other aircraft? We might remember that this attitude still persisted when Great Britain was preening itself over the 1930 achievement of the Handley Page HP 42 biplane airliner, yet the Americans were readying the sleek, monoplane Douglas DC-2 and its progeny the DC-3. At the Wasserkuppe, Lippisch was test flying an all-wing delta device.

The British Edwardian era 'attitude' and the denial of the French Deperdussin's advances can only be linked. The thought of a 'foreign' design ruling and advancing aircraft design was 'not on old boy'.

After the First World War, the Germans had been constrained by the *Treaty of Versailles* of 1919 and allowed only to glide. So, they could be ignored, could they not? Such were the attitudes of the time. As we now know, the Germans and their enforced 'gliding only' aerial existence soon jumped ahead to produce not only the new revolution in glider and wing design, but all the benefits that flowed to powered flight design. To achieve this, the Germans had to throw off their own pre-conceived ideas and think fresh thoughts, to innovate without prejudice, which surely was something the British were utterly incapable of doing in 1920.

Across the Atlantic, by 1929 the Americans had thrown off their own 'locked-in' design research psychology and, like the earlier Wright brothers, opened their minds to new thoughts, new advances in airframe and wing design. NACA took to publishing European research – principally German research (much of which emanated from the advanced glider design aerodynamics) as translated by NACA *Memorandum*. The Americans changed their attitudes in the late 1920s. Proof of this comes from the comments of the Spitfire's aerodynamicist, the Canadian Beverley Shenstone.

Shenstone toured America in June 1934 with a Vickers team of engineer designers. There they visited NACA and its laboratories and went to Sikorsky, Lockheed, Martin, and the major aviation entities of the lower Los Angeles area – notably Douglas. Of principal note, it was at NACA that Shenstone encountered the new NACA ultra-thin 2200 series of aerofoil (2200-specifying two per cent camber at twenty per cent chord) that he latterly applied to the Supermarine Spitfire. This was at the time that the British 'attitude' was in denial about the benefits of thin wings and forced the massive Clark Y section aerofoil on to the Hawker Hurricane in another example of how the British wanted to refine what they knew and dared not try or risk anything fresh, or, as they might have termed it – 'eccentric' or 'too risky'.

While he was in Los Angeles, Shenstone also visited the somewhat interesting personality construct that was Theodore von Kármán, then based at the Douglas Company and Caltech. There, Shenstone encountered a man who had just lectured on wing fillet design in Paris and was exploring this new feature of drag-reducing technology. Yet von Kármán brought ideology and immovable opinions about the benefits of his wind tunnels to his assessments and some thought his thinking was blinkered as a consequence, but the fact was he *had* been Prandtl's pupil.

As a result of being immersed in this new American drive for aerodynamic advance, this new open-minded attitude, Shenstone not only came away with ideas that further enhanced the learning of his prior 1929–1931 years in Germany, he also grasped what he could add to the revolutionary advance that was the monocoque Spitfire. Returning to Great Britain and what we can only call a generalised British attitude of superiority, Shenstone the internationalist Canadian, was moved to write the following words in an internal Vickers-Supermarine memo:

> 'The Americans are more daring than we are, or is it that their officialdom is more broad-minded than ours? Whatever it is we should do something about it.'[7]

We might ponder what Shenstone, one of the co-designers of R.J. Mitchell's monoplane of the century that was the Supermarine Spitfire, would have thought about the design of, let alone the denial and destruction of, the earlier Deperdussin *Monocoque*?

So were framed the rules, the constraints and the conditions that led to the imbalance, and to the weak position that Britain found itself in circa 1936, when, even with the Spitfire on hand, government prevaricated about ordering production of such frighteningly new technology. At least by this time, a few of the learned men and their societies had finally got the message.

Stepping Back to Understand an Ethos, a Denial and a 'Lost' Advance of the Future

Long before the Spitfire, before the Wrights, before aviation's path was defined, a precursor era existed. The startling fact was that before the bizarre and contradictory step backwards into biplane design, the dreams of early aircraft designers were not just of monoplane configuration but, in many cases, of all-wing and tailless design. We need to go back to these roots, this early genesis of aerodynamic design, to identify the lost or discarded knowledge and to understand the might of the box kite and biplane era that manifested as a deliberate altering of the course of aviation's evolution.

It seems incredible that from circa 1840–1900 a great era of monoplane, all-wing design should have manifested, only for it to be set aside by a new perceived wisdom of ungainly orthodoxy that stifled advanced aerodynamic design back into a 'stone-age' of wire, paper, wood and 'stringbag' biplane fashion – a fashion that pertained for many years at the hands of the claimed certainties of learned men, and which may have set back aircraft design by a degree only now realised as we finally enter the all-wing era.

Surely man's first flight experiments were through the all-wing design of the kite? As the Greeks, the Romans, and the Chinese, were kite-flying; others were clubbing each other with sticks whilst dressed in animal skins. Yet, by the mid-1300s, Europeans were experimenting with designs for flying machines. Windmills – or their blades – would soon also manifest as all-wing devices in the action of their aerodynamics. Windmill blade or wing design, with its focus on chord, aerodynamic centres and tip characteristics, was to provide an intriguing Middle Ages mix to the development of wings for flying devices.

Even before Leonardo da Vinci's late 1480s drawings of parachutes, helicopters and flying devices, an evidence trail of airborne or lift-developing devices is apparent. Walter de Milemete's manuscript of 1326 clearly illustrates not just an all-wing kite, but even a finned-bomb being carried beneath it.[8]

The year 1420 saw an illustration of a bird attached to some kind of rocket device. Soon afterwards, the designs of Kazimierz Siemienowicz, in Lithuania/Poland, circa 1575, manifest as evidence of triangular or delta-type wing surfaces, but what of ancient Chinese and Mayan designs for aircraft with delta and ellipsoidal wings circa 2000 BC? How did that happen? What of the Swedish Emmanuel Swedenborg and his all-wing canopy of 1714? Was this too, an early flight of fancy, or a stepping stone to all-wing thinking?

Fast-forward to 1749 and the kite designs of Alexander Wilson, thence to Bauer's all-wing monoplane with suggested rocket power of 1764, and a clear route is obvious. This was surely reinforced by Karl Friedrich Meerwein's elliptical all-wing glider-ornithopter of 1781[9] and a pattern becomes evident – a pattern of monoplane, all-wing experimentation into the act of levitation. Of interest, Meerwein had calculated his wing-loading for a self-supporting, human carrying glider. Therein, the pilot was in the prone position and the suggestion of a flap-type wing panel is evident in his papers. Cayley's sketches of 1799 clearly demonstrate an all-wing planform design for a fixed-wing type, but perhaps we can cite William S. Henson's monoplane delta-tailed, flying machine device of 1842 as the real moment of gear change towards a powered, mono-winged fuselage-less design, devoid of a tail moment-arm, and fore-body?[10]

Of note, in 1815, Cayley had shaped the first-ever tandem monoplane and then published a paper setting out an aerodynamic theory of flight in 1852[11] describing a fixed-wing glider, yet this research was ignored by the soon to be established arbiters of received thinking in aeronautics.

Further evidence of all-wing design – devoid of a fuselage – can be found in the curious tandem monoplane of Thomas Walker, the English artist, who, in 1831, 'designed' a fixed-wing tandem winged monoplane device that was 'powered' by a pilot who activated a muscle-powered 'flapper' panel that created lift and thrust action over a wing surface. The wings had crescent shaped, semi swept leading edges and wingtips. It might have looked bizarre as a form of 'ornithopter', but deep within such thinking there lay science that was to be manifested many decades later. Walker's 'powered' wing lift idea and his tandem monoplane may be reflected in later themes – notably of Bleriot.

In the early-1960s, the British, Bristol 188 supersonic research aircraft (derived from the Avro 730 studies) used a near-identical wing planform as Walker's 1831 monoplane and the resemblance to his design was uncanny across 120 years.

Otto Lilienthal – Germany's First All-Wing Pioneer

A glider pilot, or hang-glider pilot and proponent, Lilienthal achieved not just flight, but the thinking behind controlled flight and the control devices that might achieve it. He can therefore be said to have been a precursor influence upon the Wrights – who were evidentially aware of Lilienthal's efforts via publication.

Lilienthal had been convinced that powered flight would come from a 'flapping' or ornithopter type of propulsive effect and his 1899 book was entitled *Der Vogelflug als Grundlage der Fliegekunst* (Bird Flight as the Basis of Aviation). Lilienthal's glider designs were all-wing, monoplane and ellipsoid (he also designed two biplane versions of such forms). From 1891 to 1896 he made many flights (over 2,000) in his designs and even had an artificial gliding slope built from a constructed hill near Berlin. He developed 'weight-shift' control techniques as he 'hung' unrestrained from what was a de facto hang-glider.

Despite his death in a glider on 9 August 1896, Lilienthal had predicted controlled flight and thought of powered flight. The Scot, Percy Pilcher, certainly carried on the Lilienthal mantle of monoplane and all-wing thinking. Pilcher too had aimed to fit an engine to his glider, but he also died before he could do so.

Lilienthal had drawn inspiration from a number of sources, including the often ignored all-wing researcher that he consulted in Professor Friedrich Ahlborn. Ahlborn published his *Uber die Stabilitat der Drachenflieger* (Above the Stability of Dragonflies) in 1897, a year after Lilienthal's death, but from the professor's studies into the aerodynamics of flight and his close study of the *Alsomitra Zanonia Macrocarpa* seed, there had resulted his ideas for creating an all-wing planform with added stability – through adding central section mid-span length to the planform. The Zanonia seed also had an in-built wing twist – the essential ingredient of aerodynamic 'washout' that would soon become vital in wing design. Lilienthal, Ettrich and Wels, took on board Ahlborn's observations and ideas to great effect. Ahlborn's all-wing monoplane wing research was also noted by J.W. Dunne in England.

At the time of Lilienthal, Nikolai E. Zhukovskii (latterly known as Joukowsky) was the Russian expert studying hydro and aerodynamic flows and forms. He was taken with the aerodynamic benefits of the elliptical planform and with all-wing devices. In the early 1890s, Zhukovskii travelled to Berlin to observe Lilienthal's own monoplane, all-wing designs and purchased a Lilienthal glider, which he took back to Moscow. Of note, Tupolev was Zhukovskii's pupil. From this visit to Germany, came the later Zhukovskii-Kutta theorem related to calculating the mathematical expression of wing lift over an aerofoil (Martin W. Kutta having worked on a parallel theory).

Carl Steiger-Kirchofer the Bavarian and a T-tailed Elliptical Device

A long-forgotten, rarely referenced name is that of Carl Steiger-Kirchofer, who was a Bavaria-based artist and inventor with a fascination for engineering. In 1891, he published his thoughts upon birds, their flight and the relationship to that of man's flight. In his book *Vogelflug und Flugmaschine*, Steiger suggested all-wing and elliptical planforms and described experiments in gliding and control surface location and actuation, notably, differential action airbrakes and panels, to which others would later revisit. Steiger's amazing elliptical, fuselage-less and T-tailed 1891 device is a ghostly piece of future vision, yet it would be the 1940s before another German, Hans Multhopp, 'invented' the T-tail for Focke-Wulf.

In such prescient – yet forgotten works of Steiger – do we see another obscured German innovator? Certainly, in his 1891 dated elliptically winged flying machine that possessed T-tail and elliptical horizontal tail surfaces, we see an all-wing, podded device.

It is perhaps only in seeing Steiger's design as a drawing that the truth of how far backwards the biplane era that followed, really was. How much a madness and a crazed reversal of design it was. Observe Steiger's ellipsoid, T-tailed, almost all-wing, clean lined, device and then ponder on the fact that it was offered to aerodynamics in 1891. It looks more like a 1940s, art deco-inspired piece of sculptured biomorphic aerodynamics. Yet, soon after the 1890s, men were bouncing about in biplanes made

Steiger-Kirchofer All-Wing.

of wood, paper and wire. Yet again we should surely ask how and why? What on earth happened?

A French Enclave of All-wing and Monoplane Thinking

Amid the early steps of aviation, ornithopter and helicopter ideas were seeded, but one thing was very clear, early devices, early gliders – including those of Otto Lilienthal – were monoplane all-wing affairs. Lilienthal researched and perfected the ellipsoid or crescent-winged planform in his gliders circa 1888–1896. An early French exponent, Michel Loup, created a bird-like French design for a powered flying machine of 1853 which was all-wing and may have influenced the Penaud and Gauchot design of double-ellipse flying wing device of 1876.

The years 1840–1870 saw a rash of wonderfully prescient monoplane ideas. Soon Jules Verne's amazing visions would influence many Frenchmen – Robert Esnault-Pelterie and André Citroën included. Of Monsieur Du Temple de la Croix's patented all-wing machine? Well that even demonstrated *forward* sweep in the wing's planform.

That Jean-Marie Le Bris designed a glider in 1868 that was utterly ellipsoid in a high-aspect ratio planform – it mimicked the low-wing loading, highlight shape of the Albatross – must have been of note. Of particular interest, Le Bris described movable flying surfaces. Was he another forgotten pioneer of all-wing aviation? Yet the journey from the likes of M.A. Goupil's wonderfully sculpted, organically shaped, low drag, ellipsoid monoplane streamliner (with early ailerons) of 1884

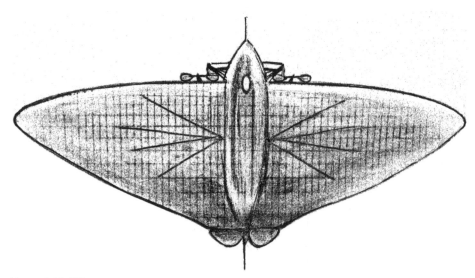

Penaud All-Wing.

– to an age of square winged, braced, fabric covered bathtubs with wings – was a strange backwards-engineered affair.

Goupil's device was a stunning, almost art deco-esque precursor piece of design. In 1883, Goupil wrote a paper on the effects of fuselage shape and area and its interaction with the wing and the corollary of resultant stability. Goupil studied fuselage forms and wing junctions and he even experimented with the design and positioning of what were, effectively, elevons – which he suggested could be slaved to the horizontal tail surfaces in order to create roll axis control – not just pitch control as elevators. Was this the true early attempt at roll axis control?

Goupil's bird-shaped airframe had the canard configuration aileron stub wings mounted low and forwards of the main wing and his test airframe actually lifted two men in a tethered static test into a strong headwind. Latterly, it has been suggested that Goupil's elevons and tail surface actuation might have presaged the Wright system.[12]

The Amazing Alphonse Penaud, a Defining Influence

The work of Alphonse Penaud has already been cited herein, but we cannot ignore him. Penaud's work did become widely known, but was also dismissed by some – those of the 'we know what we know' mindset. Yet he was, without realising it, touching at times upon the separate thoughts of Cayley. Of note, Penaud's ellipsoid test models just beat Lanchester's own thoughts into the air as test models – and Penaud's were *powered*.

Penaud was described by his contemporaries as a 'genius' and he certainly was. Unable to pursue a family-led naval career due to ill-health, he became obsessed with birds, flight, and aerodynamic studies. Penaud was the man who invented the idea of rubber-powered motors – rubber bands twisted up to unleash a torque-effect upon a propulsive mechanical propeller. Thus was born powered-model flight, which children still use today and which formed the basis of early flight testing. Penaud used his rubber band motors to test his model airframe designs; this constituted the first powered model flight testing ability.

Penaud built model helicopters and contra-rotating blades as early as 1870. In 1871, he shaped a *Planophore* model, which was a crescent, part-ellipsoid winged device with a 'tailplane' to create stability in the longitudinal axis. It was a tailplane that was 'all-moving' and the tailplane incidence could be altered. It even had de facto 'winglets', or dihedral tips, to provide stability. A tail-mounted airscrew was included. In such design, did not Penaud presage the form of later conventional aircraft and invent the first rear-engined airframe? This was the first stability-orientated planform and design and was widely exhibited after its launch in Paris, in August 1871, at the *Societe de Navigation Aerienne*. The very stable, rubber-powered model flew the unheard of distance of 131 feet, and did so in eleven seconds.

Having created what would become the standard of mainplane set in front of a tailplane, Penaud conceived a layout that modern aviation copied – and yet was dismissed by the Wright-inspired biplane, box kite configuration era with its canards, wing warping and other differences.

Penaud, like the later aero–auto exponents, Gabriel Voisin and Andre Lefebvre (latterly of Citroën cars fame), worked out locations of centres of aerodynamic pressure and gravity upon his machines.

Yet having created a defining wing layout, Penaud then went all-wing.

Within three years Penaud, with the assistance of engineer Paul Gauchot, abandoned his mainplane/tailplane configuration for a stable aircraft and delivered what we can only describe as the world's most advanced all-wing device. Between 1874 and 1876, Penaud and Gauchot suggested a tractor configuration powered all-wing lifting body as Penaud's Patent No. 111574. The all-wing was not a simple ellipse, but a minor/major chord axis modified double ellipse of asymmetric type, with forward sweep to the trailing tip edges and a smoothly curved, moulded central cockpit glasshouse that avoided offering excess interference drag to the wing's lift pattern and reduced parasitic drag.

Designed to be amphibious, the all-wing machine had dihedral, variable incidence, a form of elevon control surface design, a glass-domed cockpit fairing and, of further note, a single-stick control column device for the pilot that 'mixed' control surface functions in the manner of a modern joystick. Penaud also thought of a rubber and compressed air shock absorbing undercarriage long before the Delpeuch company, the Cowey company (both in 1915), or Messier (1925). A fully instrumented cockpit with a de facto pressure-fed barograph altimeter was also envisaged.

Of huge significance in the all-wing story, and with previous experience researching stability, Penaud's all-wing not only had double elevon type control surfaces, it even had a movable trailing edge 'tab' device on each wing. It was not perhaps an aileron, but more of an inboard tab that could act as a differential air brake to provide rudder-effect steering to the all-wing. Such all-wing stability enhancement – dated 1876 – again underlines Penaud's genius, but it also provides us with a riddle. For, if the cause of aircraft design at this time was stability and a resistance to spinning and stalling – a cause that led Penaud from a traditional configuration to the all-wing – why was his all-wing stability work effectively dismissed, his reputation destroyed and the search for stability stepped back from a monoplane and the all-wing monoplane, to the future of the biplane of box kite, flying plank, wood and paper built inheritance?

The party line of the learned men is that real in-flight inherent stability was not realised until about 1913, when flying bath tub biplanes and 'over-square' biplanes (such as the Royal Aircraft Establishment BE.2) manifested, with a natural balance in roll, yaw, and pitch axis that was deemed to be inherently stable – that is, it would remain flying 'hands-off' if correctly trimmed. But had Penaud achieved this in his 1871 monoplane model? Penaud was not of course the 'establishment', and certainly not the RAE.

The need for stability in-flight had inspired Penaud and others, and not all were just flying models, some were trying to fly and some achieved non-powered flight long beforehand (eg: Lilienthal), so differing issues of stability for model-flight and for full-size piloted flight were understood. A diversion that cost years must have been the wing warping era and within that, the effect of the Wrights and their views on stability and control design. Indeed, was not the Wright canard deliberately *less* stable and very twitchy at the controls? Even a freethinker like Voisin would struggle with the issues, but unlike the Wrights, his aircraft would make 'proper' powered take-offs requiring an act of longitudinal 'rotation', and powered landings that required approach speed and stall management by the pilot. So the first non sled-launched flights were of Voisin – not of Wright.

Although not actually realised in the 'flesh', or in flight, and remaining only as a series of detailed, intricate, mathematically calculated plans, the Penaud all-wing, ellipsoid planform offers us a significant precursor to the works of Zhoukowskii, Prandtl, Junkers, Horten, Shenstone, Hill, Northrop, and others. Of importance was that here, long before the double-ellipsoid planform works of Prandtl and the Spitfire wing of Shenstone, and way ahead of the single ellipse planforms of Baumer, the Gunter brothers, and Heinkel ideas, Penaud designed the world's first, conjoined, double ellipse effect wing planform – in 1876. Such work cannot be underestimated; however primitive later 'experts' may wish to decry it as being.

Attacked for the temerity of his different – and notably – all-wing thoughts, Penaud was soon dead by his own hand after being undermined, denied funding from his learned society friends and decried for his advanced ideas. Buried by 1880, not yet thirty-one, at least he could never be accused of having fixed ideas and of knowing what he knew and not wanting to know anything else.[13]

Other French luminaries in this era included Victor Tatin – author of the defining work, *L'Aerophile*. Tatin had, by 1879, built a monoplane of tractor power layout with a compressed air charge driving a small motor. Of significance, the Tatin design had a symmetrical elliptical monoplane wing and a delta-winged tailplane. Tatin, in the period 1880–1903, defined the monoplane and the tandem monoplane in detail – which had first been hinted at way back in 1831 by the design of Walker.

Tatin was another of the test model flyers who used rubber band power to achieve flight. In France, early tailless glider designs were also proposed by de Sanderval in 1886.

Another all-wing monoplane proponent was Clement Ader, an electrical engineer, and another man who studied birds and their flight very closely. Ader's *Eole* of 1890 was indeed all-wing, but it was too bird-like to fly, and was not a glider but designed as a powered device. A giant bat-formed 15-metre span wing and, of intrigue, steam powered, the *Eole* was more of Jules Verne and less of reality, yet it flew a short hop (50 metres) in a flight test in October 1890. So was Ader's (patented) all-wing machine indeed the first 'aircraft' to power itself off the ground and into the sky under piloted control? Despite this significance, Ader failed to grasp true powered flight with the *Eole* and it became a momentary footnote in flight. Yet once again, a monoplane and all-wing device had successfully flown; and of the biplane, there was yet little sign of its powered flight.

Yet Penaud was *the* early French aeronautical genius, one in a movement perhaps motivated and affected by many socio-geopolitical events (not least the Franco-Prussian war). In Penaud's era, the grand engineering schools of France and Germany were the genesis of an epoch-making era of engineering and design begun in the 1890s. Advances in art, architecture, science, philosophy, medicine, and, above all, in aeronautical and automotive study took place. These great steps into the knowledge of the modern age began in France and Germany, and soon focused in aeronautic terms in central and southern Germany.

By 1902, the French aeronautical movement had descended into its years of argument and inaction. Despite massive resources, the French, just like the British, failed to master powered flight and the control thereof. Seen from today, it appears an incredible situation, and one that can only illustrate the attitudes, mindset and conceits of the age and its players.

Subsequent French names of early aviation included the likes of Henri Fabre, whose first float plane was of monocoque configuration. French all-wing proponents Georges Abrial, Jean Charpentier, Nicolas Payen, and ultimately, Charles Fauvel of 'Fauvel flying-wing' fame, would all create viable all-wing type machines. Rene Arnoux was also an early French pioneer of tailless design, yet using straight-tapered or 'plank' winged planforms. His first all-wing affair, a biplane idea in 1909, was devoid of sweep or dihedral; by 1912 he had built a monoplane tailless all-wing type.

What of the French émigré Henri Coanda, designer of a turbo-propulseur ducted-fan type of early 'jet' effect engine as early as 1910, and an engine mounted in a semi-monoplane that possessed an amazing, swept surfaces design to its tail fin and tailplane. A major proponent of the monoplane was car racer and engine builder turned aircraft manufacturer, Leon Levavasseur, and his monoplane

Antoinette types (named after a customer's daughter). For a few short years, from early 1908, the *Antoinette* series of monoplanes held sway and broke the Channel-crossing record.[14]

British Lateral Thinkers

The West Country engineer William Henson's *Aerial Steam Carriage* (or *Aerial*) of 1843 was a monoplane design built in large-scale form with a swept tail design and an intriguing 'pod' for its cockpit shape. It also boasted a vertical 'fin' panel above its single wing. Yet again, here was an early designer following the monoplane and fuselage-less design configuration – in the 1840s – six decades before the leading names of the monoplane and all-wing idea were working. Sadly, Henson's Cayley-inspired ideas went no further and he emigrated to America.

John Stingfellow's 1848 elliptically winged monoplane him, conversely, to a triplane, but although that may have been a triple-winged and braced affair, even that was all-wing, with a sculpted pod for the pilot and motor.

In 1884, H.F. Phillips began his first experiments with aerofoils – notably analysing airflow in a steam injected wind tunnel. Horatio Phillips created multiple surface and camber aerofoils and was clearly taken with experimenting with curved forms. One of his design sections had a significant cranked or dropped leading edge that was a massive advance for its era. Phillips demonstrated the aerofoil pressure differential theory and his work advanced aeronautics greatly.

Whether or not we can say the same for Lawrence Hargreves is a debatable point. Often cited as an Australian, working in the scientific remoteness of Australia, Hargreves had strong English connections and was a proponent of panels, or 'flappers', that could propel a wing and airframe via a cyclical or rotating trochoidal theory. Given such, unsurprisingly, he designed a rotary cycle engine, yet it was for his rubber band powered flying models deploying lift-thrust propulsive effect that Hargreves is of interest, and notably so, because he also followed the all-wing planform route, however 'basic' his designs. From such work, Hargreves decided to create his box kite designs, thus eschewing the all-wing planform he had earlier used. We could say Hargreves 'invented' the box kite configuration, but before he did so, he followed the tandem monoplane, all-wing, curved planform idea so well profiled by the likes of Lilienthal.

It seems that the quest for stability led Hargreves to the denial of the all-wing and the promotion of the ultra-stable box kite – his all-wing gliders suffering roll axis instability (as had so many other designers' devices), for the all-wing in even its early days had stability issues and this issue was the junction, the fork in the road that led to the box kite, square winged and technically conservative design movement that the world adopted.

But crucially, Hargreves was not a pilot; apart from a tethered 'hop' he did not practice the art for which he designed machines with which to perform it. So Hargreves lacked the skills or resources to investigate the issues inherent within all-wing roll axis control by testing ideas; perhaps this explains his attempt to solve the problem via the drawing board – and his resulting conservatism of the box kite type? Pioneer or harbinger of a massive step backwards, Hargreves may have been both.[15]

Percival Pilcher was also a pioneer who toyed with early all-wing and monoplane ideas, but soon embraced the straighter, box kite type configuration that would lead to the biplane fashion as promulgated by the Wright brothers, and even Gabriel Voisin, before he turned to making incredible cars with André Lefebvre. The pair both became the 1920s fathers of modern road vehicle aerodynamics prior to the 1930s Stuttgart school and the works of Kamm, von Koenig Fachsenfeld and others in the era – after Ledwinka and Jaray.

Pilcher created a biplane hang-glider in 1896, yet his patent for a powered flying machine showed an all-wing affair. Like others, he followed the fashion and the learned men away from the all-wing, perhaps without giving the concept a chance.

In Britain, Butler and Edwards even drew a sharp, delta-wing aeroplane of 'paper aircraft' style in 1867. This was noteworthy and would not have looked out of place today, but perhaps lesser to de Telescheff's 1867 configuration for a jet-propelled delta-wing monoplane that was all-wing in its design.

We should note that the Butler and Edwards machine was of massive significance through its delta-wing planform, as opposed to its propulsive ideas. Suddenly, out of the blue, came this perfect, 1950s style sharp, swept, delta-wing in all-wing configuration. What forgotten ley line in the landscape of aviation was this amazing design? And where on earth did its modernity (in comparison to its contemporaries) spring from? Like Jacques Gerin's 1920s 'Aerodyne' – an elliptical one-piece podded car design packed with advanced ideas, the Butler and Edwards' delta-styled aircraft seems an undeniable precursor to much later events, yet one ignored at the time of its creation. Gerin, of course, had designed a large all-wing airline transport airframe by 1935.[16]

Sir Hiram Maxim built a huge biplane in 1894, but it had a dominant design feature – a large all-wing design central wing section that featured elegant swept leading edge inboard sections. It briefly 'flew' from a tethered trailer test once speed was obtained by Maxim, but he did not pursue his idea.

The greatest of the early British lateral thinkers might be cited as John W. Dunne. He was the man who built, and successfully flew, the first true, British swept-wing, all-wing, aerial machines before and after 1910. What radical genius of design inspiration went on in Dunne's mind and what cause drove him to shape his all-wing devices? If only the establishment had had the faith and the loyalty to pursue Dunne's monoplane all-wing thoughts. Instead, he was persuaded into all-wing biplanes, and then, not unlike Penaud, gave up a hopeless battle against the mindset of the great torpor of the establishment. Dunne went off to lick his wounds and write books.

The Early Jet

Study of jet-type propulsive effect – in terms of thrust action as opposed to rated power output – began in the 1860s with De Louvre's idea for an oil, or hydrocarbon derived fuel, being ignited or forced into a 'tube' or 'pipe' for consequent propulsive effect. J. Butler and E. Edwards had similar propulsive force ideas using other mediums – even steam. Add in the jet-tube ideas of Nicholas de Telescheff, and the later fan/ram-air compression effect jet tube ideas of Henri Coanda, and its seems that prior to the propeller powered biplane era, a huge advance in knowledge was on-hand.

As early as the 1880s, the Briton, Frederick Lanchester had begun his actual, flight experiments into aerodynamics, or 'Aerodonetics' as he called the subject[17]. By 1894, Lanchester had begun to build and fly models of symmetrical (and later, asymmetrical) elliptical planform. He noticed that such wings had improved glide ratios from lower induced drag and better lift coefficients than standard wings. Lanchester was not the first to explore ellipsoid wing planforms, nor the first to think about swept, crescent, or other wing planforms, but he may have been the first to build and study flying elliptical models that demonstrated differing characteristics from 'straight' wing planforms.

In 1894, even as Lanchester was flying his proof-of-concept elliptical planform model gliders, the Russian space pioneer, K.E. Ziolkowski, was designing an almost all-wing ellipsoid powered monoplane that later Junkers all-wing forms seemed to reflect. But the great period of advance prior to 1900 was only to be dismissed for years by the might and weight of European and industrial practice, and specifically in Britain by the narrow, blinkered thinking of an 'empire' mindset. From the 1860s onwards, members of the various new European aeronautical societies wanted to research new ideas, but it would not be long before the conceits of current perceptions narrowed certain minds and trends that led us to 1910 and the box kite biplane era.

Even the Austro-Hungarian arena went monoplane and all-wing, notably via the Paris-based Traian Vuai and his all-wing monoplane concept *No1*. Jacob Ellehammer of Denmark achieved (tethered) flight with his powered, all-wing semi monoplane of 1906. Again, its wing planform was highly advanced and far beyond the box kite biplanes of the day. The Danes still claim Ellehammer as a pioneer of powered flight.

Alexander F. Mozhaiski was a Russian pioneer of aircraft designer who test-flew a steam powered aircraft that was also of monoplane and all-wing configuration in 1884.

What is conspicuous are the number of French and German names within this great period of design research development – this research psychology. The English are also in evidence, as are other nationals; America's pioneer monoplane glider proponent in 1883 was John J. Montgomery, who designed gust-spoilers – or dampers – as moving wing surfaces. Still in America, Samuel P. Langley was not a pilot, but he became the country's most prolific ideas man after starting to investigate flight as late as 1887. Of significance, he was influenced by stories of Penaud and rubber-powered test-model flight. Yet steam power was to be Langley's 'thing'. By 1895, he was experimenting with tandem-wing monoplanes configuration (main, or fore planes and tailplanes). In May 1896 he stunned the learned men of the societies with a model that flew 3,300 feet and by the end of the year a later model (No.6) had flown nearly a mile.

Because he secured presidential backing (the president was McKinley), Langley became the chosen instrument of Washington-supported aeronautical research in America. Langley would receive a massive cash subsidy to build a viable flying machine – petrol powered not steam powered. With an engine designed by S.M. Balzer and modified by a C. Manly, who then took a lead role in the scheme – leading to the loss of profile for Balzer's works –[18] Langley's petrol-powered monoplane model became the world's first such machine to achieve powered flight in 1903. Langley would toy with the biplane configuration, but returned to his almost all-wing tandem monoplane ideas. Again in 1903, Langley built a full-size aircraft – the *Aerodrome*.

The non-pilot Langley made himself the first test pilot and unwisely used a catapult launch system that soon caused handling difficulties for the non-pilot and may have weakened the structure to which it was attached – the airframe itself. After two crashes, Langley walked (or swam) away from his boat-launched flying machine. Soon afterwards, he fell from political favour, lost his funding and was eclipsed by the Wright brothers. But Langley remains a 'father' of American aeronautical endeavour.

Richard Pearse – Forgotten Genius of New Zealand Aviation

In the bottom corner of the world – in New Zealand circa 1900–1906 – were the works of Richard Pearse.

Pearse designed his own flying machines, notably of monoplane configuration with all-wing layout and possessing something the Wrights did not – not just an undercarriage, but a tricycle undercarriage layout with a steerable nose wheel. Pearse's 1904 tricycle undercarriage machine was an amazing enough, yet he devised leading edge flaps, ailerons, a variable pitch and tilting engine/propeller that provided forward and downward thrust via a shaft-driven anti-torque drive shaft that was configured for a rear driven prop-rotor STOL type machine. Some claim has been made to Pearse having made a powered flight before the Wrights. This has been investigated and found not proven by reliable authorities. Despite this, we cannot deny that Pearse, who lived until 1953, was an isolated, unknown, genius of early aviation and an early all-wing monoplane proponent. Who else had thought of a tilting rotor with shaft drive mounted to an all-wing planform monoplane in 1904? It would be decades before another such machine was perfected.

Whatever the facts of the Wrights and their inventions circa 1903–1906, aside from Pearse's isolated activities, it is clear that a French lead in the monoplane and all-wing thinking output peaked circa 1900. Despite 1912 and the Deperdussin *Monocoque* and even the Dutchman Fokker's 1915, *Eindecker,* the monoplane was effectively lost after the Wrights triumphed and was only to re-emerge in British and American thinking decades later.

Of interest, all the early all-wing planform and many of the monoplane proponents created curved, organic, sometimes even sculptural shapes – the sort of biomorphic sculpted aerodynamics we have begun to see in civil and military aircraft design only in very recent years. Compound curves, standard ellipses, even modified asymmetric ellipses, wing to fuselage infill sections, swept tails, and a host of drag-reducing shapes were evident as early as 1890. Yet, within fifteen years, it had all gone, to be replaced by square-tapered 'plank' wings, struts, wires, braces, ungainly fairings and a biplane myopia that featured enormous tail surfaces, thick aerofoils and tubby fuselages; aerodynamic drag was actually created .

Advanced German Thoughts Begin to Take Shape

First there was Lilienthal, then there were others such as Ahlborn, Etrich, Wels and Kutta. By 1912, Edmund Rumpler (of Austrian descent) and his designer Igor Etrich (a Bohemian via Vienna) of the *Luftfahrzeugbau* design bureau of Lichtenberg Berlin, Germany's first aircraft manufacturing company, produced a semi all-wing *Taube* monoplane of sharply swept planform – its shape aped the early glider designs of Jose Weiss and took inspiration from Professor Ahlborn's work. The original Rumpler *Taube* boasted a revolutionary, teardrop-shaped enclosed cabin – surely only Penaud had previously hinted at such forms? Rumpler had liaised with the early aerodynmicist Hans Ledwinka in the late 1890s and had a grasp of advanced forms. He even created an early aerodynamic car in the *Tropfen-Auto.* The *Taube* name would latterly be applied to a series of Etrich-designed military aircraft.

The Rumpler design works continued into the 1920s with focus on automotive and aviation concepts, notably one where a large 'flying-wing' would carry all the cargo, engines, and fuel loads of a transport machine. Edmund Rumpler would move on to the idea of conjoined wing configurations to carry large loads on long haul flights, notably his dream of a transatlantic machine using a large all-wing – albeit still with a tail.

Rumpler evolved his thoughts into giant, twin-hulled machines that were effectively of the flying-boat school, yet with wingspans of nearly 300ft/metres. Inside the behemoth would sit over 130 passengers, a large crew, cargo capacity and over fifty tons of fuel to ensure long-range performance. The rise of Hitler to power post-1933 saw Rumpler obscured, but his ideas, adopted by others, would reappear under the Nazi design umbrella.

Back in 1910–1920 (possibly as early as 1909), over in Dessau at the Junkers wind tunnels, Hugo Junkers was researching the lift and drag equations of the all-wing's efficiencies. Junkers was, by December 1915, building his J1 – the world's first all-metal construction aircraft (a monoplane). Next, Junkers outlined his earlier testing and photographing of a host of wing shapes and he noted Prandtl's work on finite lift theories. Junker's put early elliptical shapes in his own, large scale wind tunnel, and ever the futurist, designed a sleek, spatted, monoplane prototype in 1921 that looked like a late 1930s American air racer – yet was two decades in advance of such machines. But it was Junker's who would turn his all-wing studies – and the acceptance in 1912 of his patent (applied for in 1910) – into a viable machine and then into the giant JG-38 airframe with its near two-metre wing thickness. Junkers even suggested a ten-engine blended-wing device in 1929.

At Göttingen, Prandtl, (latterly Betz and Munk et al) firmed up earlier speculations and tests into elliptic or ellipsoid wing shapes – beyond the earlier thoughts of Lanchester, Zhukovskii and Ahlborn – by developing analysis and calculus to frame that the elliptical form created lower lift-induced drag. After all, were not high performance bird and insect wings shaped such a way for a reason? Had anyone noticed the highly swept ellipsoid planform and the very stable flight of the Aboriginal boomerang?

So the way in which the lift 'worked' off the trailing edge of the wing was the area of study – with the finding that the ellipse distributed the lift loading in a more even pattern (along the trailing edge), as opposed to the concentration of lift loading near the tip and consequent higher drag of a straight or 'plan' type wing. Therefore, minimum drag was demonstrated by the elliptic wing and its lift pattern of action.

From here, elliptical effects, and then wingtip, swept-wing and delta-wing lift pattern effects were a focus of principally German study – stemming from the rapid advances in German glider design that occurred as a result of the effects of the actions of others. Soon, these new exponents of aerodynamic study, circa 1910–1925, would become the fathers of advanced wing design.

Another early German-based exponent of the all-wing idea was the Swiss-French Alexander Soldenhoff of Geneva, who later moved to Germany. Soldenhoff, an artist by profession, was fascinated by early flight and is reputed to have designed a monoplane tailless craft in 1912 – soon after Junkers. Soldenhoff built scale test models and powered full-size machines, the first of which took to the air in 1927 in Switzerland.

A piece of good fortune later occurred in 1929 when the German glider pilot G. Espenlaub (a tailless design enthusiast) flew Soldenhoff's A2 type design. Espenlaub also flew Lippisch gliders and retained interest in Soldenhoff's work. Of note, in Soldenhoff's A5 design, we see the addition of wingtip end plates and further refinements to his wing control surfaces designs. Across the years from 1920 knowledge exploded, and it did so mainly in Germany and with gliding (sailplane) design developments leading the way ahead into high speed wing design. By the mid-1930s, the young Horten brothers would add to the all-wing story.

So were set the seeds of a design philosophy that had been suggested in the 1800s, then denied and dismissed, only to be realised in a decades-long battle of giant egos and even bigger forces at work across the development of man's flight. First came the Anglo-French-American hiatus, the First World War, and the deliberate interregnum of the 1920s when the main airframe designers and manufacturers pursued the blind alley, the retardation of design that was the biplane in all its ungainly, high-drag and turbulent glory. But in Germany, another story unfolded: its effects would be shattering.

Chapter Three

Wasserkuppe

Dreamers, Visionaries and the Segelflug Sensation

If the truth of how the constraints of the *Treaty of Versailles* of 28 June 1919 backfired on the British and the French are ever questioned, one look at the glider airframes of late 1920s and early 1930s Germany, will confirm the facts. Add in that developments in such motorless flight saw a consequent knowledge transfer to powered flight, and the advances of the German glider movement – created by the effect of the treaty and its banning of a German air force and German powered flight – are obvious. Rocket-powered flight was not banned by the treaty either – now *there* was a poignant flaw.

By 1922 the world of aviation was startled by the news that a glider flight of one hour duration had been achieved. This event took place in eastern Germany upon the escarpment of the Wasserkuppe at Poppenhausen/Gersfeld – the home of the German segelflug soaring flight (gliding) movement.

There, the close neighbours that were the *Deutsche Forschunginstitut fur Segelflug* (DFS) – the German Research Institute for Glider Flight at Gottingen and the *Rhon Rossitten Gesellschaft* (RRG) – the Rhon Rossitten Works, operated as sailplane research institutes, they would merge in 1933. In time, Alexander Lippisch would lead the RRG and Professor Walter Georgii the DFS.

In Britain in the early-1920s, gliders or sailplanes were ungainly flying bathtubs with thick wings and high drag coefficients. Any attempt at tight or high bank angle turns of, for example, 30°+ bank to stay in a thermal, would result in the aerofoil losing efficiency and the glider falling earthwards in what we might term a gross height excursion. Yet at the Wasserkuppe, pilot Martens had flown the glider *Vampyr* – designed by Professor Madelung. Through a more efficient aerofoil, a change in wing loading, and a longer span of higher aspect ratio, crucial performance increases were built into the machine. Furthermore, here was the first glider to be 'smoothed over' to reduce parasitic drag, and the craft's undercarriage was retracted into its body.

This was the first ever iteration of a retractable undercarriage. Of single spar construction and smooth, stressed skin on the leading edges of the wings and fore-part of the machine; this ensured optimum aerodynamic profile for the life of the airframe. Tighter turns slowly became possible – but this was an evolving process.

Suddenly, in one go as an overnight revolution, a glider was a total aerodynamic innovation – not just in glider design but across all airframe design. In this, *Vampyr* began the seeds of the German high-speed, low-drag design revolution and it began because of the constraints enforced by the *Treaty of Versailles*. From here came the Darmstadt 'Akaflieg' Group amid the Göttingen DFS 'school'. Lessons were quickly learned. Ideas such as increasing the lift by increasing the wingspan were useless if the weight of the longer wing negated any lift benefits. A new shape was no good if its skin finish was rough. Forms had to be sculpted to cheat the air – streamlining was born – as notice was taken of the points upon the airflow's course that it would encounter as a streamed line. Smoothness was born. The Darmstadt D1 glider became a world leader in sailplane design and many other advanced German features and types followed it. Wing design preferences came and went until a planform, aerofoil and body of optimum form was achieved – far in excess of anything anywhere else in the world.

Here were learned the aerodynamics criteria that the Allies soon claimed as their own after 1946, but it was in 1920s and 1930s Germany that these advances were made. No wonder that by 1938 British gliders were often simply blatant copies of German designs.

The Germans had complained loudly at the terms of the treaty and even went so far in 1920 as to mount a Mercedes aircraft engine – wrapped in chains – upon a stone plinth at the entrance to Hamburg's Fuhlsbüttel airfield in order to symbolise a protest at the constraints the Allied Powers were entrapping German aviation within as a post-war punishment. The engine on a plinth bore a placard that protested 'Versailles 1919'. It was designed to voice concerns about the restriction of flight and flying machines, yet in reality, the terms of the treaty were little more than political window dressing for audiences in London, Paris, and beyond.

The treaty itself was very clear in its simplistic terms. A host of treaty articles framed a constriction upon German aircraft flight, manufacture and design and supplementary activity. Articles 198–202, stated that Germany must not have armed forces that included any military; or naval air force. Only 100 unarmed seaplanes and only one spare engine per aircraft were permitted as a search and rescue function for the 1920s. Article 199 ensured that within two months of the signing of the treaty, Germany would demobilise its air force and its entire staff and only retain 1,000 men within its establishments. Article 201 forbade any manufacture and importation of aircraft, parts, engines or ancillary equipment, anywhere in Germany for a renewable period of six months after surrender. Article 202 demanded all existing German aircraft to be delivered into the hands of the Allied victors. These were operating restraints, but the key treaty terms related to the restriction of design and flight of German powered aircraft. From this stemmed the move to develop motorless, glider or sailplane flight. Yet not only was glider flight permitted by the treaty, so too was the latter development of a civil airline network. Neither was rocket flight even thought about by the writers of the treaty – by default of not even being considered by the authors.

These were just three of the startling holes in the treaty and its restrictions.

Perceived wisdom has it that it was the Nazi Party and its takeover of power in 1933 that created the quick and vital advance of German aircraft design and production in the mid-1930s. This is a ruse or feint of the annals of history (on both sides, Nazi and Allied) because, long before 1933, the pre-Nazi German administrations up to the end of the Weimar period had laid, not just the foundations of military and civil aviation, but the design and construction systems of an advanced cadre of planes and pilots. Nazi-propaganda itself has contributed to creating a post-1933 development of 'Nazi' German design, but the facts clearly show how the 1920s were a massively funded and supported period of prior expansion. The drive to redesign and reset German aviation had come years before Hitler got his hands on the levers of power, even if the nascent *Nationalsozialistiche Deutsche Arbeitpartei* (NSDAP) – the National Socialist Workers Party – 'Nazi Party' existed before Hitler took control of it. However, in March 1933, Hitler's new regime ordered a 'Fur die Luft' (For the Air) policy that tasked German aircraft designers and manufacturers to submit new proposals for a new air force in a new air age.

After the First World War, Germany lacked a major defining research establishment other than foundation work going on at Göttingen. But by scattering academic researchers and supporting new aviation study 'bases' across Germany, by 1923 a massive expansion in the numbers of German aircraft being designed (as gliders) took place. From 1920, German design research expertise was seeded into universities and academic groups, which shaped the likes of the Adlershof research centre. Germany wasted no time in getting around the terms of the treaty and building a design research community. The *Deutsche Versuchsanstalt fur Luftfahrt* (DVL) – the German experimental research bureau for aviation – was the key central academic and engineering study school, but it supported outstations, or research hotspots (*Stutspunkte*), that were created across the nation and were further funded after the dissolution of the Inspectorate of Armed Forces in May 1920 through special measures within the Reichs Ministry.

From inception, the German gliding movement was co-ordinated and funded via numerous groups under the aegis of the DVL. This was no haphazard, random series of thoughts or events as were taking place in British aviation at the same time on a privateer basis. As stated in the journal *Luft-Wissen*, the official publication of the German Air Ministry: 'From its inception in 1920 the gliding movement, the entire technical work on the Wasserkuppe and later on at another place, were co-ordinated in special commissions co-operating with the DVL. The framework of the DVL – sponsored by the Armed Forces Office of the Army Weapons Office and later transferred to the Reichs Ministry of Transport – had been substantially enlarged by 1927, and since that year a special allocation was secured in the Government Budget.'[1]

And if no German air force was allowed, how was it that by the late 1920s a great reserve of airfields operating as flying clubs, where many young men trained as pilots, were to be found across Germany? In fact, over 50,000 young Germans (including women) became qualified glider pilots before 1936. Neither Britain nor America could boast such a cadre of pilots in reserve. The *Deutsche Luftsportverband* (DLV), the German aviation sport union, soon came to oversee local flying. How were such institutions funded? The answer was that while formal government funding, or support for any such activity was limited, no such restrictions applied to local funding. So town councils poured money into building local airfields and flying 'clubs' all over Germany and in doing so began the greater German flying and design and prototype testing movement. This was one of the main failings of the treaty in that it did not prevent local funding, nor mobilisation of talent and testing of ideas via the flying club movement.

Funding

Not only did city and town councils fund and build aviation facilities throughout Germany, but large corporate organisations also funded advancement – without such funding being publicly declared. Civil aviation was permitted under the terms of the treaty and this was another area of expansion that masked design developments that could easily be transferred into a military aviation capacity. A later study by Schenck,[2] stated that local funding equalled the amount given by subsidies from central government – this ran into hundreds of millions of pre-1929 Reichsmarks.

Through these bodies and groups, the hidden actions of the German High Command laid the groundwork for a military rebuilding of German air forces – for although the German armed forces may have been dissolved on 8 May 1920, the men and material, the *thinking* that lay within those forces, did not evaporate. Aviation and being 'air-minded' became a German national obsession, one that revolved around gliding and new glider designs. The DFS research group and the gliding movement based close to the Wasserkuppe soon became the fulcrum of design – not just glider design, but the consequent high-speed, swept-wing work that led to supersonics. Flight testing of new types began in earnest in late 1923 via the sponsorship of the Reichs Ministry of Transport – a peaceful name for a mechanism that went way beyond public transport in its remit. By 1927, a special budget had been allocated to this ministry from government and this allowed funding to be dispersed to the flying schools and airfields and their clubs. In 1925,

25 million (pre-inflation crisis) Reichsmarks was spent by the Reichs Ministry for Transport on 'unspecified' technical purposes.

As a comparison, in 1928–1929, the British gave a mere £52,000 in countrywide grants to their own national local flying clubs. German industry also received 'hidden' support from the German transport ministry with 13 million Reichsmarks being channelled into aircraft design and development between 1929 and 1931. The official German government figures for expenditure on aviation show a rise from less than two million Reichsmarks in 1923 to forty million Reichsmarks in 1928 and seventy-nine million Reichsmarks by 1933 – this was the admitted official figure – the real figure, that included undeclared or local and corporate funding, was likely to be double these figures. After the inflation period of 'Billion' Reichsmarks notes, Hitler took power and aviation spending in real terms had reached a figure of over 200 million Reichsmarks by 1935.

Within seven years of defeat in the First World War and the so-called restrictions of the *Treaty of Versailles*, German civil aviation was emerging as a major force; within two years after the end of the treaty's restrictions on civil aircraft design and construction, German designed and built airliners were dominant in the emergent European airline industry. A new civil air route network was created by Germany that was four times bigger than the British network, twice as big as the French network and operating on routes, whose mileage was bigger than the French and British combined, was created by Germany. Funding (pre-Nazi era) was behind the advance.[3]

Behind, or beneath, all this advancement lay the German work on motorless flight and even some powered prototype designs. This was the fundamental mechanism of advancing aerodynamics and structures knowledge to new heights in what became a uniquely German, and uniquely advanced, design research psychology from 1923 onwards. Germans wanted to fly, and wanted to fly high, long, and fast. If they were not to be allowed engines to make that happen, then they would begin by creating new engineless aircraft that could reach such new targets; this was how the advanced glider design movement began.

Advanced Wing Design

The key developments, formed by these officially funded German glider design movements, lay in wing design as a way of improving performance. The pilot training opportunities were not wasted either and by the time of German intervention in the Spanish Civil War and then the Second World War, vast reserves of trained pilots existed within German society. From advances in monoplane and aerodynamic glider design came the rise of the advanced powered monoplane and fighter monoplane that Germany excelled in by 1936. From there it was but a hop to swept-wings and supersonics – a German lead was established.

The creation of a German national glider design bureau in the DFS under Professor W. Georgii framed events. Add in the works of the other institutes, designers including Blume, Espenlaub, Jacobs, Kracht, Lippisch, Kupper, Wagner, through to the wider work of men such as Baumer and the Gunter brothers at Heinkel, and an advanced cadre of glider and powered airframe designers soon existed. The initial effort was a focus by the glider designers to create gliders that, unlike previous sailplanes, had thin wing sections and smooth bodies. The need to develop highly manoeuvrable gliders led to a concentration of aerofoil and planform design improvements circa 1925–1935. Speed, and a glider's ability to trade lift for range amid an optimum glide-ratio speed were realised for the first time – framed as a glide distance-to-descent height loss calculation – a glide ratio. What of spanwise lift and flow, yaw angles and crosswind performances of the wing and the glider? All these were vital arbiters of performance that few had researched prior to this period.

The solution to creating the fundamentals of more efficient wing design lay in chord ratio, aerofoil thinness, fuselage design, lift distribution patterns and skin smoothness (as a defined criteria) and through streamlining. By improving lift distribution, lowering lift-induced drag and other types of drag, and by researching more efficient wingtips, control surfaces and overall airflow efficiencies, the German 'school' of glider design made massive and rapid advances in airframe and aerodynamic developments.[4]

August Kupper

There can be little doubt of the influence of German glider design upon 1930s British design, research and practice. The influence of August Kupper and Robert Kronfeld have to be significant. Kupper was a Bavarian from Munich who had studied aerodynamics and quantum mechanics. He joined the *Akaflieg*, Munich, in 1927 and started to design a flying wing design which latterly became the Mu5 airframe. From Munich, Kupper was soon making the long trip to Junkers over in Dessau, where he joined the company's fluids dynamics department in 1928. Kupper was involved with the Ju-1000 all-wing prototype and observed the works of Junkers rocket pioneer, Johannes Winkler. By 1931, Kupper had gone to the DVL. Despite both working towards the same all-wing ends, Kupper and Lippisch seemed to have had a falling out, and Kupper would continue his own all-wing and delta thoughts via the Gotha 147 design. By 1939, Kupper had designed a 100ft span, swept-wing, washout-equipped airframe with his own design of 'flaperon' type control surfaces.

Kupper was friends with many British-based experts – notably Beverley Shenstone and his research colleague G. Mungo Buxton, and the British resident, but Austrian-born Jew, Robert Kronfeld. Kronfeld was also an all-wing obsessive and the pair teamed up even though Kronfeld had fled Hitler's Germany in 1933. The two men dreamed of massive commercial airline transport all-wing designs, but sadly, Kupper was killed in an aircraft accident at Berlin-Aldershof in 1935 and Kronfeld died in an all-wing crash soon after the war. Before his death, Kronfeld had mastered the art of flying the Horten Ho 4 swept-wing sailplane – and discussed its aerodynamics with his friends at the British Fairey Company.

G. Mungo Buxton and B.S. Shenstone would work closely together and Buxton's *Hjordis* glider design was almost all-wing and very smoothly finished. Like Kupper's machines, Buxton's airframe was designed to exploit the idea of dynamic soaring – using the air to gain energy in flight. Buxton then designed a fully all-wing design that never flew, but which influenced others – notably the Baynes Company. Kronfeld's designs and G.T.R. Hill's all-wing thoughts would soon come together and touch not just the Westland design output, but also the Armstrong Whitworth A.W.52 all-wing machine and the General Aircraft Company's G.A.L. 56 flying wing (in which Kronfeld would die near Lasham).

A suggested all-wing design for the Muntz Company, for a 100ft span all-wing, may have come to nothing, but can only have been of influence upon the experimental Slingsby *Carrier Wing*. By 1938, British gliders were shaped like direct and shameless 'lifts' of German glider designs – the Slingsby *Petrel* and E.O.N. *Olympia* being the two most obvious 'copies'. The British Slingsby concern closely followed Lippisch's gull-wing design trend and built eight glider designs employing such thoughts prior to 1945. The Slingsby T.6 *Kirby Kite* was a so-called 'improved' version of the Grunau *Baby* 2.

The influence of Kupper and Kronfeld upon glider design and British glider design, then upon British airframe design in general, demonstrates how far German design had got by 1939.[5]

So great were the German advances and the resultant gliders, that the world, including the British glider and aviation design establishment, descended upon the centre of these German advances at their base at the Wasserkuppe gliding centre. For here lay gliders that demonstrated massive improvements in handling, range, lift and glide ratios.

Leading British luminaries of aircraft design and glider research such as G.T.R. Hill, G.M. Buxton, G. Gordon England, Sir Sefton Brackner, Adrian Chamier (a senior British Intelligence Officer), the Master of Sempill (later reputed as an alleged enemy agent) and a host of avid aviators, began to visit the Wasserkuppe as early as 1930. The British Gliding Association (BGA) was a regular visitor to the Wasserkuppe, where it made intensive study of the German machines. The fact that later British glider designs of the 1930s were to closely mimic German advanced designs was not a coincidence. Resident at the Wasserkuppe at this time, fresh from study with Junkers, and then working with Lippisch, was the young Beverley Shenstone, who would soon present a research study on the subject and be headhunted into Supermarine via Chamier's influence.

It was at the Wasserkuppe that Shenstone would grasp the all-wing and tailless concept as the gateway to the future of aerodynamics. Buxton, too, was inspired by the all-wing and tailless ideas seen in Germany and by December 1937 had presented a paper on such designs to the RAeS. Buxton had designed the Kupper-inspired *Hjordis* as the first British high aspect ratio, smooth -skinned, thin fuselage-boom equipped glider. It had a wing taper ratio of 4:1 and a use of washout or wing twist at a total of 6°. At the Wasserkuppe were 'names' such as Gunter Groenhoff, Peter Riedel and the aforementioned Robert Kronfeld, all men who would dominate world gliding and all-wing flight testing. German glider design and German pilots led the world at this time. Buxton, Shenstone and Wills (Snr) would all have friendships with the likes of Riedel, Groenhoff, Kronfeld and others.

Of highlight, the incredibly efficient smooth skinning of the German *Fafnir II* glider (85 per cent efficiency) was focused upon as evidence of just how far ahead the German glider design revolution had become. Of note, many of these craft displayed elliptical shapes. Robert Kronfeld stunned the British gliding community with his 250ml/km flight in the Lippisch-designed *Wien* (Vienna) glider type.

Others in America and Great Britain had built monoplane gliders, but they were thick winged, box-bodied affairs. The Germans and their glider design bureaus invented the new thin-winged, sleek monoplane form. Only the blinkered could refuse to see the potential of the transfer of such knowledge to powered aircraft. The frightening realisation that occurred to just a few of the British aircraft designers – those with open minds – was that the aerodynamic advances and refinements as manifest in German design, would be transferred from glider flight to powered flight. Ironically, perhaps the British Spitfire was the first powered aircraft to incorporate aspects of such German learning into its design. It would not be the last.

Gliders such as Professor Madelung's *Vampyr* paved the way as its designer realised that a slow 'sinking speed' – an improved glide ratio – allied to an ability to stay within up-currents from the mountains and thermals from the land, were the key requirements that could only stem from improved wing design. However obvious, previous glider designers had not succeeded in solving the issues. By increasing wingspan, reducing lift induced drag, lowering wing loading, and reducing weight, the first true soaring gliders that could stay in up currents were created. Professor Madelung's glider had a higher aspect ratio than previously seen and also removed the drag inducing effects of the undercarriage by concealing it within a fairing – reducing parasitic drag. The pilot was also enclosed in a fairing for the first time. As previously noted and of particular significance, great attention was paid to the smoothness and camber of the wing's leading edge – the first time that forensic attention had been paid to this aspect of wing design.

Through such features as those brought together in the *Vampyr*, a new design culture, or design language, emerged in the glider designs of 1920s Germany. Before long, Alexander Schleicher would create his contribution to German design at Poppenhausen, thereby setting the scene for a glider design legend.

Modifications to the *Vampyr* concept by the Hannover group of glider researchers, including G. Espenlaub and works by the Darmstadt group, meant that, within a decade, superb refinements of these foundations would open the door to swept-wing, delta-wing and all-wing research in Germany. The German glider design revolution paved the way r; so were cast the roots of all-wing design. Ultimately, designs such as the *Weihe*, the *Minimoa*, the designs of Schleicher, and the *Rhönadler*, would represent the apogee of German sailplane advancement. In 1935, one of many *Rhönadlers* flying at that year's Wasserkuppe competition flew 310 miles/500 kilometres to Brühn.

Along the way there were errors, notably the creation of glider airframes that were too light, too fragile and which suffered from structural failures. These issues gave rise to a set of design parameters or rules that also laid down foundations of airframe design knowledge; issues of wing oscillation – or flutter – being of specific study. It was the need to reduce lift-induced drag that led to the next rapid innovation in the study and deployment of the elliptical wing planform. Again, the Darmstadt group were the fulcrum in this design iteration. Professor Madelung's *Vampyr* had had an aspect ratio of ten, but the Darmstadt design group produced their D1 glider design within an aspect ratio of sixteen, that was joined to a very narrow fuselage. This glider flew thirty-seven miles in 1927 and established that as the first, new gliding record. However, the D1 was heavy and this may have affected the gains found in the use of its high aspect ratio elliptical wing. Some designers reverted to wing bracing to provide wing strength in high aspect ratio wings, yet without the weight gain associated with an unbraced wing. However, this was a temporary fashion whilst wing design evolved.

In a rash of advanced new gliders such as the *Fafnir I/II*, the *Wein*, the *Rhonsperber*, *Rhonadler* and the *Condor*, German designers demonstrated advanced wing planforms, tuned aerofoils and attempts to smooth the skin of the wing and fuselage. A great deal of work went into creating wings that allowed high bank angle terms and safe behaviour in the banked turn stall region.

Wing fillets.

By 1929, glider flights of ninety-three miles had been achieved and one year later R. Kronfeld flew 102 miles. Of note, and captured in the *Fafnir II*, was design work on wing to fuselage interference and early experimentation on the issue of how a wing fillet could greatly reduce drag and preserve lift – but only if correctly shaped and set.

By smoothing or fairing-in the sharp corners between the joining of the wings and the fuselage, the effects of each upon each other – known as interference drag – can be reduced. This means that the normal turbulence where wing root and fuselage meet can be vastly reduced by trying to equalise the differing airflow speeds upon each feature of the aircraft's body, creating a smoother transition of airflows rather than creating a cauldron of them. Avoiding flow breakdown in the angled 'pockets' or corner valleys where surfaces meet can also preserve lift circulation. It was in Germany that early work on solving this problem took place – notably at Junkers in Dessau, and at Göttingen.

Specific thoughts on the advantages of wing fillets were framed with the published papers of H. Muttray between 1928–1934; culminating in *Die Aerodynamishe Zusammenfugung von Tragelflugel und Rumpf* (The Aerodynamic Aspect of Wing Fuselage Fillets) that was revealed in the journal, *Luftfahrtforschung*, 1934[6] and then was re-published in English to a world audience, as the American, NACA Technical Memorandum No. 764, 1935. By this time T. von Kármán was also studying and developing such theories from his 1930s Californian base.[7]

And for the all-wing, no wing fillet was necessary, as the all-wing shape removed the spectre of interference drag by removing the interference itself – the fuselage.

Göttingen and the Aerofoil

Delaying airflow migration, stagnation and transition, or separation, upon the aerofoil camber is vital to any efficient aerofoil and even more so in the all-wing lift pattern and effect. Moving the stalling point backwards across the wing greatly increases lift efficiencies.

Stemming from the works of the Göttingen aerofoil studies and Prandtl's early research, a series of new, non-laminar aerofoils were researched across the development of German gliding. Up until the late 1940s, most aerofoils were non-laminar in that the place or point upon the wing aerofoil of maximum lift or suction was dependent upon localised boundary layer turbulence effects and how these led to transition and separation of the airflow as it streamed over the wing. The early aerofoils did have some degree of smoothness and boundary layer efficiencies, but the key point was not how they had any such qualities, but instead it was the degree of retained smoothness over the wing's chord to the point where it separated that was the vital arbiter. Heavily cambered aerofoils, such as the Göttingen 35 of the late-1920s, had a very small area laminar smoothness just behind the leading edge, and a forward based point of maximum lift. Behind this zone, the rest of the wing had a turbulent boundary layer across the chord. This was effectively the first low speed, high lift wing, stemming from advances in glider design and handling framed in Germany.

Subsequent developments have seen wings with lower drag and smoother boundary layer across the wing to provide less drag at higher speeds – but sometimes at the expense of low-speed lift. Hence we now have a massive catalogue of aerofoil shapes and high lift devices that we can choose from for a wing application. Back in the late 1920s, it was the specific requirements of advancing the performance of gliders that led to designers taking Ludwig Prandtl's early works on aerofoils and the boundary layer, and creating a new type of wing. From these early steps came studies that led to wing sweep, and later, aerofoils of differing shape/camber. NACA would soon absorb the German research and develop its own new aerofoils, notably the thin aerofoils of the 2200 series. But it would be the 1940s before the North American P-51D Mustang fighter aircraft would boast the first production laminar flow wing.

Often heralded as the dawning of the new laminar flow age of wing design, the Mustang's wing was subject to metal dimpling due to aero-elastic panting, combat-related skin surface degradation and rough finishing, all issues that reduced its true laminar flow efficiencies once outside the rarefied and sterile atmosphere of the wind tunnel and a test section.

German designers also realised that the joints between wings, fuselages, and panels on wooden gliders could allow air to migrate through these gaps – creating a form of air leakage as a drag. They responded to the problem by refining tolerances to reduce the gaps and then sealing these joints with tapes and fillers. This was early work on skin smoothness and is reflected in today's airframes, notably in GRP gliders and composite airliner structures.

Despite the ban on powered aircraft design, the Germans sidestepped the issue and created the first glider design that had a small engine contained within its concept. This was the first true motor-glider – the *Maikafer* (Mayfly) of 1933. Although possessing a deeper fuselage (with higher drag) than a motorless glider, the DFS designed *Maikafer* contained significant advances. The principal of these were its swept, forward-spar structured, high aspect ratio wings with semi-ellipsoid planform incorporating forward sweep at the outer tip trailing edge region. The result of research by Dr-Ing Kramer, Dr-Ing Maletzke and Dr-Ing Hohndorf, the *Maikafer's* swept planform ellipsoid was an early marker in swept-wing attempts – alongside Dr Lippisch's experiments of the same year.

Alexander Martin Lippisch

'All the parts not producing lift should be put inside the aeroplane,'[8] so said Alexander Lippisch in the summer of 1931 at the Berlin test flight of his powered all-wing machine. Suddenly, German aerodynamics had stepped into a new world of swept-wing monoplane all-wing configuration – taken directly from the monoplane glider revolution of the Wasserkuppe. By 1938, Lippisch was unique in the world in his making of slow motion film footage of wind tunnel smoke flows – using the then new Zeiss-Ikon 'Movikon' camera. This gave him unrivalled 'real' airflow analysis and led him to categorically state that, in his view, mathematical assumptions would always tend towards an approximated solution. Physical findings mathematically expressed as visible outcomes of wind tunnel testing were Lippisch's great leap forward from others' abilities.

The leading creator of the new gliding era was Alexander Lippisch and he began by focusing on creating glider wings that could perform well at high bank (turn) angles through improved wing design. For a period of time, from 1930 onwards, Lippisch was to become *the* visionary of future flight – swept-wing, all-wing, and deltoid flight. He and his machines were famous long before the fact that Concorde's wing (and a host of others) stemmed directly from Alexander Lippisch's inventions – the Me 163 and DM-1 prototype being recognised stepping stones in the history of aviation that came from his pen. After being seized in 1945 and taken to NACA for verification, Lippisch's delta-wing research prototype airframe DM-1 (and DM-2 ideas) would form the basis of the delta-wing supersonic generation to come.

By the summer of 1945, Lippisch, having fled from Vienna, was 'by arrangement' in the custody of the Air Technical Intelligence branch of the US Army Air Force, first in Paris and then transferred to Kensington, London, prior to onward travel to Wright Field, Dayton, Ohio, USA. Lippisch was relocated, along with several of his co-researchers, including E. Sielaff and F. Ringleb. From 1947 through to the 1950s, Lippisch worked for several US aircraft companies, notably General Dynamics-Convair, Collins, and a period with the US Navy's research department. This led to the XF-92 and then the first USAF delta-winged airframe, the F-102A 'Delta Dagger', the Convair XF-92, and the B-58 'Hustler' delta bomber. Lippisch set the foundations of modern swept and delta-wing design in a pre-Nazi Germany.

Back in the 1920s, little could Alexander Lippisch have known what horrors and what successes the future held in a sky not then cast with flying triangles.

A young Alexander Lippisch witnessed Orville Wright fly in a demonstration in Berlin in 1909. He was captivated by flight and studied the works of Ahlborn, Dunne and Etrich. By 1921, Lippisch was designing gliders and working with G. Espenlaub. Soon afterwards he would create a rocket-powered airframe for Fritz von Opel and also receive the financial backing of Herman Kohl. Lippisch would latterly create the DFS 194 as the world's first successful liquid fuel-powered rocket design (flown by H. Dittmar). Of note, Lippisch was, from the start of his career, fascinated by all-wing and tailless configurations. By 1925, he was directing research at the Wasserkuppe Rhon Rossitten Gesellschaft. Lippisch experimented with models, but understood the confusing issues of the aerodynamic scale effect between wind tunnel testing of models and real, full-scale aerodynamics. He made a special study of test smoke flow to refine his theories. From small test models, to one third and then two-thirds scale models, thence to full size, he undertook a step by step research evaluation, yet his thinking was never limited or prejudiced by convention.

By 1930, he was creating the swept-wing and deltoid Stork and Delta D-type all-wing configurations. Prior to that, Lippisch's stepping stone to advanced wing design was his role in the 1920s development of more efficient gliders – the only type of flight allowed under the infamous paradox of the *Treaty of Versailles*.

Ultimately, Lippisch worked on three main themes to advance wing design and glider performance:

1. He reduced the rolling inertia of the glider by tapering the wingtips to reduce weight and area, and by mounting the wings directly into the fuselage. This concentrated weight in the body of the aircraft near its centre-line and centre of gravity. Given that up to 50 per cent of the glider's weight is in its wings, this was a vital factor.

2. He applied 'washout', or wing twist, along the wings to tune localised aerodynamic effects and control surface effectiveness. This reduced the wingtips angle of attack to the air (incidence) and ensured that the ailerons and tips stalled *after* the main wing – greatly reducing lift losses and the risks of spinning via wing drop. The previous lack of aileron effectiveness at slow speeds and in tight turns or banks had been a major factor in the poor manoeuvrability of early gliders. By using new, thinner aerofoils and refined cambers and smooth skinning, the Göttingen designers shaped new gliders and new aerofoil sections of great efficiency. Research into lift patterns and span loadings, with specific focus on trailing edge and tip/aileron design, revealed much to Lippisch and his pupils – notably Shenstone. The Hortens would also note such works, as would Multhopp.

3. Because of the new way of both shaping the wing planform and twisting the wing's aerofoil section, and because the ailerons were now a more effective shape, a change to the rolling effect of controls surfaces and wings was created. By making the wingtip region that contained the ailerons more effective by being wider, yet thinner inboard, much greater control response was delivered

but not at the expense of control force effort. With a large, high aspect ratio wingspan came the need for ground clearance at the wingtips: this led to angling the wings upwards to increase wingtip clearance. So was created the first dihedral effect – with all the bonuses of increased flight stability that it also offered. The gull-wing effect was tried out on wing design at this time as a similar dihedral 'tweak'.

The fashion for a long thin fuselage, with a consequent long tail boom, or 'moment' arm fulcrum, also came about at this time because it improved yaw angle response. By making tail fins smaller and by making the rudder a larger part of the vertical fin, less weight and reduced inertial effects were imposed upon the airframe – improving yaw axis responses in terms of handling. In terms of the pitching axis, little added research was needed because glider design by default places the airframe weight close to the pitch axis. Lippisch also set about studying where the best place to mount the wing – on or into the fuselage – would be. This would turn out to be a crucial design aspect, not just to glider design, but to powered aircraft design, and notably, swept-wing design. He realised that lowering the wing below the shoulder line of the fuselage and smoothing the join between fuselage and wing could drastically reduce drag – the spectre of 'interference' drag being of note. Some experimentation in shapes, notably as to how to fair-in the pilot just in front of the leading edge and wing root area, was undertaken.

Lippisch brought all this work together in the *Fafnir I* with pilot Gunter Groenhoff. This pairing of advanced design and superb piloting skills led to world record breaking flights, principally the 170 miles flown in early 1931. In an interesting piece of modification, more advanced aerofoils with *less* camber, gave better high speed flight characteristics and lower drag, with only minimal losses to low speed handling. By adding speed and penetration, these new aerofoils delivered the first true, long distance glider flight capability. This let glider pilots fly fast and long between the newly discovered potential of thermal flying – principally (but not always) under and between clouds. For cloud thermal and non-cloud thermal (ground rising) flying, new techniques were developed, as were the wings to permit such flight. The Lippisch *Fafnir II* (also tagged *Sao Paulo*) glider developed its aerodynamics to permit such flying. *Fafnir II* was the first glider with its wing faired into the fuselage (preserving lift) and with all the new lessons of aerodynamics blended into its structure. Here was the first mid-wing to fuselage mounted high aspect ratio airframe. *Fafnir II* achieved a glide ratio angle of 1.27 at 50 mph and flew 232 miles in a world record flight in 1934.

This was all advanced stuff – unique in global design at the time – and frames the nature of the German advances in aerodynamics. Yet hidden within this research there lay the seeds of the revolution. Leading these research fields was

Lippisch, who spent his summers flying test models and then full-sized iterations of his ideas, and his winters in his design room within the wooden building at the Wasserkuppe, known as the Ursinus House and named after Oskar Ursinus. There was born the swept-wing era and the all-wing revolution. Also soon to be present at the Wasserkuppe would be the young Hortens and their all-wing devices.

By constant development and by applying what he learned through the glider design revolution, Lippisch penned a series of advanced ideas circa 1927–1933. He experimented with canard, elliptical, and then all-wing and tailless forms. Today's commercial airliners have sprouted winglets – which have their roots in Lippisch's experiments.

In late 1932, Lippisch's observations on the engineering and design needs of the tailless aeroplane were published in *Flight*[9] – with the opinion that large all-wing tailless types had a future. Lippisch proposed a five-engined, four tons gross weight machine to be a practical proposition. Of interest in terms of subsequent claims that the delta was a 1940s invention, this 1932 commentary makes clear reference to the delta form and its aerodynamic issues. Of particular note in terms of the delta-wing's historical chronology (putting aside the earlier prototypes plans of Butler and Edwards), as early as 1932, Lippisch's experiments were leading him away from highly swept-wing planforms with near constant chord. Instead, he moved towards a triangular planform with a moderately swept leading edge, and of note, a trailing edge that was straight yet which incorporated a touch of forward sweep towards the wingtip. This, stated Lippisch, was how to control the centres of pressure and lift patterns to create fore and aft stability. By adding a reflex curvature of the centre line to tune pressure differentials, and the splitting of trailing edge devices into three or more zones of action and effect, the 'elevon' effect was again suggested.

All of Lippisch's later craft were monoplanes with swept-wings and special control surfaces. Prior to his untimely death, Gunter Groenhoff was the pilot of the moment, whose skilled assessments of handling and the effects of modifications helped Lippisch refine his ideas. In the *Storch* (Stork) series of glider (and latterly powered) airframes, Alexander Lippisch defined the swept-wing and the delta-wing in an all-wing iteration. An early backer of the all-wing was the aforementioned Hermann Kohl, who had supported the highly successful Berlin demonstrations of Lippisch's later powered *Storch* series. A 24bhp engine powered *Storch VII* flew 300km in the world's first powered, long-distance flight of an all-wing tailless type.

From the *Storch* came the development of the more triangular delta shaped planform with which Lippisch would achieve true international status. By devoting hours on calculus, testing and sculpting, focusing on the effects of trailing edge sweep (+/-) and form, Lippisch created the delta-wing by solving the issues of span loading lift distribution, vortex patterns and trailing edge and control surfaces issues.[10] Within less than a decade, such advanced research would be manifesting itself in the non-deltoid but swept-wing Me 163 and Me 262 rocket and jet-powered machines respectively. In the all-wing Me 163, Lippisch dispensed with horizontal tail surfaces but insisted on retaining the vertical fin for stability. But through his DM-1/DM-2 designs, Lippisch would lay the foundations for the delta-shape and a generation of American, British and Russian aircraft – touching the Vulcan, Concorde, Convair 104, Mirage, designs by MiG, Sukhoi, and other types. Lippisch also investigated VTOL, disc aerofoils, hydrofoils, sea-skimming craft and a host of aero and hydro-dynamic devices and effects – including the boundary layer. In his tutoring to a young Beverley Shenstone between 1929–1931 and constant contact thereafter, Lippisch also touched the development of the Supermarine Spitfire's wing. Let us not forget that Lippisch was welcomed with open arms at the RAeS in London in December 1938.

The Me 163 was not, of course, born inside Messerschmitt's bureau; it arrived as a concept in Lippisch's mind and his DFS 194 work. There followed a degree of internal communications problems between the two men and their teams. Given the political issues involved, it is perhaps no surprise that Lippisch left Messerschmitt's employ and in the spring of 1943 joined the leading research body the *Luftfahrtforschungsanstalt* (LFS) in Vienna. Cleverly, Lippisch sold his design patents to Messerschmitt before leaving.

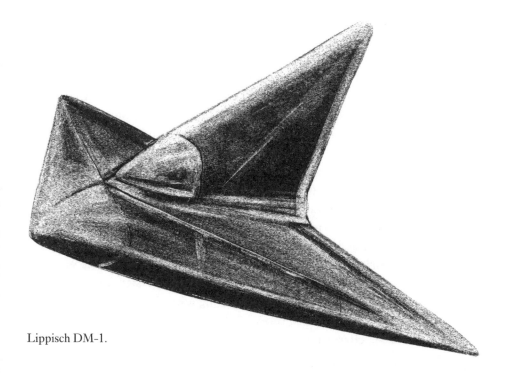

Lippisch DM-1.

There can be no doubt that Alexander Lippisch was *the* defining thinker of advanced wing planform aerodynamics post-1930 and that his effect upon the history of flight is hugely significant, yet little framed beyond the aerospace cognoscenti and narrow world of his subject. Like his lifelong friend Beverley Shenstone, Lippisch did not seek fame and fortune, nor celebrity 'designer' status. Lippisch was not as well educated as a student and only achieved his doctorate during the war, but it was his abductive, disruptive, lateral thinking that led him to invention and success. He was not a deductive, assumptive analyst relying on known-knowns, but instead, an inductive, explorative researcher and an often animated character full of energy and of constant ideas, according to Shenstone.

Shenstone wrote of his friend: 'Lippisch was always talking, always smiling, animated. He was encouraging, listened to everyone's ideas and then had the ability to bring everything together and add to his own views. He was open-minded and explored many new pathways. He would talk to each of us individually. His processes led him to his advanced thinking despite some lack of resources. If no wind tunnel and or smoke indicators were available, we used snow to illustrate airflow patterns from small flying models. He was indeed a remarkable man and a massive influence.'[11]

Lippisch's time working in Augsburg for the corporate and political mind of Willi Messerschmitt may have been difficult, but it was productive. There, he also linked up with designers from Junkers and Arado to produce, at the Berlin Air Ministry's edict, Horten research as a Junkers-built all-wing 'Amerika Bomber'. Thanks to his friends in Great Britain and America, and notably thanks to Beverley Shenstone, Lippisch was known not to be a Nazi and recognised as a genius to be embraced post-May 1945.

The profound effect of the Wasserkuppe-based segelflug revolution was seen in the works of many German designers, but Lippisch, and then the Hortens, took it to dramatic heights and then came a direct knowledge transfer into Allied aviation practice. The wider effect was also significant – swept-wings, as then applied to jet-powered airframes, surely stemmed from the unique research.

Even the famous German sculptor, Antes, got the nurflügel bug and developed in the 1930s, an all-wing design of profound shape. Looking like something from *Star Trek* forty years in the future, or perhaps a Luigi Colani future-vision, the Antes-designed swept, part-parabolic all-wing was a giant transport aircraft. He suggested ten engines and a huge payload and range stemming from the one-piece body. A flying model of this amazing curved, almost-biomorphic device was test-flown – demonstrating great stability. Of great interest, the design featured a novel open void within the parabola of the central wing area; this wing opening made room for 'pusher' engines whose prop-wash flowed over a trailing edge 'blade' – creating a stabilising effect similar to a horizontal tail surface.

Chapter Four

The Boys from Bonn

The Horten Brothers and Dreams Beyond the Perceptions of the Moment

Some people say the Horten brothers were geniuses, that they were the men who defined the all-wing concept, other people say they were eccentric, or of little consequence. Upon careful reflection, the former of the two statements appears be nearer to the truth than the latter. A touch of unfair prejudice entered the telling of the Horten story a long time ago. However, not everything the Hortens touched turned to gold – they had their failures, or 'learning experiences' along the way.

Often now perceived as two brothers, there were in fact three Horten brothers – Wolfram the oldest being killed in 1940 over the English Channel. Yet without Wolfram and his Luftwaffe contacts and help, the two younger brothers, Reimar and Walter, may not have reached the attention of Ernst Udet, the Luftwaffe, or the annals of German design. Walter Horten survived the Battle of Britain as a Bf 109 wingman to Adolf Galland.

Proud Germans, proud to be part of German aviation, and just like anyone else anywhere, citizens who supported their nation at war, the Hortens were not 'Nazis', despite claims of such caricature made by some. The brothers were not active evangelists for the Hitler creed and yet, like so many designers, they were streamed into Luftwaffe enrolment. However, they were hardly the 'pin-up' SS members or active party supporters that some of their colleagues were accused of being. Indeed the Hortens, like Lippisch, had intended to leave Germany in the late 1930s and post Second World War Reimar applied to work in England and for Jack Northrop in America, but to no avail. Reimar Horten, the genius designer, dreamed of vast all-wing airline transports and cargo machines, but his dreams were channelled by the German war machine of which he was a citizen. Walter, the practical engineer, would, in a post-war environment, go on to be a leading figure in the new Luftwaffe and in NATO.

Of significance, Richard Fairey of the British Fairey Company had flown the Ho 4 and soon sought out Reimar Horten for possible employment in Britain in 1947 – again to no avail.[1] The RAeS would award Walter Horten its bronze medal in 1963 and in 1993 an RAeS gold medal would be awarded to Reimar. Clearly, none of these things would have happened if these two men had been the rabid Nazis of the ilk sometimes ascribed to any German who worked for the Nazi war machine.

Reimar only went to Argentina in 1948 *after* requests for employment in England and America had failed, he was therefore not part of a 1945 'Nazi' framed 'escape' to South America with which some commentators have caricatured and confabulated his move. Why Argentina? Because there lay opportunity and funding under Peron's Government to create a new aircraft industry – Focke-Wulf's Kurt Tank had alighted in Argentina; there was also a pre-existing German community from prior to 1945 (just as there was a pre-existing English and Welsh community). As far as we know, neither were the Hortens in the Russian zone, nor in any sense' missing' or unaccounted for in 1946–1947, as has been alleged by some.

Born into a well-to-do academic Bonn family, Reimar and Walter would, in a sensational manner, pursue the all-wing (totally tailless) goal in a framework well beyond the norms of learned-by-rote aerodynamics practice at the time. Gurus of aerodynamics like Prandtl and Betz were left far behind by the radical new thinking of Reimar Horten and his brother Walter. Old, wind tunnel-based assumptions about lift distribution and aerofoil behaviour were challenged by the Hortens on a seemingly intuitive yet mathematically suggested basis. These young men did not go to the correct university to be taught what to think and what not to think by those immersed in their arrogance of their own certainties and perceptions. In academic terms, this would place the Hortens outside the protection and help of the learned men and their societies, but this would also leave them free to think the thoughts that they did. As philosophers of design, the Hortens did not ascribe to certainties of opinion before they started work – for that would have been entirely self-limiting, as it is in other arenas. Quite where Reimar and Walter got their mental inspiration from is an enigma. Ahlborn, Dunne, Junkers, Lippisch, Cheranovskii, and others, must have been known to them, but the Hortens stepped beyond even those boundaries. After all, even free-thinking Lippisch still insisted on a vertical empennage – a tail fin – even if he had removed the horizontal tail surfaces in his deltoid all-wing planforms. Had the brothers ever even seen a swept all-wing, ultra-thin aerofoil, smoothly finished and perfectly balanced boomerang?

The incredible story is that these young Horten boys simply started building wooden gliders to their own designs and, led by Reimar's mind, evolved these into defining, tailless, all-wing forms. Their swept-wing work influenced the development of later, generalised, swept-wing theories. How and why this happened to two teenage boys in Bonn is the enigma, but the outcome was clear. For, in the all-wing designs and lift pressure distribution patterns and control surfaces of the Horten all-wings, lay the answer to the refinement of the all-wing concept and the swept-wing itself. Neither should we forget that using early forms of plastic ('*Troilitax*' of Dynamit AG in Troisdorf), the brothers designed and built the world's first radar-absorbing, low-signature airframe. 'Stealth' technology started with the Hortens in the 1940s, not in America in the 1980s.[2]

In the early 1930s, as young teenage boys, the two younger brothers, egged on by their older brother's enthusiasm for gliding, started visiting the Wasserkuppe and flew their model designs. Then they took their B and C licences in basic gliders and began to think not just like designers, but also like pilots. So began the Horten 'Ho' series of sailplanes – many built at the family home with family funding. Although the boys' father was a Bonn University academic professor, he could think beyond the constraints of his class and allowed his sons to go wild with their ideas, an act for which we can only be thankful. It seems that Reimar and Walter absorbed all that was best about advanced German aerodynamics and then added their own, intuitive future vision. It is easy, and quite fashionable, to underestimate their work and effect. They made mistakes along the way and had airframes that behaved badly and did not deliver what they wanted – but that was how they evolved their theories of the all-wing. Getting the vital handling components of the yaw and the stall, correctly tamed in the longitudinally and vertically challenged all-wing concept was not plain sailing but it did lead to successful all-wing sailplaning and then powered all-wing flight.

The first Horten, the Ho 1, had an all-wing triangulated wing planform, which was an angled version of an ellipsoid, featuring forward sweep to the trailing edge and backwards sweep to the leading edge, both meeting in a sharp-pointed tip.

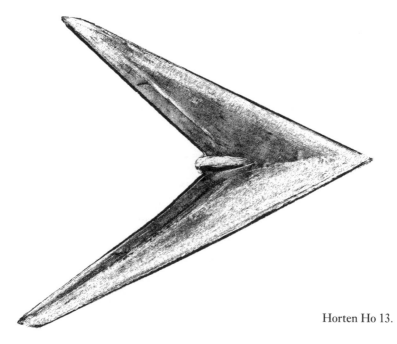

Horten Ho 13.

In 1934, Ho 1 took a prize at the Rhon Wasserkuppe summer competition as the most innovative design. By the time the Ho 2 and Ho 3 had been presented in the following two years, the Hortens had created stunningly futuristic all-wing forms and even gone so far as to motorise the Ho 3 with a small pusher-propeller. By 1938, the younger brothers' work had won a Lilienthal prize for design innovation and a DM 5,000 bursary. Also in 1938, Hannah Reitsch was test flying the Ho 3. From there it was a short hop for Reimar and Walter to be absorbed into the junior officers' rank in a technical arm of the Luftwaffe. The senior design statesmen that were Ernst Heinkel and Willi Messerschmitt would talk to the young Horten mavericks about their all-wing inventions with a view to possible production, but the talks came too little.[3] Walter and the key-designer Reimar were, it seems, not the types to be absorbed into a design office and be told what to do.

Early in the design process, Reimar had studied[4] the concept of wing-twist, or washout, and he ensured that all his wings stalled inboard first – reducing the danger of outboard (tip) stalling and resultant spinning. He also worked out, via calculus and actual sculpting and testing, the best shapes for preserving curvilinear lift distribution and lift behaviours across the entire aerofoil and chord interaction. A 'bell' shaped lift distribution pattern across the span was the key to Reimar's wing designs. In such mathematics, Horten studied localised airflows, boundary effects, skewness, kurtosis effects and spanwise flows and lift patterns to create an efficient and consistent lifting 'zone' on the wing, yet one tailored in effect to deviate from the low-induced lift of the ideal elliptical lift pattern. Out at the wingtips, Reimar seems to have used negative and positive washout and advanced tuning to build differing flows that were a compromise between low drag and better local flow patterns. Every centimetre of aerofoil lifting surface was calculated and examined to create a new level of tailored airflow and lift behaviour control. Perhaps only Lippisch and Shenstone were the other exemplars of such, prior to the Hortens, and the Supermarine Spitfire wing shows many boundary layer and lift pattern novelties that the Horten work mirrored. The sweepback discoveries of Lippisch, Multhopp, Busemann, and others can only have informed Reimar Horten's experiments.

The significant problem for any sailplane is yaw behaviour, and for the all-wing sailplane that has no vertical component via a vertical fin or rudder and relies upon wing behaviour and control effectiveness, taming the yaw and induced effects, was key. Advanced ailerons and elevons and flaps – all designed to create low-drag, low slip, low yaw flight – were the crucial ingredients. At one stage, Reimar fitted a swept canard-type foreplane ahead of the main, swept-back all-wing. This was utterly revolutionary and did not see series production in a delta-wing configuration until the Tupolev Tu-144 and the Saab Viggen delta types flew.

By bringing a forensic approach to accurately predicting these aerofoil and planform characteristics in a semi and full-scale prototype – not in a wind tunnel using models – Reimar Horten advanced the art of wing design. Automatic, lift-restorative, nose-drop and recoverable stability were features of Reimar's wings. Tuning outboard wing flows, spanwise flow, elliptical lift patterns, yaw behaviour, creating new locations and shapes for wing-mounted control surfaces (elevons) and almost approaching laminar theories, were all key Horten works. Reimar's principles on lift distribution patterns and sweep and about effects were, to coin a modern phrase, leading edge. They were, in fact, revolutionary and years ahead of their time.[5]

By 1940, the Hortens had been offered Luftwaffe support and provided with a rank, location and supplies to work from via a special technical arm known as *Sonderkommando 9*. Even early Junkers Jumo and BMW Hirth jet engines were made available to the Horten bureau, which was based at Göttingen and eventually would find itself cast across numerous locations, latterly at the Oranienburg research airfield close to Berlin and Reichsmarschall Göring's seat of power at Carinhall.

The Key – A Specific Wing Design – What Reimar Did

The key to yaw controllability – stopping the all-wing rotating around its own axis, and the key to curing its potentially lethal stall characteristics lay in wing design and tailored lift behaviours.

Reimar's outboard wing twist theory was applied in degrees – both linearly and parabolically distributed. The aerodynamic centre profile was calculated by integration of the product of local loading and the distance of the local aerodynamic centre behind a convenient spanwise datum along the wing's lifting surface – in a defined line. Load distribution was first calculated by Weissingers method for a sweptback wing, and this was added to by a Reimar Horten developed modification of Hans Multhopp's technique – which extended the lifting line theory to take account of chordwise pressure distribution and the influence of this on local induced airflow velocity along the span. Trailing edge design (perhaps after Lippisch's works) was also critical to Horten wing performance. Airflow was made to change direction and behaviour over the specially shaped ailerons/elevons that could act as de facto rudders and stabilisers. Reimar got his wings to fly with no in-flight deflection of these surfaces – unlike other all-wing designers. To have to have had the ailerons pitched up to produce a lift or nose-up trim would have been a drag-inducing disaster, but it took months of work to achieve perfection.

Reimar conceived a centre-wing lift pattern that produced a unique 'double centre' of pressure reflex profile that lay just aft of it – the core of Reimar's wing lift 'bell-curve' theory. Post-war testing of an American-modified Ho 4A by Mississippi State University utterly ruined this vital aerodynamic feature and the 'false' bad results of a destroyed lift-to-descent (LD) coefficient, then became erroneous 'fact' – via OSTIV – officially repeating of them. The university had reshaped the Ho 4A cockpit bubble and greatly lengthened it chordwise – ruining all Reimar's shaping and panelling work at this critical lift zone.

Reimar Horten looked at the formulas of Prandtl, Weissinger, Schrenk and the later modifications and expansions of those by Multhopp.

- Reimar Horten designed set 'points' upon the wing to create mathematically predicted airflow effects from – trailing edge upper and lower airflow mixing and formation of lift induced drag and wake turbulence and circulation vortex behaviours being the critical area of study. Vital study went into the aerodynamic centre of pressure and whereupon the wing this could be set and worked from. This was the stuff of 'span loads' and after Multhopp offered a new view of assessing and predicting this in 1938, Horten realised it might be the key to refining his wing design work. With the Horten 'bell-shaped' lift pattern with minimal lift at the wingtips, the values differ from the early theories of Prandtl and Schrenk, but, with a new method, the wing and its span loads could be further tailored.

- Horten worked out localised induced drag at each 'point' along the wing. The design and effect of control surfaces was critical to the all-wing and here Reimar really excelled – surely beyond anything that Northrop came up with. Northrop used powered surfaces (via hydraulic ram actuation) to ensure control surface authority, whereas the Hortens did not – they tuned the local airflow patterns to 'work' for them upon the control surfaces – this even enabled Reimar to create unique 'active' airflow patterns over elevon and aileron-type control surfaces and wingtips. This was Reimar's vital breakthrough in stability, drag management and, above all, control surface effectiveness and stall behaviour. It was all done by hand with no computer and no wind tunnel. It was nothing less than incredible, but few were aware of it.

- Part of the specific task for Horten was to assign wing twist and washout in a way that meant that the benefits of such stability enhancement did not lead to an unacceptable rise in drag. Using twist or washout to compensate for the sweepback angle had to be seen against the aim of using linear twist at a set point. More or less twist, dependent on sweep, was the conundrum: inboard or outboard twist? And how to mate any such effects together? Reducing drag in one wing area might raise it in another – how to balance all this was the key. These issues were the essence of solving part of the all-wing equations.

- Reimar Horten came up with his 'bell shaped' (as opposed to elliptical) span-loaded lift distribution – this 'bell' profile has a downwards acting 'load' at the wingtips, yet extra lift near the centerline. Modifying wing washout twist to have positive and negative zones along the wing was Reimar's secret technique. Northrop, by contrast, applied simple, single washout, linearly. Reimar's airflow design work moved certain aerodynamic effects rearwards upon the aerofoil, giving a de facto change to the incidence and creating local airflow velocity and lift changes with a sort of cloak of air at the wingtips as a form of vortex layer control. Was this effect an early attempt at an 'active' wingtip airflow thrust component, as later framed by the 1970s aerodynamic 'winglet' effect of Whitcomb, or the fin-sail blade works of Spillman? At the central mid-span of a Horten all-wing planform, another unique, tuned lift distribution pattern created a 'bubble' of centre line, curve linear lift distribution, adding to the lift coefficient.
- By concentrating on the tuning and taming of lift patterns, spanwise flow, localised flows, control panel effects, and yaw behaviours, Reimar Horten's wing designs contained advanced techniques and performance. Of significance, Reimar's swept-wings did not require chordwise vertical wing fences to deal with adverse spanwise flow. This was the mark of his success – the resultant swept, device-free 'clean' wing without wing fences, nor leading edge device and with no resultant loss of lift coefficient. A successful Horten swept all-wing did not suffer from spanwise flow, instability, wobbling, wing drop, or roll approaching the stall, nor violent spin tendencies.[6] There was indeed a special factor involved and perhaps Northrop failed to achieve the same effects.

Although never revealed to the CIOS/RAE Wilkinson Report, other experts (according to C. Wills whose gliding champion father, P. Wills and, R. Kronfeld, had interviewed and known the Hortens and even flown their craft) were certain that Reimar had invented some kind of amazing localised airflow and lift effects at the tips and over the ailerons and elevons that was balanced by the central lift zone and shaping over the main wing and engines. The possibility of the use of boundary layer effects and flow reversal (forward or sideways 'active' airflow) and an early appreciation of later winglet-type effects and factors at the wingtips and over the control surfaces – created by Reimar's genius, has to be considered as his unique achievement.

Horten's New View on All-Wing Airflow

The part clue to achieving this may have lain in the work of Schrenk – who postulated that a modified 'lifting line' theory (after Prandtl) included the effects of wing planform taper and aerofoil twist as a whole effect that included control surface location, area and deflection. Missing from Schrenk and Prandtl's works was, of course, the factor of wing sweep – which is where Reimar Horten's own researches are likely to have then been informative.

As with the wing works of Lippisch and Shenstone (assisted by Professor Howland), advanced mathematics is required amid an actual understanding of airflow. No amount of small-scale testing in a wind tunnel could, in the 1930s or 1940s, have revealed the localised effects of design features and airflow effects. This was why Reimar Horten was adamant (as had been Lippisch) on actual flight testing in real air of actual physical surfaces that avoided the 'scale effect' of wind tunnel work. Why else would Reimar have fitted his development airframes with cameras, and also arranged photographic chase aircraft to monitor tuft-testing in flight? There can be no other reason and therein lay the secret of Reimar Horten's step by step real-life aerodynamic learning – outside the wind tunnels then so favoured by the establishment.

Wills, Shenstone and others were convinced that Reimar Horten had advanced the art of swept-wing and all-wing aerodynamics. And, as the aerodynamics expert and Horten aficionado, A. Bowers framed[7, 8] all this was advanced work – even compared to today's computational fluid dynamics (CFD) achieved by electronics. Such computational dynamics modelling still leaves us having to estimate unknown features and effects – especially in turbulent airflow regions upon airframes. Given such reality, the true achievement of Reimar's hand-calculated and flight tested wing lift pattern works can begin to be appreciated. There was no CFD digital assistance in the 1930s.

Further Horten expertise is evidenced by how much effort Reimar put into his stall research – after all, the all-wing (like the Delta) can have adverse, rearwards-acting stall behaviours (as Northrop and Hill discovered). Cockpit cameras and chase plane cameras captured Horten flight testing where woollen tufts were fitted to indicate airflow behaviours – this was vital evidence of actual effects and not a mathematical hypothesis dependent upon wind tunnel issues. Reimar was very proud of his airframes stall behaviours – flight tested by his expert test pilot brother Walter.

An example of the daring of the Hortens' swept-wing research was demonstrated by the Ho 10 (or Ho X). This was an arrow-shaped flying wing with sweepback of over 50° that was reputedly inspired by Busemann's statement in 1935 at the Volta Conference, of the beneficial effect of sweepback on delay of the shock stall. Such views echoed Horten thinking. Initial work on the Ho 10 consisted of experiments with flying models weighing about 8 to 10kg. From these tests the brothers deduced the C.G. position needed for satisfactory flight with low aspect ratio and high sweepback, and found that they got good results with 4° dihedral – even with no empennage.

The next step was a piloted glider weighing 400kg. The wing section was a symmetrical DVL low drag type with maximum thickness at 45 per cent chord. Wing washout was 12°, dihedral 4°. Small nose elevons were fitted, but no trailing edge flaps. Rudder control was to be by Horten's unique wingtip rudder bars or panels. The undercarriage was of tricycle layout giving zero ground incidence, but clearance for a 15° nose-up pitch attitude at take-off; the front wheel was to be retractable but the rear wheels fixed.

After an exploration of low speed control problems on the glider, the next step was to have been a powered version with an Argus AS10C pusher engine. The final version was a suggested jet-propelled aircraft, with the same general dimensions, weighing 7,000kg. A single jet engine was proposed and a top speed of 1,200kph was expected with 1,300kg thrust; the thrust was to be improved to 1,500kg.

The Ho 11 was a research glider with an extremely high aspect ratio of 32.4:1. Constructed of wood and metal, the aircraft was considered by Walter Horten to be the highest performance sailplane of its day – one that required an experienced pilot. From there, the Horten series featured ever more sweepback, more skin smoothness, more aerodynamic tuning (also taking into account effects of aero-elasticity in flight). The Ho 13 of 60 degree sweepback is a sensational example of futurism from the Hortens and its planform is closely aped by the F-117A 'Stealth' fighter. From 1937, the Hortens raced ahead and their airframes went from sailplane to powered configuration – with pusher-props buried in the trailing edge, to jet engines mounted inside or below the wing. Even old Professor Prandtl had to admit his wind-tunnel testing-reliant conservatism had been challenged.

With *Reichs Luftfahrt Ministerium* (RLM) funding, Horten design advanced rapidly. Wood, plastic, alloys, special glues, advanced moulded surfaces, and composite construction were all introduced. A prone-pilot position was also featured in the Ho III – which achieved a nine-hour flight duration on one occasion. The Ho 4B (registered and known as LA-AC) was a real advance in terms of shape with its Plexiglas moulded central body section and wing performance. This was the machine that found itself at the RAE Farnborough in 1945 being displayed to the cream of British aeronautics. The Ho 5(B), or Ho V, was the first airframe constructed largely of plastic, using synthetic materials in a composite construction. Plastic film was used for wing covering, moulded plastic in the wing rib webs, and plastic laminate for main spar booms and stringers.

The highly curved Horten Parabola evoked utterly new thinking in terms of shape. Only one was built, yet its design was echoed just a few years later in the 'Roswell Incident' reports. Reimar Horten produced a diverse range of ideas, from small hang-glider types to very large transport aircraft configurations.

A total of forty-four Horten airframes were constructed. Later Horten designs and the Argentina output that was the 1954-designed IAe 48 delta-wing, show design milestones that surely caused the likes of Convair, Dassault and others to take note. We can, however, look to the Ho 9 V2/ V3-B or Ho 8/Ho 229 twin-jet all-wing airframes as the defining moment in the creation and then the seizure of German all-wing design. Ho 9 V-series is *the* precursor to today's all-wing and blended wing aircraft. The fact that the Ho 9 V3-B was carted off to the United States of America in 1945 and studied closely for years rather proves the point. Through the Horten 'Amerika Bomber' design studies of late 1944 and early 1945, an extraordinary story emerges.

Given that Reimar Horten had proposed a large, transport-purposed, six-engined all-wing jet in late 1944, the interest in the Horten work of Jack Northrop should have been no surprise. Northrop was already developing his large all-wing ideas programme.

CIOS – Find the Hortens!

A British CIOS/BIOS (Combined/British Intelligence Objectives Sub-committee) team discovered Horten airframes (Ho 3/Ho 4 sailplanes) at Rottweil, on the Neckar River, approximately 60 miles (100km) south-west of Stuttgart, Germany. US teams located and secured the advanced twin-jet Ho 9. The British BIOS team included international gliding champion Phillip Wills, whose connections in aviation and government were of the highest order. Philip's son, the famous glider pilot, Christopher Wills, confirmed to the author the facts of large numbers of German sailplanes being scooped up (partly under Operation Seahorse) and transported from Germany to Great Britain, Canada and the United States in 1945–1946. The highest priority was given to seizing and securing Horten, Messerschmitt, Focke-Wulf, and Arado airframes. From July 1945 to mid-1946, such machines were transported to new homes (including to Wright Field), where they would be studied with forensic attention.[9]

Horten Highlights:

Ho 1
Glider built in Bonn, 1931–1932.
Span – 41ft. Flying weight – 440lbs.
Wing area – 226sq. ft. Gliding angle – 1/21.
Weight empty – 264lbs. Sinking speed – 2.8ft/sec.
Won Rhon glider contest. Destroyed purposely by fire.

Ho II
Both glider and powered version were built in Bonn, 1933–1934.
Span – 54ft. Flying weight – 830lbs.
Wing area – 344sq. ft. Gliding angle – 1/24.
Weight empty – 605lbs. Sinking speed – 2.6ft/sec.
Had good flying qualities and did not spin. The nose dropped (classically) at the stalling speed.

Ho III
Glider built in Tempelhof (Berlin), 1938.
Span – 66ft. Flying weight – 750lbs.
Wing area – 403sq. ft. Gliding angle – 1/28.
Weight empty – 550lbs. Sinking speed – 2.1ft/sec.

Ho IV (RLM 251)
Glider built in Konigsberg in 1941.
Span – 66ft. Flying weight – 750lbs.
Wing area – 203sq. ft. Gliding angle – 1/37.
Weight empty – 530lbs. Sinking speed – 1.8ft/sec.

Ho V
First plastic-built all-wing airframe: Outer wing panel was of metal construction. The pilot was in a semi-prone position.

Ho IVB
Glider built at Hersfeld. It was a plastic wing version of the IV. The leading edge was made of 'Tronal'/'Troilitax' – an early plastic manufactured by Dynamit A.G. Troisdorf.

Ho V
Built in Ostheim, 1936–1938. Powered by two Hirth HM 60R (2x80 hp) engines. Also built at the Peschke factory in Minden, 1941–1942 and flight tested in Gottingen, 1943.
Side and single cockpit versions. A plastic version with flush cockpit was also built. The wings of this airplane were plastic.
Span – 53.3ft. Flying weight – 2,750lbs.
Wing Area – 452sq. ft.
Weight empty – 2,310lbs. Max. Speed – 150mph
Landing Speed – 47mph.

This airframe was built for the purpose of carrying on preliminary research for the Horten fighter.

Ho VI
Glider version of Ho-IV with a larger span and less dihedral was built at Hegidienberg and flown. Design was abandoned because the wings were too flexible for practical handling on the ground.

Ho VII
Basically similar to the Ho-V. Powered by two Argus AS10-C (240 hp) engines. One airplane had been built at the Peschke factory at Mindenand and tested at Oranienburg. A second was completed in 1945. A characteristic feature was the use of a 'rudderbar' spanwise and protruding from the wingtip as a directional control. Outer wing panels were of the same aerodynamic shape as those of the Ho-V. At the center line the section was 16 per cent thick, with 1.8 degree camber (zero Cmo) graded to 8 per cent symmetrical tip sections. Wing twist was 5°; 2° linearly and 3° parabolically distributed. The aircraft trimmed with elevons neutral at 260kph.

Ho IX
The remarkable twin turbojet proposal with composite construction that defined all-wing design in Ho IX B/V iterations (see below). Also suggested as an Ho IX C with the addition of a vertical empennage after the school of Lippisch. Generally cited as the Ho 9V2 and Ho 229 V3 series. Sadly, expert Horten test pilot, Erwin Ziller, was killed in the crash of the Ho IX twin-jet, due to suspected starboard engine failure, in February 1945.

Ho X
A version of the Ho-III with movable wingtips for lateral control.

Ho XIII (A)
An amazing 60 degree sweepback planform proposal for a supersonic jet/rocket assisted fighter. Flight tested for over ten hours as full-scale non-powered glider as the Ho XIII (or Ho 13 A). The design then evolved into a more deltoid planform as a 'C' model. A 70 degree sweepback scale model test glider was built in 1944. No one else in the world was exploring such swept-wing possibilities.

Ho Parabola
Glider with parabolic planform. Not test flown during the Second World War, but cited in reference to the Roswell incident. Destroyed by fire.

Horten Ho 229.

Ho IX (or Ho 9 B V2 – Ho 229 V3 series):

This series of airframe developments of jet-powered, swept-winged, all-wing fighter proposals – using Jumo 004 engines – were the glittering prize. This was the amazingly advanced stepping stone design that was seized by the Americans in May 1945 and shipped to the USA.

Beginning life as a derivative of the twin-engined Ho 8, the Ho 9 VA was an engineless, glider test airframe that proved the design concept prior to receiving jet powerplants, and then subject to a series of modifications that led to the Ho 9 V2 and Ho 229 V3 twin jet airframes. The series only appears to have become cited as 'Go 229' in the confusion of the CIOS seizing of the type and its production status intent at the Gothaer Werke AG.

With its swept-wing, curved planform, chamfered design, advanced aerofoil, and buried jet engines, it looked like a design project from the 1980s, not the 1940s. The Ho 9 concepts were built under the protection of the RLM and of the Luftwaffe *Sonderkommando 9* and can be said to be the culmination of over a

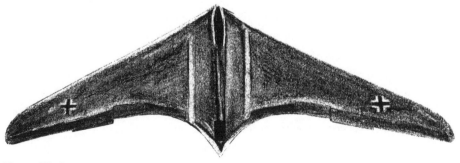

Horten Ho 8.

decade's research into tailless wing lift theory and design. The wing loading was 40lbs/sq.ft. The maximum speed with full loaded at 20,000ft was quoted to be 720mph, the landing speed 90mph, and the endurance 4.5 hours. The airplane was flight-tested at Berlin-Oranienburg. Take-off runs of 1600ft were obtained on initial flights with light load. It was estimated by the Germans that a take-off run of 3000ft would be needed with full load. Of note, the top speed was 250mph higher than the contemporary Me 262 and the fuel duration three times longer. Of particular interest, the use of wood and plastic in the construction was significant. The wing was very smoothly finished to criteria that were far beyond the normal standard of the time – a special lacquered finish ensured maximum skin efficiency.[10]

As late as January 1945, a desperate Göring ordered ten – then twenty – airframes as mass production runs via Gothaer construction of the latterly, and it seems, erroneously tagged 'Go 229'. Gothaers' were keen, it appears, for the design to be taken out of the brothers' direct control and rebranded. Gothaer's seems to have tried to sideline the Hortens and adopt the concept as its own with 'improvements', such as the Ho 8/Ho 9 '229' model variant. In 1945, the advancing Russians would seize the Gothaer factory and secure Horten-originated all-wing research. The Allies would seize several Horten originals from the salt mine at Salzdettfurt, where they had been hidden. The Ho 229 V3 was secured by American forces at the Gothaer works at Gotha-Freidrichroda in April 1945 and transported in June 1945.[11]

According to the CIOS interrogations, Reimar had started work on more than just plans for his large airline transport at Gottingen. Details of the six BMW engines, set in an all-wing planform of 157ft (49m) span – arguably perhaps the most incredible of the 1940s Horten designs – could be seen on the Ho 13 pure glider designed for aerodynamics research, yet it looked like a modern fighter with high sweepback planform, and ultra-thin aerofoil of the smoothest skin criteria.

That the Hortens had leapfrogged perceived practice and entered the unknown was certain. The world's first jet-powered flying wing was of Horten design. Yet oddly, for many decades afterwards, it was assumed that their work had been an interesting, yet passing footnote in the development of the aeroplane. All that changed from the 1980s onwards, when, starting with the B-2 and F-117 airframes and then onwards to today's 'blended wing' fashion, the knowledge of the Hortens manifested itself in a new all-wing movement – one that used many of their secrets.

We can argue that others, notably J.K. Northrop, G.T.R. Hill, and J.W. Dunne, achieved much in the same field, but we can also note that it was 1941 before Northrop really succeeded with larger, thicker, more stable, all-wings – whereas the Horten designs used a tuned, thinner aerofoil of lower drag and with all the consequent benefits. We can also debate whether the Northrop wings really tamed the all-wing airflow behaviours in the manner that Reimar Horten had? Throw in Horten's advanced, low-radar signature, composite wood and plastic construction, sailplane, and powered configurations, sweepback of 60°, and the nature of what the brothers from Bonn achieved so long ago, suddenly seems far more important than previously realised.

The Devastating British CIOS/RAE Report – the Wilkinson Paper[12]

Back in 1946, however, an agenda seems to have been at work. An Anglo-American Combined Intelligence Objectives Sub-Committee (CIOS)/Royal Aircraft Establishment (RAE) report on the Horten design work appears to have set out to undermine their ideas and work. Was it a fair hearing? Or was it a policy decision, or a result of ego and jealousy? We may never know, but it could be construed as having been a way of helping to shield the reality of the Horten achievement so that greater powers could seize their ideas and keep them unseen for decades amid a global technology race between east and west.

In this scathing CIOS-led RAE report on the work of the Horten brothers, who were held in London and Farnborough for several months in 1945, a later luminary of British aviation, gliding, design, and the airline business, K.G. Wilkinson, interviewed the Hortens (and referred to a CIOS interrogation with one, *single*, opinionated, mathematically unskilled example of their workforce). Wilkinson then dismissed their ideas and works as apparent flights of fancy; stemming, it seemed, from what felt like a British attitude of the Hortens being men 'without the proper background, don't you know'.

The language of the report speaks volumes for its principal author's attitude: and cites a view that the Hortens investigated issues that took their fancy and that their methods had the temerity to favour observed physical aerodynamic results over the theory upon which the British preferred to trust![13]

Such words mask the fact that Reimar Horten's actual flight-tested observations of a prototype are clearly being suggested as inferior to theoretical calculations! Incredibly, this was stated in the knowledge that the Hortens had equipped their flight test airframes with woollen tufts and flown alongside the airframe in a Fieseler Storch, which photographed the tuft patterns in real flight! It seems to be being suggested by Wilkinson that theory would have overruled any actual flight findings. Wilkinson and others were locked into their certainty that wind tunnel tests of theoretical ideas provided the best results. Even the likes of Prandtl and Betz had had to actually visit the Hortens to grasp a different possibility. Wilkinson, it seems, resisted.

Yet the report was not, as some have portrayed it, solely the work of the one man whose name headed its title – Kenneth G. Wilkinson of the RAE Farnborough.

Astoundingly – given his connections to all-wing research (including German designers, B.S. Shenstone and Professor Parkin's Canadian all-wing group) – Professor G.T.R. Hill was also a part-time member of the CIOS report team led by Wilkinson. Furthermore, ex-Wasserkuppe pilot and Horten Ho 4 pilot, Squadron Leader Robert Kronfeld, was also present, as were Messrs Power from General Aircraft Ltd (builders of an all-wing proposal) and Watson (Armstrong Whitworth), who were working on their own all-wing machine under chief designer John Lloyd, and a Mr Lee from Handley Page – also builders of all-wing proposals. What on earth led these all-wing men to decry the Hortens? Maybe they, individually, did not; perhaps one single editorial influence was at work?

Of little known fact, was that the British sought out the Hortens on several occasions in 1945–1946. As early as April 1945, a CIOS team got to Bonn to interview the brothers about their designs – that was before Hitler's death, the Third Reich's demise and V.E. day. Some urgency in speaking to the Hortens was therefore evident. Having been arrested by US forces on 7 April, by May, the Horten brothers were en route to the RAE – via a detainment in Kensington Palace Gardens London. Interviews began on, or around, 17 May and lasted until the 31 May. As a result of such, a British team, including Wilkinson, went back to Germany in June 1945 with the Hortens to try and secure Horten airframes – to little avail.[14]

The funding for this exclusive visit included specific air transport movements and operational support. Then, in September 1945 (the Hortens now back in Germany), the *British Tailless Advisory Committee* also took itself off to Bonn for more discussions about Horten all-wing designs. Even a member of the Fairey Company sought out Reimar Horten in 1947. Given such efforts and expense, it seems odd that the resulting official report of the British authorities should be so dismissive of the brothers' work. We have to now ask, what games, what agendas were at work?

If we suggest that without the Horten's contribution and Lippisch's own efforts, would the world's first all-wing fighter that was the Me 163, have ever existed? Who built the first jet-powered all-wing? The Hortens – not Northrop and the Americans. Can we not offer this as some effect of the Hortens works? If so, they once again step beyond the parody of being 'glider enthusiasts' that the likes of Wilkinson tainted them with.

The answer as to why, may lie in the fact that the maverick Hortens had not done their sums in a wind tunnel, but had the temerity to build and actually fly a test model; and then the full-size airframes – *in real air*! Even old Professor Prandtl (and later Dr Betz) had been to speak to the young brothers in the 1930s. Prandtl was immersed in the blinkers of wind tunnel-only research. Having seen amazing low-level stunts performed in a Horten all-wing machine, Prandtl had

had to change his opinion about the so-called lack of stability he had assumed afflicted the all-wing.

The likes of Wilkinson and von Kármán, who had both interviewed the Hortens in London, were apparently trapped into a prejudged mindset of some arrogance. It was a familiar and typical conceit. From such a standpoint, Wilkinson and his ilk were perhaps never going to understand the Hortens. And was Reimar likely to divulge his wingtip airflow researches to such people and could we blame him if he did not?

In his work on the Hortens that stemmed from direct input from the brothers, David Myhra[15] perhaps hints at a possible scenario of Reimar Horten's views about Wilkinson. We might feel that Wilkinson was, potentially, a man locked into an academic ego or agenda: given recent events and the resurgence of the all-wing, many concur with Horten and Myhra's opinions. When questioned, other experts such as Wills and Shenstone all had a positive opinion of the Hortens and Reimar's wing design ideas and the testing thereof in flight, *not* in a small wind tunnel affected by scale effects and flow interferences. The Horten work on aerofoil tuning, sweep, washout and other lift criteria were groundbreaking. How could the CIOS report ignore this – other than deliberately for reason of either ignorance or requirement?

Such was the devastating effect upon the Hortens' reputation by Wilkinson's report that the American view of their ideas was tainted. By 1949, Reimar had removed himself to Argentina and Walter returned to Germany, only later to become a senior Luftwaffe and NATO general in the new Germany of the 1960s. If Wilkinson was correct, and the Hortens' all-wing work was a blind alley, we have to ask why the RAeS awarded them gold and bronze medals respectively several decades later for their all-wing work, of which most was researched in 1935–1945. We should also ask why, in 1945, Horten all-wing and parabolic airframes were shipped to America and studied, only to be reproduced (Northrop not ignored) as the basis of all-wing military aircraft and drones, let alone forthcoming airliners, in recent years?

Clearly, under the American and British 1945–1946 views of the Hortens, other agendas were at play and Kenneth Wilkinson, a man so correctly respected for his later gliding and airline transport works, may, or may not have been dancing to a prejudged outcome set by higher authority. Either that, or was Wilkinson an alleged bigot of an academic who had prejudged the issue via the potential contamination of von Kármán's certainties and a chat with one ex-Horten worker? What of the esteemed Professor Hill and others on the Wilkinson team? What agenda was afoot? Was this a politically-led report framed to shield the reality of the Hortens' achievements while British and American all-wing work raced ahead, or was it a veiled attack by academics upon the maverick of genius – genius later awarded RAeS recognition and medals?

Intriguingly, the Horten airframes that the CIOS teams did secure from various locations in Germany disappeared for over a year – only to then emerge in America – a brief appearance at Farnborough notwithstanding. It is recorded that by 1947 several Horten airframes (Ho 3; Ho 4; Ho 6) had been taken to Britain, Canada, and, of note, the Northrop works in California. It is reasonable to state – not the least in light of Horten-related technical reports and photographs that emanated from Wright Field, Dayton, Ohio, at the time – that the Ho 3, Ho 4, Ho 9 V2 and Ho 229 V3 airframes were taken to Wright Field and studied at the secret facilities there, before the Ho 4 being sent to Northrop.

Whatever is the truth of the events around the 1945 interrogations of the brothers and the hunt for and locations of the airframes, the CIOS 'Wilkinson Report' slated the Hortens. Similarly, a US Army report of the brothers when first interviewed in Germany by US agents, suggests that, to the interviewer, the brothers were eccentric or abnormal, with the actual phrase being 'exceedingly peculiar and can be easily classified as eccentric and individualistic'.[16]

We can ask when did individuality or superior thinking become 'peculiar'? We can safely suggest that the brothers' brand of 'abnormality' was superior intelligence to the 'norm' that obviously needed to be undermined by those less blessed and that the interviewer and author of that report, and his masters, were perhaps not equipped with the highest of abilities in assessing the brainpower of Reimar and Walter Horten. Reimar Horten can only be cited as the man who made ultimate all-wing design viable across a wide spectrum, Walter the man who engineered the ideas into airframe reality. Thankfully, through working with expert advocates such as P. Selinger and D. Myhra, Reimar and Walter Horten managed to tell their story for those who wanted to listen. The views of C. Wills (see chapter 11) also provide a confirming narrative to Horten genius.

The Horten brothers' story has suffered numerous reinterpretations, and some recent broadcast documentary claims are best left uncommented upon. A particularly interesting example of the enigma surrounding the Hortens can be found in a recent book about Area 51 by Jacobsen,[17] who clearly frames an evidence trail from Operation Harass documents[18] as cited, that suggests that, circa 1947, the Hortens were in some sense missing and that they were searched for, maybe even hunted for by US authorities over a number of months. Jacobsen frames a view that some kind of manhunt for the brothers took place. Were the Hortens in the Russian Zone? Had the brothers sold out to Russia? Unless someone has missed something it seems inconceivable – although Horten research may have been gleaned by the Soviet authorities via their holding of Gothaer's and Heinkel's, Horten research documents.

Horten Ho 18.

Such suggestions of a Russian connection, or a 'missing' period, do seem very odd indeed when we reference the CIOS/BIOS/RAE reports that stemmed from the Horten brothers seized in Gottingen, Germany, on 7 April 1945, then being transported to London in May 1945, where they were interrogated by numerous figures for several months. As we know, Kenneth Wilkinson interviewed them from 19 May to 31 May 1945, and after that the brothers (and one of their Ho 4 airframes) were seen at the RAE Farnborough a few weeks later. In June, a special return trip to Germany to secure Horten research saw Wilkinson and the CIOS team take the brothers to Bonn and attempt to visit several of their former workshop locations. Wilkinson was on hand in Germany as the two brothers were driven to various sites. This team, with the Hortens, then returned to London.

Many weeks later, under the terms of Operation Matchbox, the brothers were to return to Germany and begin to assemble their works for possible use by the Allies, the RAE overseeing their research in a post Fedden Mission mindset. The potential of Reimar's large, all-wing transport airframe and his jet-powered parabolic fighter (with jet engines mounted at the wingtips), both being the reputed focus of events.

The publication of the damning Wilkinson Report seemingly put an end to British or American interest in the Hortens and their works. By mid-1946, Reimar was back in Germany studying at the University of Bonn for his PhD and Walter was in Germany pursuing private business interests. As late as 1947, Reimar was back in London at the behest of the British Fairey Company and only after that avenue failed and possible Chinese interest,[19] did he begin his journey towards relocation in Argentina via his relationship with Focke-Wulf's Kurt Tank.

Yet, on 18 July 1946, at Chance Vought Aircraft in Stratford, Connecticut, USA, the engineering department was logging a translated document: 'Excerpt from LGB-164/Advance Report "Ten Years Development of the Flying Wing High-Speed Fighter" '. This was a technical paper that had been presented by the Horten Brothers at the wartime-German, 'Flying Wing Seminar' on 14 April 1943. So the Hortens' works were *still* in the minds of the Americans in 1946, despite Wilkinson's efforts. In Canada, the National Research Council (Professor J. Parkin et al) and the Soaring Association of Canada (via D. MacClement and B.S. Shenstone) were closely studying German glider and all-wing design and the war-prize gliders seized from Germany. In California, the men of Northrop were examining actual Horten airframes.

Given all these events – that are documented by the paper trail of the CIOS/RAE papers, Myhra's interviews with the Hortens, and the Wills, and Shenstone recollections, etc. – any new 'evidence' suggesting that in 1946 or 1947 the location of the Horten brothers was unknown, or in any sense, unreferenced, or that they were actually working for the Russians – leading to a 'hunt' for them by US authorities, can, unless reliably challenged, only be seen as either a ruse of paperwork, a deliberate feint created at the time (perhaps to further defame the brothers' reputation?) or a red herring set amid Operation Harass. Factually, such suggestions are at odds with the Allies' contact with the Hortens from the day of their arrest on 7 April 1945 – onwards.

From 7 April 1945 to late 1947, the British and American authorities and other Allied interests had known the brothers' locations and movements. How can they possibly have been missing or working for the Russians? The suggested paper trail of Operation Harass, or any related project, to 'find' the so-called 'missing' Horten brothers, can only be either a deliberate false trail, or a gross administrative error – the right hand not knowing what the left hand had just done - or a result of mixed messages and false trails laid by one party or the other. Unless of course, there is something we have not been told.

Would Walter Horten have become a senior NATO officer amid the rebuilt Luftwaffe if he had been a Nazi, or a Soviet worker? Of course not. Would the Royal Aeronautical Society have awarded bronze and gold medals to Walter and Reimar, respectively, if they had been tainted by a past of Nazi or Soviet activism? No.

One thing must be obvious, the boys from Bonn were neither Nazis nor Soviet stooges, but they became the proud German fathers of successful, swept-wing, low-drag, safe handling, all-wing planforms. Their ideas, notably Reimar's all-wing, swept planform, lift behaviour and trailing edge studies, have, shall we say, been 'used' by the western powers and form the basis of today's advanced guard of all-wing/blended knowledge and also contributed to the wider, swept-wing revolution of the late-twentieth century.

Chapter Five

The Learning Curve

From Silent Flight to Supersonic Speed

rom the Wasserkuppe, from the academic bodies, from the flying clubs and from the greater effect of the segelflug revolution in Germany, came the technology of the new. The development of glider design in Germany immediately touched powered airframe design knowledge and trends. The wider effects would go supersonic and reach orbit.

From such roots came the German arsenal of aerospace technology. There, lay key airframes that would shape the future, not then cast, upon the skies of the Cold War and beyond. Principal amongst these machines were the swept-wing, all-wing, jet and rocket-powered machines that formed the basis of the future of man's flight – not that the public or most military men knew that at the time.

Amid the cadre of advanced aerodynamics research were men such as Benz, Gothert, the Gunters, Henschel, Hertel, Horten, Jensen, Junkers, Kupper, Lippisch, Mittelhuber, Multhopp, Pohlmann, Voigt, Vogt, and many more. They worked for *Flugzeugbau* (aircraft design bureaus) and airframe manufacturing companies that soon embraced swept-wings and all-wing concepts. From experiments in forward sweep, to variable geometry planforms, to delta shapes and a mixture of all-wing and tailless combinations, advanced German design was years ahead of the competition.

Hugo Junkers had been an early exponent of the all-wing via his 1910 patent application for such a craft, but even Ernst Heinkel would adopt the all-wing planform in the wake of Junkers' and Lippisch's thinking.

Junkers

As early as 1910, Hugo Junkers stated his belief (latterly echoed by Lippisch) that any part of an airframe that did not produce lift ought to be inside the wing.[1] What is more, only the *Treaty of Versailles* prevented Junkers from proceeding with his all-wing machines – they would surely have been metal-built. As it was, he produced the mammoth Junkers G38 – the world's first, large all-wing type. As the constraints of the treaty were eased, by 1929, Hugo Junkers had built another large, passenger carrying all-wing prototype design in the strangely entitled J 100. Soon afterwards came the more conventional Ju 52 tri-motor.

The Junkers F13, with its corrugated duralumin panelling, has to be cited as the world's first 'proper' all-metal airliner. Surely the F13 was the precursor to the formula that gave us the DC-2, DC-3 and beyond? And surely the slowness of the British school of design can be framed by the post-F13 existence of the Handley Page HP 42 dinosaur of an airliner?

One of the ironies of Hitler's egotism and his failure was that Germany had no large, long-range four-engined bomber fleet – a very strange omission in the Reich's conceit of its own existence. This was not because the design technology did not exist, but because Hitler's micro-management of policy was psychologically as flawed as the man himself. In the Junkers company, a design for the Ju 90 – a swept-wing, four-engined bomber by Ernst Zindel – did exist and could have easily given the German war machine an Atlantic-capable long-range bomber. Russia, Britain and America, would all have had to take such a threat very seriously indeed, but incredibly, Germany lacked a long-range bombing strategy and the Ju 90 – the airframe that would have provided it – was cancelled.[2] In the Ju 287 we saw what was the world's first swept-wing, jet-engined, heavy bomber design.

Hugo Junkers was no Nazi and refused to deal with the Third Reich of Hitler in 1933. Unsurprisingly, Junkers AG Dessau was nationalised – seized from the Junkers family, and by 1935 Hugo himself was dead. Hugo Junkers and his nascent design team had visions of a globally encompassing airline transport network served by their designs. Yet his name lived on in the Reich's war machines and the company retained an interest in the all-wing, this led to a series of Second World War proposals for all-wing airframes from Dessau.

Having looked at forward wing sweep via its Hans Wocke influenced Ju 287, the all-wing ethos of Hugo Junkers still lived on in the wartime company. Using its own knowledge and that gleaned from Horten researches via the Lippisch and Messerschmitt relationship, Junkers drew up Project 130–140 as a series of jet-powered, all-wing designs for a long-range bomber. By this time, Heinrich Hertel had moved from Heinkel to the Junkers Company and brought his all-wing and tailless works with him. By late 1944, the German Air Ministry had decided that Junkers would build a production standard version of the Horten Ho 18 – this was to become framed as the 'Amerika Bomber'. Thus came together, Hertel, Zindel, Wocke, and Voigt as co-designers of a Horten-referenced airframe – yet one which would be given a vertical tail at the insistence of the aforementioned team. Several of these men, and Bruno Baade, would find themselves east of Moscow before the end of 1946.

Events precluded the reality of Project 130–140, and the same events curtailed the swept, almost all-wing Ju 128 fighter prototype.

It was Junkers who also persevered with Rudolf Diesel's engine design and pioneered all-metal construction for airframes via the use of Duralumin. In Hugo

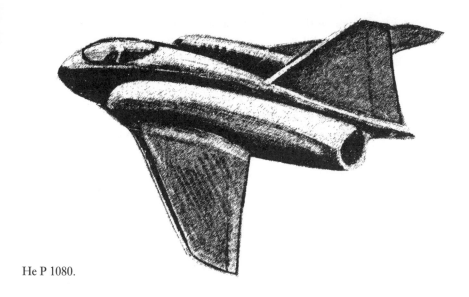

He P 1080.

Junkers, we also see the beginning of viable, metal-built, all-wing flight, diesel-cycle engine design and axial flow jet engines. When the Soviet Army seized the Dessau factories in July 1945, there were still nearly 150,000 employees. Amongst these were several top Junkers designers – notably Brunolf Baade and Hans Wocke. From their works came the very first pylon-mounted engines beneath a wing and, fuselage-pylon mounted engines; at a time when Allied jet designers were following the wing-root buried engine philosophy. Also in Russia was Heinkel's designer, Siegfreid Gunter and the DFS director Professor Bock. Dr Anslem Franz, who had been responsible for axial-flow jet engine development at Junkers in Dessau, had escaped the advancing Russians and within not too long a period, re-emerged as a leader in a design bureau in the United States of America.[3]

Put simply, the total effect of Germany's design and manufacturing pioneer, Hugo Junkers and his Fluzeugbau und Motoren Werke AG, cannot be underestimated and post-Second World War Russian aviation would soon benefit from those Junkers designs and employees that had not escaped its reach. Can we conjecture that today's European (EADS) blended wing proposals owe part of their heritage to Hugo Junkers, the Junkers' Professor Hertel and the all-wing design he penned for Junkers and his post-war employer that was SNECMA of France.

Heinkel

The Heinkel Company was as much a part of German aviation as any other household name. If Blohm and Voss, or Focke-Wulf had specialisations, so too did Ernst Heinkel. Perhaps Arado had a similar advanced thinking, but Heinkel was a one man band – or so the marketing went – but in fact its design team lay behind the 'name'. Ernst Heinkel was a man who, like Junkers, refused to embrace Nazism, yet remained a pragmatic survivor – unlike Hugo Junkers.

Few people realise that Werhner von Braun started his career with Ernst Heinkel Flugzeugwerke GmbH.

Heinkel loved speed and he loved monoplanes. From early collaborations he co-created the famous Albatross B.1 in the First World War and after establishing his company in the early 1920s, soon signed up the Gunter brothers, Walter and Siegfried, to create a series of sleek, advanced monoplane designs. The Paul Baumer-inspired, Gunter-designed, Heinkel He 70, took many world speed records and set new standards. However, it was categorically *not* the basis of the Supermarine Spitfire's ellipsoid wing as some have tried to suggest in contrast to the dated and vital evidence that exists.

Heinkel had an open mind and was willing to try new ideas; it was Heinkel who supported German jet engine development under von Ohain. In the form of the He 111 bomber, aircraft design also took a step forwards. However, it is the fact that the world's first rocket-powered airframe of 1938 and the world's first turbojet aircraft took flight in 1939 under Heinkel's tutelage and brand that is the mark of the man and his company. This jet-powered flight was nearly two years before the British Whittle machine. Heinkel had put his money where his mouth was and built the jet-powered He 162-178 series. The He 178 was the world's first turbojet-powered airframe to fly. The He 162 *Volksjager* also pioneered an engine pod, mounted ventrally atop the fuselage. Heinkel took huge jet airframe steps, which led to the He 343 – a four jet-engined airframe design – as early as March 1944.

However, being rich and supremely confident meant that Ernst Heinkel's opinions were an issue if they conflicted with those of the Nazi High Command – and they often did. Therein may lie some of the reasons why he and his firm were latterly eclipsed in terms of contracts and design development funding. Yet Heinkel's record is illuminated by swept-wing developments, jet engine success and an interest in delta-wing and all-wing planforms. He showed interest in the Hortens work and teamed up with Lippisch. Heinkel's Project P.1078 was an advanced gamble of swept, cranked wing design and jet-power. Delta works at Heinkel also came under the influence of Heinrich Hertel – another 'grandee' of design.

From this airframe came Heinkel's tailless experiments, notably the P.1078 B/C series, which was a tailless, cranked wing device with an unusual, 'double-bubble' fuselage designed to reduce frontal area and improve visibility. In the P.1079 A design, Heinkel's Gunter-led design team created a fan-tailed shape that was latterly closely aped by the Supermarine 508 and Fouga CM.107 Magister. Given that the French had scooped up the Heinkel design and factory assets not in the Soviet zone, this was hardly a surprise. Ultimately, Heinkel would produce the P.1080 delta-winged, twin-jet, T-tailed fighter design – to which later British types from Fairey and Gloster (the Javelin) bore uncanny resemblance. Heinkel himself had been detained for over ninety days in Kensington, London, in 1945 by the combined Anglo-American CIOS/BIOS teams.

An interesting twist in the tale lies in the securing of Heinkel factory assets in Marienehe and Rostock, and of top designer Siegfried Gunter and other leading Heinkel design team members such as W. Benz and A. Jensen, by the Soviet forces in 1946. The British and Americans showed little interest in Heinkel's chief designer, but the Soviet's did and lured him from Berlin. From there we can trace Soviet delta-wing and all-wing jet fighter design to the present day. One quick comparison between the 1950s Soviet output and even recent MiG-29 or Sukhoi designs shows an undeniable and very obvious lineage of Heinkel legacy. Across sixty years, beyond the Cold War, the stunning MiG-29 represents proof of Germany's design brilliance. Having ignored Heinkel and Gunter in the summer of 1945 under Operation Paperclip, the Americans would pay a high price – facing later Cold War Soviet airframes of Gunter and Heinkel genetics.

Heinkel as a corporate entity was absorbed into the VFW concern and its legacy disappeared into today's German aviation industry's roots.

Focke-Wulf

Stemming from the commercial liaison of Professor K.H. Focke and G. Wulf, Focke-Wulf was a company steeped in tradition ideas and designs, and yet in the work of Hans Multhopp it nurtured one of the greatest aerodynamic designers and stylists of the twentieth century. By the early 1930s, the old firm's general design office management was in the hands of a certain, Dr Kurt Tank, an engineer rather than an industrial designer or aerodynamicist. From airships to four-engined transports such as the highly effective long-range Fw Condor, which surely was a wasted device under Hitler's and Göring's planning, Focke-Wulf did create design legends – not least the feared Fw 190 single-engined fighter. Yet Focke-Wulf did not readily embrace the all-wing. This may reflect Kurt Tank's conservatism, yet he and Focke-Wulf did indulge in stylish swept-wing, jet-powered airframes. Of significance, the company produced the Multhopp Ta 183 fighter design – copied the world over post-1945, and with its employees, Multhopp and Winter, detained at the RAE under the CIOS/BIOS programme, Focke-Wulf employees left a legacy upon British swept-wing design – notably as the ER 103 and EE P103 Lightning. Focke-Wulf designs for the 'Triebflugel' found their way to Convair, and to Lockheed post-Operation Paperclip in the form of those companies' VTOL design studies such as ' XFY-1' and XFV-1'. Respectively, swept-wing, pylon-mounted engine design was also born (via Multhopp) in the Fw Ta 283 athodyd research airframes.

Like Dornier and others, Focke-Wulf was not, however, a member of the all-wing club until the last desperate demands of the Nazi regime's RLM demanded advanced 'wonder weapons'. Thus was considered the Focke-Wulf all-wing planform – the 3/1000C. Embracing swept-wings for a larger bomber airframe and aping Horten inspired practice – notably in engine location – Focke-Wulf served up a Lippisch design with two jet powerplants and a curious glazed nose shape. Yet, by 1944, the large bomber idea had belatedly come and gone for the German air force and its supplying industry.

Gothaer

The old Gothaer Waggonfabrik AG Company, known as 'Gotha' after the name of its location, had built biplane bombers in the First World War, which led to the company being cited for restriction in the *Treaty of Versailles* – a unique honour. However, by the 1930s, a resurgent Gothaer company, through the designer August Kupper, had made early investigations into the all-wing planform and the swept-wing. Igor Etrich's monoplane for Gothaer in the First World War might be cited as a precursor of advanced wing design for the company, but by 1936, 'Gotha' had built the Go 147B all-wing prototype. Kupper had been one of the original all-wing glider designers in the early 1920s and Kupper had built the 'Owl' all-wing glider by 1929, with a wingspan of 55.8ft/17m. With research via his work at the DVL, Kupper achieved wing-sweep of nearly 40° (38.7) in the Go 147. Sadly, this great proponent of the all-wing was killed in a crash of his machine.

By late 1942, the aptly named Dr-Ing Rudolf Gothert of the DVL, joined Gotha and brought with him a new enthusiasm for swept-wings and all-wing planforms. Gothert had been a founding member of the DFL and used its wind tunnels to further his wing design work. In what seems a moment of serendipity, the Air Ministry ordered the Hortens to produce their Ho 9 via a construction contract with Gotha; the Hortens lacked the ability to take on large scale production. So a Horten design became a de facto – yet erroneously cited – Gotha production type under Gothert's direction – Dr Gothert being a specialist in aspects of all-wing control surfaces, elevon and aileron design. The jet-powered Ho 229 (or Go 229) would also be built in small numbers by Gotha, but Gotha's designers made changes to the Ho 9 design. Yet the mistakes over the type's nomenclature seem to occur post-war. We can imagine Reimar Horten's feelings at scaled-size, wind tunnel measurements by Gotha being cited as the reason for suggested changes to his design and the negative outcome at full-scale, of such changes.

The proposed Gotha all-wing became the P.60 and its variants, and received a production contract in 1944, yet this would be overtaken by events. The P.60 was the first airframe to use twin, rear-mounted jets that were vertically stacked as part of the fuselage and tail assembly. This idea was copied after 1945 by the English Electric P.1 'Lightning', and the incorporation of the engine in the tail was seen in later tri-jet airliners – notably the DC-10 of the 1970s. The P.60 was a formidable blend of Horten and Gothert ideas, but the war ended before the first airframe was completed. Of significance, it was at the Gotha works in Freidrichoda that advancing American specialists found and seized the Horten Ho 229 V3 swept planform all-wing jet fighter and it was towed across Germany by truck and despatched by ship to America for forensic study. It is now in storage at the Smithsonian Institute's Silver Hill facility.

In mid-1945, under Operation Paperclip, Rudolf Gothert was interned as an intellectual by the American authorities at an airfield near Paris, yet soon returned to Germany, only to then find employment back in France for three years for the Sud-Est Aviation concern, where he worked on a large all-wing airline transport design study not dissimilar to Reimar Horten's ideas for such a type.

Messerschmitt and the Me 262: Swept-Wing Brilliance

Eighteen degrees might not sound much, but it was a revolution at the time. Some commentators say that the Me 262's wing sweep was used to aid C.G. issues stemming from its engine position. This argument seems to suggest that the benefits of wing sweep were an unintended and perhaps unconsidered consequence – as if to decry the knowledge of wing sweep and its application. It is unlikely that a man such as Messerschmitt would countenance the costs of such advanced design simply to alter a C.G. The Me 262's advanced swept-wing handling must have been considered at its application, not as an accident. After all, the Me 262 had the advantage of wing sweep over the competing straight-winged Heinkel 280. The shape of the Me 262's fuselage was no 'accident' either – its unique flattened and chamfered sculpted form represented advanced aerodynamics, not just unintended consequences stemming from using a triangular section fuselage that had room for the retractable main undercarriage. One glance at the Me 262's ungainly rival, the Gloster Meteor, with its slower speed, slower rate of climb and turn and its lower wing energy and higher drag, soon explains why the RAF kept the Meteor out of German skies for any last minute combat against the Me 262. In comparison, we see in the Me 262 the true advance of German aerodynamics over Allied thinking.

Me 262 easily got Mach 0.84, yet by 0.86 would show signs of compressibility and pitch issues over the tailplane. In level flight the 'standard' Me 262 reached a cruise velocity of 541mph (870km/h) and was therefore 120mph (193km/h) faster than any Allied prop-driven competitor.

Messerschmitt's quest for speed came from his early days as a glider pilot and then powered airframe proponent. His Bf 109, stemming as it did from the mind of glider enthusiasts, relied on power, brute force, lightweight construction and some very small-wings to achieve its high speed at the expense of wing loading and turning ability. The 109 was always fast and so too were subsequent Messerschmitt machines. The Me 262 also stemmed from late 1930s work at the DFS and first flew with propeller-power, yet by July 1942 the jet-powered machine (then with tailwheel undercarriage) was achieving 470mph (755km/h).

The penultimate version had to be the 43 degree wing sweep applied to the Me 262 HG-2, with its much more powerful new engines replacing the original Jumo of 1,984lbs thrust per engine, replaced with HeS 011 turbojets of a combined 5,730lbs of thrust (1,594kgs). Even faster was the Me 262 bi-fuel with a rocket pod mounted to the rear. This gave a three-minute climb boost of more than 3,500lbs of extra thrust.

Did the Me 262 also influence civil airliner design? One glance at the Vickers jet Viscount with its underwing engines provides an answer, and a close look at the Boeing 737 sees amazing similarities in wing planform, engine mounting and flap layout, and jet pipe designs and layouts.

Me 163 (Komet): All-Wing Excellence

Although labelled as a product of Messerschmitt of Augsburg, the reality is that the all-wing configured Me 163 had its roots in a Lippisch design first backed by the DFS as the DFS 194 research airframe. This glider-test airframe became a rocket device that could get to a cruise speed of 516mph/830kmh, using its volatile, bi-fuelled, Walter HWK 509-equipped powerplant. Higher speeds were attained later (see below).

All-winged and rocket-powered, the Me 163 could zoom to just under 40,000ft/12,200m in just over three minutes. Combat missions were flown but duration was the limiting factor.

Stemming from his 1930s work into wing sweep and all-wing layouts, yet still possessing a vertical tail – but not, of note, any horizontal tail surfaces – the Me 163 was the stepping stone to really high-speed flight. An ardent all-wing enthusiast, Lippisch remained firm in the belief that the all-wing required a vertical fin for stability. In this he occupied different ground to the Hortens. Having toyed with joining forces with Ernst Heinkel, Lippisch did, in January 1939, join Willi Messerschmitt's company at Augsburg and brought advanced swept-wing and all-wing knowledge to the Messerschmitt bureau – which made the most of it.

Messerschmitt was overjoyed and his 'battle' with Heinkel took another turn. Now that the wily, politically astute Messerschmitt had Lippisch and his 'Department Lippisch' on board, Göring would not fail to be impressed and further funding must be forthcoming, reckoned Messerschmitt.

The DFS research airframe was soon modified from prop-power to glider and then to rocket-power. Yet development stalled at the mad hand of Hitler's ever-fluid war plan. Even in mid-1940, Hitler demanded quick-fixes and approved only design work that would produce airframes within less than twelve months. High-speed research of the likes of the Me 163 would take their time. Willi Messerschmitt provided funding to keep the Lippisch team on the go and the DFS 194 research airframe soon became the Walter rocket-powered Me 163 and benefited from research from Peenemünde in a series of flight tests conducted by Heini Dittmar. Dittmar was a leading test pilot and a confirmed all-wing advocate. Achieving a speed of 620mph/1,000km/h at the transonic gateway to supersonic flight was the goal of the team and even in early flights the later Me 163B was touching Mach 0.87. Yet at the same time Lippisch continued with his delta-wing planform obsession and was creating plans for the P.11 and P.12 delta airframes, which were in rational reality the basis of the delta knowledge and shapes that later manifest in a post-war environment.[4]

From various Lippisch-penned DFS research airframes came the wing sweep of the DFS 194 and Heinkel supported Project X – what became the Me 163. Early variants had varying degrees of sweep along the wing and 'washout' – twisted wingtips to reduce tip-stalling. Up near 580mph these features produced adverse effects via compressibility, but Lippisch soon learned to alter the wing sweep from 23° at quarter chord, to vary from 20° at the root to 32° of sweep near the tip. Built from wood and equipped with various engine options, the records show that an Me 163C reached 702mph on 6 July 1944 in the hands of Rudi Opitz.[5] Despite its service ceiling of 39,500ft, one Me 163 flew to 52,000ft. The Me 163 had a climb rate from take-off that would take decades to be matched by any American or British machine.

To achieve such performance, Lippisch had equipped the little wooden rocket machine with ultra-smooth skin surfacing, a wing fillet, a tuned wing and only a vertical tail. Hours of work into controlling and tuning spanwise flow, interference drag, stability and boundary layer effects were seen in the Me 163. At very high Mach numbers pilots found that the Me 163 tucked its nose under and became uncontrollable, yet without doubt the aircraft was the defining moment in transonic flight design. It was almost there in terms of solving the compressibility problem. If we ignore the vagaries of its explosive T-Stoff fuel mixture and its limited range, it becomes the gateway to the future that the Allies seized upon.

Luminaries of Advanced German Design

Ludwig Prandtl was indeed the 'father' of early aerodynamics, yet he was a man partly constrained by theory, wind tunnels and convention – the 1940s would expose his constraints. Cast with the likes of the Russian Zhukovskii, and the Englishman Lanchester, Prandtl was the main pioneer of the new art of the science that was airflow study. As such, he was the leader of German aerodynamics but also of global appreciation of the science. Although a senior figure, Prandtl was perhaps not as conservative a thinker in the manner of some of his contemporaries and he encouraged free and perhaps even 'wild' thinking. From such traits came the effect of Prandtl's students – notably in Hans Multhopp's works (which touched the Space Shuttle) and in the elements of von Kármán and others. Prandtl was open-minded enough to go and talk to the young Hortens and observe what they had achieved *without* wind tunnels or degrees in mathematics.

Prandtl discovered and defined the theories of the lift distribution and boundary layer behaviours. Few know that he also worked for the great pioneer Hugo Junkers and that, thanks to Prandtl, Junkers AG had one of the earliest and largest wind tunnels in use soon after the 1920s dawned. Prandtl did not just create the calculus and theories of applied aerodynamics; he researched new thoughts and ideas. As early as 1910, Prandtl was refining wing planform ideas into distorted, forward swept elliptical shapes and 30° swept elliptical shapes.

In the 1920s, Hermann Glauert, who had been born in England of German parents, studied under Ludwig Prandtl and then returned to England, where he published translations of Prandtl's defining works, into English. These books, including *The Elements of Aerofoil and Airscrew Theory*, became the standard texts of aerodynamics for many decades. Men like Adolf Betz, Max Munk and Adolph Busemann followed in Prandtl's footsteps and they were the men who helped give birth to the swept-wings of the 1930s. Throw in the works of Vogt, Voigt, the Gunters, Hertel, Blume, Koisin Kupper, Kracht and others and a cadre of aerodynamics men of the calibre to influence global practice becomes obvious in 1930s pre-war Germany.

Ludwig Prandtl's early works effectively built the foundations of the new science of aerodynamics.

Adolph Busemann went on to become one of the key leaders in 1930s swept-wing research work in Germany and presented his theories upon the international stage in a series of papers and lectures, notably at the Fifth Volta Conference. Even von Kármán was initially wary of the swept-wing research, but Busemann worked on the building of the world's first transonic wind tunnels in Germany in 1939. Busemann was grabbed by the US authorities under Operation Paperclip and worked at NACA prior to securing a professorship at the Colorado State University.

Theodor von Kármán was born in Budapest, Hungary. In 1906 he attended the University of Göttingen and received his doctorate under Prandtl. In 1913, he attended the University of Aachen, where he met Hugo Junkers. In the early 1930s, von Kármán moved to Pasadena, California, to become director of the Guggenheim Aeronautical Laboratory at Caltech, which became the centre of aerodynamics in America at that time. Admired by some and not by others, this man was clearly clever, yet in his narrow view that insisted wind tunnels provided answers verifiable to full-scale flight testing, he occupied controversial and risky ground.

Max Munk was born in Hamburg; he was one of Prandtl's most gifted students. He also received his doctorate from the University of Göttingen. As a Jew, he took the decision to leave Germany very early on and moved to the USA. He rose to prominence at NACA Langley, Virginia, and created a new type of wind tunnel.

Ignaz, or 'Igo', Etrich, was from Trutnov, in what was Bohemia. From education in Leipzig, Etrich was another early thinker affected by the work of Professor Ahlborn on the *Zanonia Macrocarpa* seed and its all-wing, tailless design. Etrich noted that Lilienthal had followed such all-wing concepts. Etrich, with family backing, would design a series of small aircraft of advanced planform from his design bureau in Vienna and then in Berlin with the Rumpler concern.

Hans Multhopp – Key Shaper of Modern Aerodynamics?

Of all the men of Germany, Professor Prandtl's student, Hans Multhopp (alongside Alexander Lippisch), arguably, has to be the man of potentially the most influential aerodynamic genius that touched the post-war world. Ironically, in 1945, he was in British hands at the RAE Farnborough, but the British in their arrogance of certainty, let Multhopp dangle, as if they were not really bothered, and he was snapped up by a very grateful America.[6, 7] Decades later, in October 2014, an American unmanned orbital re-entry vehicle – a mini-space shuttle – returned from a secret orbit mission. This small craft, little-publicised and hardly known, looked very futuristic indeed, yet in its design it was a near-identical copy of one of Hans Multhopp's 1950s 'lifting body' all-wing devices that he dreamed up for the Martin company as orbital re-entry vehicles – the precursor of the manned and unmanned NASA 'Shuttles'.

Hans Multhopp, of Lower Saxony and a graduate of Göttingen, was one of the leading young aerodynamics geniuses of his time, an early builder of advanced gliders and also worked in the first of Germany's new wind tunnels. A student of Ludwig Prandtl, Multhopp had true future vision. He joined Kurt Tank's Focke-Wulf outfit at Bremen in 1938 aged just twenty-five. Although steeped in aerodynamic calculus, Multhopp had an eye for form and design – perhaps best exemplified by his creation of the T-tail concept.

Hans Multhopp may have framed the T-tail, but he also knew that the tail offered drag and weight at the expense of its functional efficiency. Multhopp had realised that placing the tailplane high up away from the wash from the main wing meant that it was more efficient and could be made smaller and lighter than a conventional low-set tail. Thus, Multhopp too was an early advocate of the tailless and all-wing concept and this led him to develop his own theories in the field, which were a stepping stone to later all-wing works. Of significance, Multhopp researched lifting all-wing, tailless body theories and forms, work that ultimately shaped the Space Shuttle (albeit a machine festooned with a vertical fin).

Regarded by many as Ludwig Prandtl's leading student, Hans Multhopp was a freethinker and his years working under Kurt Tank at Focke-Wulf may not have been easy. However, from that design bureau stemmed the seminal Focke-Wulf Ta 183. Although deemed a 'Ta' design, this was an advanced, swept-winged airframe that contained much of Multhopp's ideas – notably the highly aerodynamic efficient T-tail (later used worldwide in military and civil aircraft design). Experts now agree that the most advanced and most influential airframe that was not a delta, nor an all-wing type to come out of Germany, was the Multhopp penned and calculated Ta 183. It was closely copied by Saab (J29A 'Tunnan') in the defining Mikoyan (MiG-15/17) and it influenced American and British designs.

An often forgotten Multhopp design signature was his decision to suggest two rear-mounted podded engines on pylons in the swept-wing Focke-Wulf Ta 283 design – a machine powered by a ramjet athodyd gas turbine technology. The machines of these men and their employers were the gateway to today's understanding and practice of aerodynamics.[8]

Of Alexander Lippisch we cannot deny that his 1930s delta and swept-wing experiments informed the Messerschmitt Me 163, and the Me 262. Then came the less well known Me P.1101 which truly was the precursor of many things American, European and Russian post-1945. Neither should we forget that the Heinkel He 178 was the first jet to fly in 1939, or that twin-engined He 280 was also a precursor. An He 280 (V7) with its engines removed was used as a glider in high speed flight research trials in Germany and achieved 578mph in a dive – the world's fastest glider until the Space Shuttle in its landing configuration, over sixty years later. Although the He 280 lost the race to become the world's first operational jet fighter to the Me 262 – which became the chosen instrument – the Heinkel's learning curve was fast and steep. Of men like Voigt and Vogt, Multhopp, Tank, etc., the learning curve was significant.

Of Discs, Bells and Anti-Gravity

Any discussion on the subject of disc flight and anti-gravity is laced with risk. For around the subject lie cliques, agendas, conspiracy theorists and denials. For a scientist to discuss the subject, it can lead to ridicule and career-long detrimental effects. After all, perceived wisdom denies the disc flight and anti-gravity story. In the disc-flight story lie problems and prejudices.

To suggest success in creating discoid 'vortex' airframe success, or anti-gravitational shielding, or an anti-gravity effect and airframe use, is a rash thing to do – not least as a number of physicists are involved in the investigation of anti-gravity and no outsider should surely be allowed to usurp their certainties. Throw in the fabled 'Nazi' anti-gravity story and the whole subject becomes a high risk arena. The theoretical, let alone commercial issues of a success in defining an anti-gravity mechanism would, without doubt, be earth-shattering. Yet certain facts are known within the 'anti-gravity' establishment – even if they are not admitted to in the journals of learned men and their societies, or public discourse. NASA and Boeing have investigated anti-gravity, but a pre-existing narrative has been established around the subject – just as it was over Operation Paperclip, UFOs, Nazi technology and the Apollo programme. If, as the American Physical Society tells us, that anti-gravity is a 'physical impossibility'[9], then all outcomes are, of course, prejudged and pre-narrated.

Yet the facts are that anti-gravity experiments have been taking place since the late 1930s and the German Nazi war machine spent many millions of its money on researching the possibilities of anti-gravity, the separate, Coanda effect, disc flight, metallurgy and propulsive technology. This is fact and by 1946 the American Government was also funding related research in Canada with Alexander Lippisch as a consultant.

Henri Coanda had earlier observed that if airflow is powered it will, via the boundary layer effect, follow the contours of a body over which it can be forced to flow. Evolving such theory by 1941, Germany was pouring money into researching the effect – the 'Coanda Effect' and a Coanda 'disc' research programme was later absorbed via Wright Field, Ohio, and Malton Airbase, Ontario, in a post Operation Paperclip environment. Yet it had been as early as 1936 that Professor Heinrich Focke had designed and patented a lifting body that contained two (enclosed) rotors that drove the airflow over the body and also provided thrust action. Earlier still, a German amateur enthusiast named Arthur Sack, from the Leipzig region, had built a circular model aircraft – a 'flying saucer'. This was officially endorsed in June 1939 at the Nazi's National Air Contest in Leipzig. The Sack disc was seen performing a 100metre flight and even featured in the British aeronautical media. Flying discs and flying bell-shaped machines, were also all-wing or wing only –

the Coanda effect alone was a low drag, high-lift marker of ultimate aerodynamic efficiency.

The roots of vortex-motor and energy-field research are often (possibly mistakenly) ascribed solely to Viktor Schauberger, whose own lifting body research work led to the fabled 'Repulsin' mechanism and effect.

A self-taught inventor from an agrian background, Schauberger had been working on such energy field devices since the early 1930s and had applied for patents to cover his research into a propulsive effect – an 'engine' that created not just thrust from its power, but a new effect. By sucking air into an especially shaped chamber and creating exhaust venturis, a multi-dimensional vortex is formed and then used across surfaces and 'air tunnels. Such airflow control via implosive forces (as opposed to traditional jet-type explosive forces) of water and gaseous boundary layers, were the very core of Schauberger's early, self-taught works. However, the capturing and channelling of an element and the use of shaping and charging effects were the central heart of Schauberger's turbine-related thinking. Such 'ram', 'chamber', and 'efflux' forces (notably nozzle design) were to become vital in von Braun's rocket motors and in the development of the jet engine itself. Some might conjecture as to whether Schauberger's early research was a precursor to the research that informed the jet and rocket motor and disc aerofoil design. Others might dismiss him as a woodsman who dreamt a lot and achieved little.

However, the research of Schauberger (and his studies at Prague University) *had* kicked off study into the pattern and energy of the disc effect. Schauberger created analysis of water and air flow and of altered states of active lift – but then so too had 1930s hydroplane enthusiasts like Lippisch, Tietjens and others. But Schauberger stepped from studies of hydrodynamic flow to magneto-hydrodynamic flow and in doing so sowed the seeds for the bell-shaped anti-gravity flight experiments that the mysterious, SS figure of Hans Kammler may well have delivered to the Allies. Was the Heinkel company the Berlin Air Ministry's chosen implement in developing or assisting the Prague researchers? It has been suggested that this was the case, but Heinkel's soon to be scant resources were all focused on jet engine, rocket motor, and airframe developments. Schauberger would end up working for Messerschmitt, but all the 'discoid' and anti-gravity work would soon come under the control of the SS and from thereon come the tales of 'occult' and possibly delusional behaviours associated with the events and later versions of the story told by others.

Schauberger, like other Austrian and German experts, was forced to become a party-member and to work under SS direction. This did not make him a Nazi, and of note, in 1934 he had refused to supply Hitler's new regime with intellectual data. Sadly, the 'occult' background of the Nazi Party, which manifested in the early-1920s, means that any discussion of the disc technologies immediately gets labelled as the ramblings of the delusional, the mad, or the fantasist. Of note, Schauberger was imprisoned by both the Nazis and the Americans – ultimately he died an early death. Finding peer-reviewed 'proof' of his claims and those claims about him remains an obstacle, but the evidence trail of anecdote and beyond, exists.

Early disc or all-wing circular planform aircraft researches were dated pre-1920 and, by 1925, a Professor Winifried Otto Schumann of Munich Technical University School had designed disc-shaped aerial devices. At the same time as early disc-body research, based on parabolic and elliptical effects, the Hortens' were moving towards the creation of their semi-disc parabola-shaped machine – not a Coanda-effect type – but, nevertheless, a parabolic flying wing. Both Sack and the Hortens had the interest of, and backing from, the Luftwaffe's General Ernest Udet. Through Udet's support, the true beginnings of German wartime research into the separate arenas of all-wing, disc, and bell planform technology began. Lippisch would soon research the concept, and VTOL, further. This technology was obvious and relatively simple and it did not involve UFO's, aliens or mass hysteria (yet).

Researchers into the Nazi disc research programme have often cited the names of Schreiver, Miethe, Habermohl, and others. Ascribing actual status, qualifications and referenced location to such names is fraught with difficulty and numerous authors have built or confabulated, claim upon claim. The evidence trail has become clouded by false spoor and the disc-flight story has suffered as a result. Claims of actually achieving discoid anti-gravity flight prior to 1945 are splattered around various authors on the subject's narratives, but the evidence is anecdotal. However, upon his deathbed, Viktor Schauberger is said to have insisted that disc-flight was achieved in the 1940s.

Yet, as the post-Roswell 'UFO' created myth manifested across America, 1950 saw the likes of Rudolph Schreiver tell the media, and principally *Der Spiegel* of 30 March 1950, that Prague University academics had suggested flying disc technology during the Second World War and that all this research had been taken from Prague by the Germans. But does such a claim make a truth? Who were Schriever and Miethe? What was their exact status? Was one of them even qualified to comment? Here lay the origins of the all-wing 'flying saucer' in all its reality and myth, respectively.

Of note, anti-gravity and bell-shaped devices have become the focus of recent discussion – with much of it being framed in a 'conspiracy theory' framework hooked up on the UFO phenomena. This allows experts and academics to dismiss certain aspects of the anti-gravity ' device narrative as the work of overactive minds amid the UFO supporters. Yet the facts are very simple, for anti-gravity research was established in Germany prior to 1939 and was seized under Operation Paperclip, only to become a seventy year research programme around such all-wing, parabolic designs – only recently alluded to by NASA.[10]

In simple terms, the concentration of giga-electron-volt potentials, created in a high vacuum atmosphere has the ability to not just provide flight, but also to provide stability to a device. This is achieved by 'charging' a body as an electron capacitor and creating a 'gauss' effect of magnetic field activity – an energy change – this becomes separate or insulated from background levels. This effect was in part, proven by creating a 'degaussing' field around ships (using charged wires) in order to set off mines at sea before the ships own hull was close enough to do so, thus avoiding explosive damage.

Expanding this theory in a lifting body creates an electron-charged, magnetic, plasma-altering effect and this forms a diode that differentiates between the charge body and the surrounding atmosphere. From this comes the 'anti-gravity' effect of a different atmospheric layer or 'cloud' that then levitates the device concerned via a magnetic buoyancy within the device from what we term a 'plasma' effect. Electrostatic ion-moving effects can be manifested in electrogravity experiments known to most physicist students. The 'plasma' effect and magnetic levitation occupy shared ground – as does the gyroscopic effect. Studies in hydromagnetic displacement and lines of force energy fields all go back more than 100 years, yet it was German and Czech scientists that focused such studies in the late 1930s. Creating a plasma-charged super conductor that will repel external forces became a negative gravity reversing device. If, as is accepted, a magnetic force can attract a body to the earth's surface, surely a *reversed* magnetic force device can repel and move such a body *away* from the earth in a weightless state. If this is so, 'anti-gravity' effect or 'flight' becomes a reality. Any such device would have remarkable properties.

In an intriguing tangent to the 1930s study of theoretical physics, gas flow, ion charging and related gaseous boundary layer effects (based at Princeton University), one of the leaders of 1930s nuclear spectrography was a certain Allen Goodrich Shenstone. A.G. Shenstone was also a decorated wartime scientific intelligence officer, senior member of Canada's National Research Council and intriguingly, uncle of the Supermarine Spitfire's Lippisch-trained aerodynamicist, B.S. Shenstone – who during the Second World War could be found at the Air Ministry in London, or at the secret research facility at Wright Field, Dayton, Ohio, prior to working with his old friend Lippisch on 'disc' designs at Avro in Canada. Intriguingly, another Princeton expert, Dr H.P. Robertson would lead Operation Paperclip's advance team in 1945 and go on to frame the disc-flight and 'UFO' psy-ops programme in the early 1950s.

Applying knowledge about plasma force fields to magnetic 'polarised' effects came about during 1940s nuclear and other experiments in Germany, and built a core knowledge base that was in advance of US findings at that time. Electromagnetic 'pulse' effects created by chemically created explosive disturbance

The Fafnir glider, the
world's smoothest
sailplane, 1931.
Note the wing fillet.
Groenhoff in cockpit,
designer Lippisch
in crowd at the
Wasserkuppe.
(*Photo B.S. Shenstone*)

Right: Lippisch,
Groenhoff and others
manoeuvre the scale
model of the all-wing
onto the launch track at
the Wasserkuppe.
(*Photo B.S. Shenstone*)

Below: Lippisch's
all-wing aerofoil ready
for launch. (*Photo B.S.
Shenstone*)

First flight test of the Lippisch all-wing at the Wasserkuppe. Note reverse-angled sweep to ailerons to add forward sweep at tips. (*Photo B.S. Shenstone*)

All-wing excellence. The Lippisch D.2 in 1930. (*Photo B.S. Shenstone*)

Wasserkuppe 1930. Alexander Lippisch standing; Gunter Groenhoff in cockpit. (*Photo B.S. Shenstone*)

Lippisch D.2 full-scale all-wing test airframe readying for flight, Wasserkuppe. (*Photo B.S. Shenstone*)

Horten Ho.4 all-wing scale test model in flight. (*Photo L. Cole*)

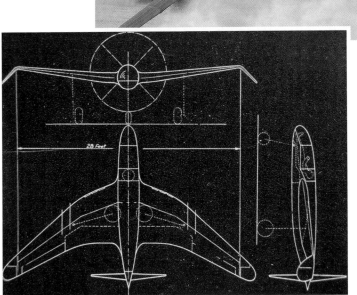

B.S. Shenstone's 1938 all-wing design for a fighter airframe. Note anhedral wing-tips and cranked swept-wing. (*Photo L. Cole*)

Me 262. Smooth skinned and swept-winged. The aerodynamically tuned flat undersurface is very obvious here. (*Photo T. Hart*)

Me 163. All-wing reality that opened the doors of perception in Allied minds. (*Photo T. Hart*)

Lippisch DM. 1 Delta. The airframe was studied in the USA and became the basis of all subsequent Delta outcomes. (*Photo L. Cole*)

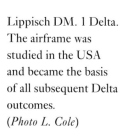

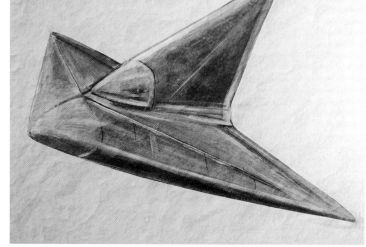

The first American iteration of Lippisch DM.1/DM.2 research was the XF-92 Delta as a outcome of Operation Paperclip. (*Photo NASA*)

Avro's Vulcan shows off its Lippisch-derived delta-wing. Note revised leading edge shape. (*Photo T. Hart*)

Me P. 1101 was the next swept-wing step from the Me 262. The Fedden Mission and CIOS teams inspected the airframe in 1945 prior to shipment to the USA. (*Photo L. Cole*)

Bell's X–5 was
a direct copy of
the Me P. 1101
that was found at
Oberammergau.
(*Photo NASA*)

DH 108 swept-wing
research airframe
after the Lippisch,
Messerschmitt and
Horten ideas.
(*Photo D.H.*)

The DH 110 that
closely resembled the
Fw P.6 Flitzer. Note
twin booms and
'beaver tail' exhausts.
(*Photo T. Hart*)

EE P.1 Lightning that so closlely aped the Multhopp and Winter designs for the RAE in 1947. (*Photo T. Hart*)

HP Victor displays the crescent-wing design taken from Koisin's Arado designs. (*Photo by T. Hart*)

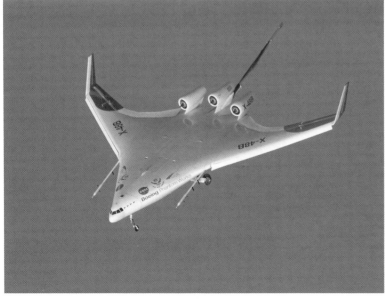

Boeing and NASA designed this blended-wing body X-48 B airframe. It is cited as a new invention and the future, but surely it is an all-wing reinvention. (*Photo NASA*)

Left: 1933 Maikafer or Mayfly designed by the DFS, was the world's first swept-wing, ellipsoid high aspect ratio airframe. (*Photo B.S. Shenstone*)

Right: The futuristic Horten Ho.4a built 1941 at Konigsburg, seen in England 1946. (*Photo by VGC Chris Wills Collection*)

Horten Ho.15B or IAe 34-M with 18m or 59ft span, seen in 1950s Argentina. (*Photo VGC Chris Wills Collection*)

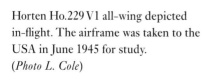

Horten Ho.229 V1 all-wing depicted in-flight. The airframe was taken to the USA in June 1945 for study. (*Photo L. Cole*)

were only discovered when the means to view and analyse such events came about in the 1930s. The creation of electromagnetic disturbance during atomic explosion and electron experiments should not therefore have been a surprise to experts circa 1941. Using such science, the Germans built a series of disc and bell-shaped electron-charged lifting body devices that have now become framed as the 'Nazi Bell Project'. With its space flight potential, such 1940s research was embraced by von Braun at Peenemünde and became part of the great cache of aerospace science that the USA seized under Operation Paperclip.

The NASA Apollo Space programme was the first iteration of von Braun's rocket thrust work, but the application of Nazi anti-gravity knowledge in space vehicles and in flying devices, has never been fully revealed across its seventy-five year history. Work on such science by the US Air Force, NASA, and its contractors – notably Bell Corporation and North American Aviation – and touched by the likes of Lippisch and others, proceeded throughout the 1960s. And of the reputed sixty-three German scientists who, in 1944, were working on the orders of the Nazis to develop the anti-gravity effect as part of Hitler's last gasp of 'wonder-weapons', the reader might ask what happened to them and their precious, advanced knowledge? The suggested answer is that they were all murdered by their employer – the Nazi Party – at the Führer's direct orders in early 1945. Clearly, their level of knowledge must have represented a threat even to the delusions and disease of Hitler's deteriorating condition. And yet Dornberger, von Braun, and their team of 500-plus rocketeers, were not assassinated – and the mystery of why, and of Hans Kammler's possible role in saving them, remains an unknown.

Within the anti-gravity story lies another example of how German science was seized and re-purposed into the technological future that became today and tomorrow amid a pre-narrative of denial by the powers of the state. None of the weird origins in the occult of the disc flight programme of the Nazi Party, or the confabulated anecdote cited as 'evidence' ever since, alters the fact that, at the end of the war, the Allies, and principally the Americans, grabbed every aspect of the disc aerofoil/anti-gravity research works. They took it all off to Wright Field for analysis and thence much of it went to Avro in Canada as the basis of a US funded research programme.

So there is 'fact' in the anti-gravity' story – be it a combination of force or energy field, aerodynamic (Coanda) effect, or the more obscure 'earth energy' characteristics often cited, and German research furthered all aspects of these possibilities to create a viable flying disc. Some say that this was achieved as a jet-powered Coanda effect (later 'copied' by Avro), others lean towards the possibility of German and then American success in creating a true anti-gravity aerial device.

Avro Canada, Lippisch, Shenstone, Frost and a Disc-Flight Story

A ruse of feints were applied to the rocket, all-wing and disc technologies that arrived in America from the summer of 1945 onwards. Without delving into conspiracy theory, the nature and course of the story can be easily framed.

Fascinated by the possibilities of the rocket science, all-wing, and flying disc technology, forensic study of German machinery took place at Wright Field (now Wright-Patterson AFB). There, from Hangar 18 and beyond, a whole series of experts and academics were gathered to assess the German technology, and the German scientists themselves. A familiar name, Beverley Shenstone, was a Wright Field regular from 1941–1945, his fluent technical German and friendship with Alexander Lippisch and Junkers luminaries being just the tip of that particular iceberg.

Soon after the gathering of the technology and the technologists in 1945, there manifested the great 'UFO' mass psy-ops game where a false trail was laid by the authorities in order to conceal their examination and flight testing of all-wing and disc-technology airframes. Thus began Project Grudge and then Project Bluebook. The infamous Roswell 'UFO' event can rationally be framed as nothing less and nothing more likely than the flight testing of Horten Ho 9/Ho 229 derived designs amid the relevance of delta-wings, parabolas, discs and boundary layer controlled devices. Little green men from planet alien are unlikely to be the cause of the Roswell affair – or 'incident' as it is best described.

A longer term ruse was the setting up of publicly acknowledged scientific experiments to design and build disc-shaped craft. The British A.V. Roe (Avro) company would soon be busy creating Lippisch inspired delta-winged prototypes that led to the mighty 'Vulcan' delta-wing bomber, but Avro (Canada), which was a large and successful Canadian company, was soon to be associated with the flying disc 'Silverbug' and 'Avrocar' programmes. Were these a double-edged device to publicly demonstrate a PR-friendly face of the new heat of technology, or a cover for something more? Such devices could hardly 'fly' and should not be held up as UFO 'cover-ups' by theorists. Indeed, the Avro machines were unsuccessful and no amount of UFO hype can change that fact.

Obscured behind the 'Avrocar' and 'Silverbug' experimental devices, lay the real work – the true advance in Coanda-effect disc airframe design and anti-gravity work that stemmed directly from what had gone on in the forests of Bohemia under Nazi control from 1938 to 1945.

The names of Schauberger, von Braun, Miethe, Klein, Schreiver and others, are often cited in stories of advanced technology and many claims and counter claims exist. Confabulation and fantasy are not unknown within the tale, and the story is now occluded by hype, theory and deceit. What we can say with certainty is that a very large amount of money was poured into flying-disc research by Germany and then by the Americans via Avro of Canada from 1946 onwards. This culminated by the mid-1950s in a series of disc-flight related events. But where did the money come from and why?

There was a mass migration of British design to Canada and America in the immediate post-war years and Avro's Malton, Ontario, base was a hive of jet, all-wing and disc flight thinking. Was this just a natural consequence of the pace of events from Operation Paperclip onwards, or was it something else entirely?

Famed delta-wing inventor Alexander Martin Lippisch was also a vertical take-off and landing (VTOL) enthusiast and had worked on many VTOL ideas. He had also researched the boundary layer – as had his close friend and slightly younger associate, the aerodynamicist Beverley Shenstone. Of note, Shenstone had published a paper on boundary layer control before the war.[11]

The pair had worked on advanced designs together since 1930 and, as late as December 1938, Shenstone had hosted Lippisch at the RAeS in London, where Lippisch had lectured. The pair would meet next as the Anglo-American CIOS/BIOS/FIAT Paperclip teams raced (with Shenstone's assistance) to rescue Lippisch from Vienna and transport him to safety in London and then Wright Field. Alexander Lippisch's influence on the science of circular or disc shaped 'wings' was significant. Lippisch's VTOL and disc airframe ideas came to the fore at Wright Field, and then in his contribution to the Avro project. Also based at Wright Field were R. Hermann, H. Schmitt, H. Heinrich, F. Doblhoff and E. Zindel. These experts in aerofoils, airframes and supersonics did not work in isolation – there was knowledge transfer between the all-wing and swept-wing designers and the supersonics and rocket teams. The Peenemünde men were not an isolated cadre.

As early as 1941, Lippisch, in his VTOL researches, had tested disc shapes in a wind tunnel at Göttingen and, by 1943, the Prague-based disc research centre had, say many commentators, test-flown a six metre span powered disc device. This work also focused on gyro stabilisation techniques – which later became a core factor in the German 'V' series rockets and in the consequent Saturn and Apollo programmes. So wing design, aerodynamic lift, allied to VTOL, stability and flight, metallurgy, powerplants and rocket flight, were all studied by the Nazi-funded German experts, and much of that knowledge was transferred to Wright Field from 1945 onwards. No rational observer would surely suggest that having seized and secured such knowledge, nothing would be done with it. And would such science be separated and isolated? Would the disc-flight, rocket-flight and aerodynamics knowledge be linked and not studied in isolation?

The Money

By 1947, the American Government had reputedly delivered the massive sum of $5 million to the development of VTOL, all-wing and disc flight. Washington had decreed that this development must take place outside the United States. The location chosen to further this research was Canada, the company was Avro, and once again a familiar named cropped up as one of the funding's lead scientists – Beverley Shenstone. He walked away from his employment high up at ministerial level in the Canadian Government and went to work in the Canadian aircraft industry for Canadair and then as a director with Avro at the stunning 1940s salary of $13,000 CDN per year.

As early as 1943, Shenstone had been offered a job by Ralph Bell, who was the Director General of Aircraft Production and Munitions Supply in Canada and, after several delays, Shenstone took the job. This was to be short-lived as Shenstone was then recruited into a role as technical advisor to C.D. Howe – Minister of the Department of Reconstruction. From there it was a short hop into the Canadian industry. Shenstone was the top expert and regularly commuted across the Atlantic to visit Rolls-Royce and other major facilities in Great Britain at a time when Atlantic commuting was only for the privileged VIP or government official. In 1946, Atlantic airline services were in their infancy and the ticket cost equated to many months wages for the average man.

The arrival of a large amount of American Government money and the knowledge of Alexander Lippisch as part of a disc-flight development programme at Avro, allied to the presence of the boundary layer and aerofoil expert Shenstone – who also had strong links to Wright Field and Lippisch, and had intimate knowledge of German all-wing technology, aerodynamics and metallurgy – makes the whole recipe begin to look too much like a coincidence of conspiracy theories. However, this *was* the structure and it was strengthened by Shenstone's very close links to his old mentor Professor Parkin, who by now was heading the Canadian National Research Council's work on all-wing and tailless aircraft and researching composite construction materials. It was as if all the ducks had been lined up in order – entirely by coincidence of course.

Yet, most unexpectedly, Shenstone would suddenly leave Canada and the advanced research in 1947 to return to a role in the British industry. According to Shenstone family records, he had just designed and commissioned the building of an advance 'eco' house in Canada and turned down repeated high-level approaches to return to the British aircraft industry – including an offer from Vickers to be its next in line chief designer. Even Shenstone's former employer, Sir Wilfrid Freeman, had lobbied Shenstone to return to Britain. The British establishment was desperate to get Shenstone back – why? Were they concerned he would give America the lead in design?

Shenstone had stated that he did not want his wife or young sons exposed to the privations of post-war Britain. Shenstone's family were also lead figures in the Massey-Harris agricultural machinery industrial concern: this was old Canadian money. Even Professor John Parkin – Shenstone's old tutor and now head of the Canadian National Research Council's All-Wing Research Committees group – was present; he had been made godfather to Shenstone's eldest son.

Shenstone was also on numerous Canadian-based engineering and government committees: he was a member of the Associate Committee on Aeronautics, member of the Canadian Aeronautics Institute (CAI) and a member of the Aerodynamics Sub-Committee – both at the National Research Council of Canada – and chairman of the Technical Committee of the Soaring Association of Canada. Shenstone was also consultant to Avro on the 'Lancastrian' project and the Canadian delegate to the Airworthiness Division of the nascent International Civil Aviation Organisation. He also worked on the 'North Star' airliner conversion.

Clearly, Canada was home. What on earth would make a man abandon all this and follow a course he previously refused to take? What occurred to suddenly result in a serious change of mind that saw Shenstone and his family head back to bankrupt, disheveled, ration-book Britain and the worst winter in a century? What shook Shenstone up so much that he immediately left Canada and the Avro disc project working alongside his old friend Lippisch on their boundary layer and VTOL work? Was it a personal issue, or a clash at Avro? Or was it Shenstone's previous military intelligence gathering role which, like that of his uncle, A.G. Shenstone, had touched several relevant fields? Did Beverley Shenstone discover something about the disc-flight or anti-gravity technology that affected him so deeply that he choose to remove himself, or was it something more simple? If it was, he gave up a great deal in Canada that he had worked hard to establish.

No one really knows why he left, however there are those who feel that Shenstone's very high level official status as an expert, and as the man who had shaped the Supermarine Spitfire's wings, may have been relevant. He was also one of the few men who had been on board HMS *Prince of Wales* with Wilfrid Freeman in August 1941 at the *Placentia Bay* meeting between Churchill and Roosevelt, and had advised the British Government on wartime German aviation technology. Did any aspect of his knowledge of advanced German design and Nazi-era science and technology lie behind his utterly paradoxical and rushed departure from his Canadian homeland in 1947? Why would such a man abandon boundary layer studies and disc-flight design work? The answer remains an enigma and there would be a riddle in the tale.

After Shenstone's unexpected departure, the next glider pilot, all-wing expert and aerodynamics guru to go into Avro and the disc development programme was the highly respected aerodynamics and airframe designer John C.M. Frost. He would oversee Avro's advanced aerodynamic research facility and register patents in his field, yet he too would take his secrets to the grave.

Avro Canada began to research jet power, axial flow, radial flow, ducted thrust, Coanda effect thrust lines and surfaces, boundary layer issues, and built a series of disc-flight airframes. One was the 'Silverbug' and the other the Disneyesque 'Avrocar', which was publicly unveiled as a prototype that could just about hover a few off the ground and proceed forwards at a few knots. Behind this comedic PR-stunt facade, those five million US dollars were burning a large hole in Avro's hangars as the company researched serious, disc-flight devices – or as some might want to construe, 'flying saucer' type airframes.

Officially, the U.S Government terminated the Avro-based project, absorbed the research back into America, and ended the arrangement. Behind the scenes, the advanced research teams threw everything they could at developing the disc-flight and so-called 'anti-gravity' technology of the Nazis.

A strange twist now occurred. Enter again stage left, Beverley Shenstone – Lippisch-trained designer. Shenstone was also closely linked with the intelligence services via his mentors, Professor John Parkin and Air Vice-Marshal E.W. Stedman – who was a Canadian national defence intelligence figure. Via their actions and joint RCAF/RAF arrangements, Shenstone (an RCAF trained pilot) had spent time working at Junkers and with Lippisch in pre-war Germany, and had been acting for the British and the Canadians gathering information and sending it back to the Air Ministry in London and to Parkin and Stedman in Toronto. The fluent German-speaking Shenstone reported to the British authorities – military and intelligence grade – and only years later was his intelligence gathering role realised.[12] Of interest, during the Second World War, Vickers chief designer, Rex Pierson, wrote to Shenstone (by then an Air Ministry Director) stating that: 'If the Germans had known what you were up to, you would have been shot.'[13]

During his time inside the German aviation industry in 1929–1931, Shenstone had met many influential people and been befriended by two aristocratic nobleman who were avid glider pilots at the Wasserkuppe and aeronautical design students who went on to officer rank in the German military during the war. There had also been a close friendship with Peter Riedel, who by 1940 was, according to Shenstone, allegedly a German intelligence gathering agent in New York prior to Reidel's escape from Nazi hands. These friendships persisted until 1939. Soon after the end of the war, Shenstone was approached in Canada by some of these former pre-war friends and, just as with his friendship with Lippisch, continued the contact. Shortly afterwards, German men of aristocratic status from senior German noble families (and their immediate kin) appeared as immigrants in Toronto and began new lives in Canada. We do not know if Shenstone had anything to do with such events, but at least one of the noble lineage immigrants to Canada had been close to Shenstone in his 1930s Wasserkuppe years. That man, a member of an ancient Bavarian noble family, sought out Shenstone and asked him for help while being released from a British prisoner of war camp in 1945.

The aristocratic German connection was furthered soon afterwards when a reputed former SS-ranked technical liaison officer, Count Rudolf von Meerscheidt-Huellessem, is said to have had dealings in 1949 with the Canadian Government regarding disc-flight technology developed by Germany in the war. It seems the count was looking for a new life and a new home – and specifically approached the Canadians – as opposed to the Americans.[14] It is unclear what occurred, but it is suggested that the offer from the count was reputedly declined. But would his alleged work inside the German advanced aerodynamics, powerplant and metallurgy of the Nazi disc programme *really* have been dismissed? It is possible but unlikely. And the count *did* end up as a Canadian citizen. Had he handed over his information to a German-speaking Canadian aeronautical expert? Why did the count approach the Canadians, instead of the Americans who had run Paperclip? Was the answer, via Shenstone, and/or his aristocratic German links? And why had Allen Dulles, CIA Director, and brother of John Dulles of 'Sputnik' denial fame, set up a research facility in Canada?

These alignments in the story, may tie up some of the evidential loose ends without ever falling into the trap of conspiracy theory. Without even beginning to discuss the names of Miethe or any other contentious figures, the plot line is clear: Operation Paperclip – seized science – Lippisch – his friend and Canadian Government official the leading figure of Shenstone – the intelligence services – Avro – the American, British and Canadian Governments – a German count who had reputedly worked within the Nazi disc programme, *all* congregated on Toronto just after the war. Given such significant alignments, it is unlikely that the disc-flight research programme was a hoax, a conspiracy theory or a piece of professionally engineered 'psy-ops' delusion. And the alleged five million US dollars was a very, very large sum in 1946 – bankrupt Britain's Dominion of Canada would surely have welcomed such an amount.

In this plot of circumstantial evidence, where advanced aerodynamics and propulsion research saw rocket scientists, all-wing and airframe experts thrown together via Wright Field, and then in Canada, we may have a strong lead to the rational reality of the secrets of disc-flight research from 1945 onwards.

Japan and Russia

There was a close relationship built between Germany and Japan during the war, and of note, Heinkel provided support to Japanese fighter design with at least two employees from its design office seconded to Tokyo. A great deal of intelligence traffic and weapon design details were traded to Tokyo by Berlin. It is also known that from the early 1930s, a major British aviation figure had been supplying British design knowledge to the Japanese.

The Japanese were also very interested in the all-wing concept and built a series of viable all-wing designs. In the last desperate days of the Pacific war, Japan also looked at building versions of the Messerschmitt 163 tailless design for flight testing and Mitsubishi designed both powered and non-powered prototypes. Prior to the Second World War, the Japanese Army's aerial research department supported experimental all-wing designs by Dr H. Kimura. The first all-wing to fly in Japan had been an experimental model built as early as 1910. By 1941, Kimura, assisted by a designer named Naito, had drawn the 'Kayaba' company's gliders as viable 35ft wingspan Japanese all-wing planforms that flew more than 250 test flights. Of interest, several of these demonstrated use of advanced 'cranked'; or near crescent wing planforms and it is postulated that this research can only have come from German wind tunnel and research work.

Kimura, with co-designer J. Washimi, also designed an advanced 'Mk 3' all-wing in 1941. This KU-3 was a two-seat experimental craft and, of note, now had no vertical control surfaces – it was a true all-wing type.

Of the Soviet all-wing programme, less is clear. The first Russian all-wing research went back to 1900 and the work of Nikolai Zhukovskii at the world class aerodynamic institute in Moscow. It was here under Zhukovskii that Tupolev learned his craft.

Having had access to German aerodynamic and rocket research from April 1945 as the Soviet forces invaded Germany and scooped up scientists, it was inevitable that the Russians under the USSR would explore all-wing and tailless configurations.

Early explorations into seized German research took place in 1947 by the Chetverikov 'RK' research project. Unsurprisingly, re-manufactured Rolls-Royce Nene jet engines (as given to the Russians by a naïve British Labour Government in 1946 under a useless document of non-existent Intellectual Property Rights protection), were to power the proposed airframe. Wingtip fins as de facto winglets – yet performing a different aerodynamic purpose featured in the Russian design – to prove a rudder steering effect. Despite several years of research, the project failed to proceed to the airframe building stage and a brief stop was called to the all-wing in the Soviet Union. However, Russian designers had had access to a great deal of Lippisch's delta research and had also secured nearly a dozen top German wing designers who would remain at work east of Moscow until 1956 when, via various negotiations, they would return home to what was now East Germany.

Several years later, attempts at a Soviet all-wing would re-emerge in the form of the research project led by a Moskalyov for the Leningrad Engineering Academy. This would be a supersonic, jet-powered, nuclear weapon-carrying airframe with a massive 30,000lbs payload capacity. A speed of Mach 4 from at least six jet engines and a 100,000ft service ceiling seemed incredibly ambitious. As the design progressed, such parameters were reduced to more achievable goals, but the cranked wing with sweep of 72° inboard and 42° outboard was retained in what became tagged the 'DSB-LK' project. By 1961, with massive costs and the order from the USSR to ramp-up conventional aircraft design as the Cold War evolved, advanced Russian all-wing design was cancelled and this project was curtailed before it achieved prototype build stage. There is, however, much anecdotal evidence that a smaller, Lippisch-type deltoid all-wing, with a vertical tail fin, was designed and extensively flight tested in the remote eastern USSR.[15]

Chapter Six

The All-Wing Thing

A Flying Wing Fashion

In 1946, out of the blue – or rather out of Germany – there suddenly came the arrival of the flying wing or all-wing (nurflügel) movement as a recognised and so-called 'new' technology. Penaud and Junkers were as if invisible from their 1890s and 1910 islands in the sky. Pre-war thoughts of all-wings and things in Britain, France and America had been put on hold while the machinery of war mechanised its way to conventional engineered victory. Post-war flying magazines and engineering journals were to become busy with articles on the all-wing and the tailless configurations. The 'all-wing thing' became all the rage as an in vogue fashion topic of the moment.

The esteemed *Flight,* the aviation industry's journal of choice, ran regular articles about what it called 'flying wings'. *Flight* told its readers that there were many advantages to the all-wing concept and that these were structural as well as aerodynamic. Placing the cargo, passengers and fuel load inside the wing as a self-supporting body saved great amounts of weight and costs by deleting the usual fuselage. *Flight* also claimed, on 9 January 1947,[1] that the saving in drag losses of an all-wing device was a minimum of thirty-three per cent. Quite how this exact figure was arrived at, we are left to ponder, but it was a significant figure – as was the claim that an all-wing airliner would appear with an all-up weight of approximately 300,000lbs. Readers were also informed that when the all-wing concept was to finally appear as commercial reality, it would be powered by gas turbine engines buried within the wing. However, the experts at *Flight* still claimed that the issues of stability in the all-wing concept had yet to be fully resolved. But they realised that the bigger the all-wing, the greater the load and range advantages. Although citing British and American all-wing developments such as the work of Dunne, the Armstrong Whitworth AW52, the Northrop XB-35 and the Handley Page Manx, *Flight* could not avoid the names of Lippisch and Horten as the high priests of advanced all-wing development.[2]

Suddenly the all-wing was all the rage.

All-Wing Aerodynamics – a Brief Explanation

What *was* the advantage of the all-wing flying machine?

Without going into extreme forensics, we need to know just what the benefits of the all-wing idea were and are. Why would so many men dream of the all-wing – often in a tailless, monoplane, biomorphic form or configuration?

The answer lies in the efficiencies of the shape and configuration. By removing the causes of interference drag, by reducing lift induced drag and by reducing profile – or body-generated parasitic drag through the removing of the fuselage and tail, the overall amount or coefficient of drag can be reduced by the order of between forty and sixty per cent. This is a massive reduction in drag that gives rise to numerous other benefits in terms of weight, range, payload, powerplant, and speed.

The American all-wing pioneer, J.K. Northrop, stated in his 1947 Wilbur Wright Memorial Lecture to the RAeS[3] that for a large all-wing aircraft (given equal wingspan and weight comparisons to a conventional configuration aircraft) the advantageous ratio of minimum parasite drag coefficient for all-wing aircraft to that of conventional types was approximately 1:2. Northrop suggested that if a conventional high speed airframe had a drag coefficient of C_D 0.023, the range of drag coefficients for all-wing types vary from C_D 0.010 to C_D 0.0113. He also framed the lift coefficient advantages from the all-wing. Northrop thought that with development and jet engine power, an all-wing might have forty per cent less drag. He also noted the need for less power to achieve the same speeds as more power hungry conventionally winged types. At the crucial take-off and landing weights, the all-wing also offered a better wing loading for a given weight and span, so this too was another advantage of the all-wing. By spreading the structural loadings and payload throughout the all-wing, Northrop opined that better efficiencies in weight saving and consequent increases in range were obvious. Weights and their ratio effects (such as fuel load upon wing loading) at take-off and landing are also advantageous to the all-wing design.

Profile, parasitic, lift-induced, interference, and other types of aerodynamic drags, are the focus of flight. Aerodynamics, itself borne of hydrodynamics and aeromancy, is a science based in mathematics, yet a glance at Concorde, the Spitfire, a Boeing 747, a Horten glider, or a fast military jet, will show us sculpture and art defined by a fusion of form and function that defies calculus and manifests as a physically sculpted device designed to give lift and to lower drag. 'Streamlining' may have been borne into an industrial design consciousness from the art deco period and a new global era of design circa 1925–1935, but a look at machines like Penaud's 1870s all-wing, or Steiger's elliptical monoplane of 1891, show us exquisite sculptures of advanced thinking and low-drag effect.

Even the development of cars was touched by aerodynamics in the period 1925–1935, with the likes of Voisin, Jaray, Ledwinka, Gerin, Lefebvre, Bertoni, Andreau, Bel Geddes, Sason, Paulin, von Koenig-Fachsenfeld, Tjaarda van Staernborgh, Farina and Bugatti, almost all using aviation knowledge to create lower drag car body designs in age of aero/auto-mechanical investigation. The first aerodynamic car body built upon a Citroën – that marque famed for aerodynamic excellence – was that of the design of aero engineer Pierre Delcourt in 1928. Surely, one look at Gresley's aerodynamic 'Pacific' A4 Class streamlined locomotive design will reveal the aeronautical and automotive art deco influences upon its sculpted form and curved side fillets.

Fuselages or bodies create drag, as do tail fins. Surely if they are removed, the weighted effect of self-created drag can be reduced – thus increasing performance. Similarly, the act of a wing creating lift leads to induced drag stemming from the creation of lift itself. If wing design can be made to have lower lift-action induced drag (as found by elliptical practice and thinner aerofoils), then induced drag can also be reduced. Removing the fuselage can also reduce the combinations of drag where fuselage and wings meet – interference drag. Removing the fuselage also saves weight. Removing the tail fin and tailplane also reduces drag and saves weight. Drag creating cross sectional area is also reduced.

By reducing all types of drag and weight, lift coefficients, speeds, ranges and performances are improved. Wing loading, the vital factor of aircraft handling and performance, can also be improved through the use of the all-wing and its lower drag/better lift attributes in comparison to traditional mainplane, tailplane and fuselage configurations. The all-wing can also carry far more payload – people or cargo – in the depth of its wing box and fuel capacity is also increased. In-flight strength and crash safety are also much improved in comparison to normal designs due to far higher torsional rigidity and the lack of the exposed fuselage cabins fore and aft of the wing with their lack of deformation zones. Above all, wing strength and resistance to failure is significantly higher in the all-wing construction technique with Hugo Junkers being the early pioneer of such discoveries and applications.

As the Hortens framed and the Americans adopted, the other 'secret' of the all-wing concept was its lower radar signature. The all-wing and its true tailless planform and profile reduce radar returns by having not just less mass, but a differing shape: radar returns are thus significantly lower. The world's first, all-wing, 'stealth' aircraft was a Horten all-wing, jet-powered and built of wood, alloy, and early plastics. It was, of course, spirited off to the USA and its advance shielded for decades until the Americans were ready to frame such technology as stemming from their own fundamental brilliance – rather like getting to the moon.

For the all-wing, however, the aerodynamic issue of removing the tail surfaces – the 'moment arm', or stabilising fulcrum effect, has often been cited as the great negative of the all-wing theory. A badly designed all-wing will try to turn around its own axis, never mind rear-up upon itself. But careful design can reduce the problems. Indeed, an all-wing with a tail surely seems a half-hearted aerodynamic exercise.

In the highly swept-back, all-wing planform, the difference between chord-wise definition provides a de facto longitudinal length to the lifting body. Because the swept-wing planform provides a considerable longitudinal divergence from the normal, unswept, uniform chord of a tapered or 'plank' type wing, a greater front-to-rear length is achieved – adding stability and the resultant effect is created by the sweepback of the wing itself – replacing the 'normal' fuselage and tail arm effect. More sweepback means more longitudinal effect. Allied to tuning of the all-wing lift pressure distribution pattern, span loadings and taming spanwise flow, the issue of lack of stability in a longitudinal axis can be addressed. Similarly, the lateral or roll axis stability and any combined roll and yaw ('Dutch roll' type) effect can be tuned out despite the lack of a tail with which a deftly applied rudder input, allied to an aileron flick, would normally resolve: Some designers include a vertical tail on all-wing devices as a 'halfway house' measure. Lippisch added them, as did Northrop and Hill.

Twisting the wing (known as washout) means it has a differing angle of incidence to the oncoming airflow – beginning at a location upon its span or length in relation to the wing's main angle relative to the airflow's motion (travelling forwards into the airflow's effect). This washout, or twisting to the wing's effect can, if correctly applied, add stability without a resultant massive increase in drag created by the washout 'twisting' against the airflow itself. By specifically twisting the wingtip region of the wing in a certain way, a dihedral or anhedral effect can add stability in the same manner as having tail feathers. Spin resistance is improved by wingtip washout as it keeps the wingtips 'flying' after the main wing has begun to stall. Stall instability therefore occurs inboard on the wing and does not provoke a spin. Focus on the trailing edge airflow behaviour, localised flow, and induced drag, allied to work on control surfaces, can create a trade-off between lift, drag and airflow behaviours to create the best design. Reimar Horten's stunning work on these factors, notably via dual axis wing twist and modified flow patterns, was his significant but little-realised act of all-wing genius.

So a swept all-wing planform can offer better longitudinal stability than an unswept all-wing straight tapered 'plank' wing design, yet the French, Fauvel-Abrial-Arnoux school of unswept, straight all-wing planforms, has solved many inherent problems without the need to use highly swept surfaces. However, straight all-wing designs can require more emphasis on vertical surfaces to provide control and stability and are therefore less likely to be totally not tailless. Thus the drag of vertical tail fin and tailplane surfaces are created.

Aerofoil thickness and section is also crucial – using differing types of blended aerofoils with very carefully calculated merging of the aerofoil section along the span is another crucial arbiter. From this came Reimar Horten's tuned lift distribution theories.

Swept back wings can suffer from migration of the airflow across the direction of travel and action – known as 'spanwise' flow – turning across the length of the wing. Therefore spanwise flow is inefficient and can reduce not just lift, but also dangerously degrade stability and performance, especially at lower speeds such as those found on landing approach. To cure such spanwise flow (with its low-speed instability) the aerodynamicist can build 'fences' across the wing's top surface to channel or funnel the air back into a chordwise flow across the aerofoil (particularly, at speeds close to the stall). These crude fences do, however, cause drag and reduce the coefficient of lift because they reduce wing area – cutting aerofoil lift. So they can cure spanwise flow, but at the expense of reducing the lift coefficient by varying amounts. (The Russians had to apply several wing fences to the swept-wings of the Tank/Multhopp derived MiG-15, as their designers lacked aspects of swept-wing knowledge, other than that they had seized from Germany in 1945.)

Other techniques to counteract spanwise flow can see nasty little angles, triggers, and stick-on devices applied to the wing leading edge or even its under surface. These devices do work – but at some cost to performance. Of significance, the true all-wing will have a strongly swept planform, but will be devoid of such devices because the designer will have calculated the flow so well that spanwise effects are designed out, the lift distribution pattern solved and low speed handling unaffected – as Reimar Horten achieved. Certainly the works of the Hortens, Lippisch, the Arado 'crescent' wing of Rudiger Kosin, and of Shenstone on the Spitfire wing, must be cited as superb examples of the art of tuning wing flows without resorting to wing fences or leading edge devices, yet at the same time ensuring safe wing performance across the speed spectrum from take-off to landing.

Techniques of skewness and kurtosis – the calculating of shaping, cambering and sculpting of the wing aerofoil to avoid unwanted or untuned, localised changes in aerofoil shape and airflow speed, lift, drag and boundary layer behaviours were the vital effects applied to the Spitfire, and to the Lippisch and Horten all-wing, swept, and delta-wing planforms – and latterly to a range of civil and military aircraft – notably Concorde itself. That wonderful double curve of Concorde's wing, which reverses itself towards the tips, stems from such discoveries about airflow on the delta planform. Under such effects, every wing rib, every wing skin form, has to be tailored and tuned to a forensic degree to avoid unwanted aerodynamic effects. Such issues, of 'source' and sink' and localised curvature and streamwise flow, will deeply affect the wing's performance and abilities.

In all-wing design, a debated parameter that is shared with elliptical and delta planforms, was discovered to be the combined issues of trailing edge design – often as a partial application of forward sweep or such effect – to the trailing edge and wingtip and aileron regions of the wing. Adding forward sweep as a raked-forward shape to a trailing edge of a wing was not easy. However, the beneficial effects of such properties were to delay the tip-stall and thus create ailerons that 'worked' better and offered control response beyond normal parameters, and wingtips that stalled after the main wing – reducing the likelihood of a wing wobble or a spin. Lippisch's early designs for swept and delta-wings, clearly show reverse-curved bulges in planform to the tips and ailerons – adding *forward rake* to a *rearwards* swept form. Forward sweeping of the entire wing also works and was first tried in Germany, yet presents issue of loading and twist upon the wing structure because forwards sweep makes the wing bend under motion.[4]

Lanchester, Dunne, Prandtl, Lippisch, Shenstone, Mitchell, Hill, and the Hortens, were some of the early proponents of the study area of trailing edge vortex and aerofoil lift wake pattern efficiency. The aerodynamic behaviours of ellipsoid and delta-wings are linked to the behaviours of swept all-wing design. Lift pattern, stalling behaviour, in-turn efficiencies and aileron and elevon surface design are the crucial parameters to these types of wing and trailing edge/aileron design. The locations and shapes (and consequent effects) of control surfaces or panels upon the all-wing tailless aircraft can be the defining issue of its success or otherwise. As far back as the 1870s, Alphonse Penaud was studying this factor with his all-wing's twin 'tabs' and surface devices.

Swept, all-wing planform, aerofoil, and lift pattern distribution were the key areas of German advancement that stemmed from all-wing, swept-wing and delta-wing gliding and design developments between 1925–1945. There was a reason why the Horten wings, the Messerschmitt 163 and 262, contained the advances that they did, and the reasons lie in wing research that began with gliders.

Correctly calculated and correctly applied, the 'gain' from the percentage of drag reduction and benefits in-kind of a properly designed all-wing planform in comparison to a standard wing is massive. Removing the tail, the fuselage and other addenda, reaps huge rewards in aerodynamic and resultant performance terms.[5] This is the essence of the all-wing and tailless revolution that was first studied across the nineteenth century – before the coming of the straight-winged biplane and its resultant losses and retardation of design and technological advance.

Within the combination of science, maths, natural design, and aerodynamic sculpture, lay the roots of the all-wing and it secrets that were for so long either denied, or stolen. In terms of safety, despite claims by many, the all-wing is not less safe than the conventional wing, fuselage and tailplane configuration. Indeed it is an odd twist that the biplane era which manifested as a cause for safety and stability, resulted in biplanes that were often far more likely to spin and flick stall than a well-designed all-wing. Furthermore, with the tailplane at the rear in a biplane or monoplane, the main wing can stall first, that removes the main lifting component from the aircraft – a serious event. In the canard, fore wing planform configuration the smaller, lesser wing stalls first – leaving the main lifting wing 'working' and the machine in a natural nose-down stall recovery attitude with the loss of lift being upon the small fore wing. But the canard fore wing or tail first configuration was also dismissed by the learned men and their biplane obsession. So the apparently 'safer' normal or conventional aircraft design, with the tail mounted rearwards, had all the potential to create a serious main wing stall and spin situation.

For the all-wing, things are different. Although its stability is often derided or doubted, this is a falsehood if the all-wing is correctly conceived and built. For the all-wing is stall resistant. Pre-stall effects lead an all-wing into a gentle porpoising oscillation that gives the pilot plenty of warning and time to intervene. Whereas the delta-wing can rear up and fall over backwards in extreme cases at the stall, a well-designed all-wing will not. The all-wing *can* stall irrecoverably rearwards if it is of thick aerofoil and moderate sweep, but the deft application of flaps should produce a nose-down pitching effect of stall-recovery. In the Northrop YB-49 all-wing bomber, a combination of characteristics produced an airframe with difficult stall and spin characteristics leading to the addition of vertical surfaces. Of all designers, perhaps we can cite Reimar Horten's work on all-wing lift patterns, pressure, control surface design, yaw, and aerofoil behaviour as paramount in progressing the all-wing theory. Film footage of Walter Horten performing very low-level loops in a Horten flying wing during late 1930s testing reveal an amazing level of performance and control – including close to the ground. Even if Walter Horten was a talented aerobatic expert pilot, the capabilities of the Horten all-wing were outstanding. You had to see it to believe it.

If correctly conceived and constructed, all-wings are not dangerous, difficult or unstable – nor unsafe.

Chapter Seven

High Speed Flight Secrets

Not only did the rules of the *Treaty of Versailles* backfire on the French and British in terms of unpowered aircraft design, the treaty also backfired because it did not prohibit rocket study. Neither did those who drew up the treaty realise that by banning powered aircraft design and production that a massive impetus to advancing the art of glider and wing design would result.

The prohibition of powered aircraft design for military use by the enforced rules led the Germans to their advanced glider designs – which they then applied to their motor-powered designs in a huge leap of technological advance; the learning of the glider era was also available to the German rocket men. Having been banned from powered flight development, it was obvious that the Germans would advance non-powered flight: perhaps it was not quite so obvious that they would forge ahead with rocket motor design. Somehow the *Treaty of Versailles* overlooked this tangent.

Although military aircraft production was banned for many years, the treaty did allow for a later commencement of civil aircraft manufacture. Even in this field the German designers raced ahead and by 1930 German airliners flying for German airlines were outstripping British, Dutch and French airliners on a route mile and fleet basis.

Thanks to the treaty and its constraints, the stepping stone to swept-wings, delta-wings and high speed flight was the process via which glider design was advanced in Germany through the creation of new techniques in aerodynamics. Previous mathematical assumptions (upon which many learned men had based their reputations) were overtaken by actual wind tunnel and flight testing. These new lessons translated into elliptical, swept and delta-wing thoughts that were subsequently the subject of wartime development. High speed flight study in Germany stemmed from glider study in Germany, and high speed flight study and realisation in the USA and Great Britain used these German research lessons to make their consequent leaps. In a parallel thematic development, German high speed flight research via high speed wind tunnels led to German rocket flight – which itself led to American and Russian space flight. The Mach number was the definition of the aerial vehicles speed ratio of speed, to the speed of sound (varying with air pressure, after the work of Dr Mach).

DFS 346.

There was a reason why most Allied post-Second World War jets and rockets looked like German wartime prototypes and it was not a coincidence.

The key realities of German high speed research are now the fundamentals of high speed aerodynamic knowledge, but in 1945, they were the startling discoveries that shocked the Allies, who immediately seized, not just the designs, but the unique high-speed wind tunnels of German science. The work carried out between 1935–1945 in German aerodynamics institutes represented the true basis of modern flight. At the *Deutsche Forschungsanstalt fur Segelflug* (DFS) at Darmstadt in the 1930s, swept-wings were the focus. The DFS design director Felix Kracht was a leading exponent of swept and all-wing design that stemmed from his organisation's research, which resulted in a series of research airframes that were jet or rocket-powered and had sharp, thin-section swept-wings and T-tails. Of note, the Felix Kracht-penned, rocket-powered DFS 346 can be seen as a significant stepping stone to, and influence upon, post-war transonic and supersonic airframe design.

Vogt and Forward-Sweep

Even forward sweep of the wing planform was achieved via the DFS and then the works of Richard Vogt for Blohm and Voss. Swept-wings – stemming from glider design advances, would also appear on rockets. Dr Richard Vogt, after graduating from the University of Stuttgart and joining the Dornier Co. in 1923, was latterly to become known for his advanced airframe and wing designs. Vogt designed a large number of aircraft for Blohm & Voss including a defining, large flying boat. In 1946, Vogt went to the USA under Operation Paperclip. Vogt's P.202, designed in 1944, had a 'Swivel Wing' which was later aped up in the work of R.T. Jones at NASA and the AD-1 'Oblique Wing' in 1980. Working at Boeing, Vogt continued to design unusual aircraft – such as nuclear-powered bombers in the mid-1950s[1]

Such advances included key areas of research and outcomes that defined advanced, world-leading knowledge of aircraft design in Germany. The vital stepping stones into the future were concentrated around core research themes:

1. **Sweepback:** This is the difference between the angle by which the wingtip lies behind the centre line of the wing. By creating highly swept-wing planforms, with theoretically ideal sweep rates of +/-35° and 60°, German researchers (notably Lippisch, Voigt, Busemann, and Betz) discovered that swept-wings (note, of *forwards* as well as rearwards sweep) would delay and reduce aerodynamic drag and compressibility effects at speeds close to the supersonic 'barrier' of Mach 0.85–Mach 1.00. Wing sweep delays drag rise and shock wave formation – so sweepback delays the Mach number at which compressibility effects (see below) appear in the wing's airflow – by altering the values of such effects. Sweep, considerably reduces the rise in drag due to the secondary effects of a shock wave stalled condition. Actual, rather than theoretical values can only be achieved by wind tunnel versus flight testing. Gains from sweepback can be considerable. Drag rise with an unswept-wing versus drag with a swept-wing varies greatly. J.R. Ewans, Avro's chief aerodynamicist, stated as late as 1951[2] that at a sweepback of 45°, drag rise occurred at Mach 0.83, whereas drag rise at unswept zero degrees occurred at Mach 0.7.

   The German way of expressing the formula was to say that sweep-back increased the Mach number at which drag rises from one mathematical value to another (M to M$\sqrt{\sec\varphi}$). The benefit of sweep was first postulated by Lippisch and at the Volta High Speed Congress in 1935 by Professor Busemann, thence in 1939 by Professor Betz – a pupil of Professor Prandtl.

   The more the sweep angle, the more the aerodynamic benefit at high speed. In 1946, as this research was confirmed by seized German findings, wing aerofoil thickness was also crucial – just as it had been on the Supermarine Spitfire's thin wing of 1936 that was set against British expert opinion that such wing section thinness offered little benefit – a huge error in 'learned opinion' that cost the Hawker Hurricane much in terms of performance – as Sir Sydney Camm openly stated.

   Sweepback (and forward sweep) were, along with the shape (planform) of the wing, vital to high speed stability – notably longitudinal stability. The effects of the tail, or of tailless configuration were crucial to studying and resolving these effects, so a great deal of German research went into studying and resolving stability issues of wings and missiles. It was this effect that created the later 'sound barrier' effect mindset where control problems stemming from drag rises and then from airflow compressibility effects upon the wing were deemed the issue. Richard Vogt's work on forward sweep and then the asymmetric sweep of the oblique wing revealed many potential benefits, but have yet to be fully developed, despite the NASA AD1 prototype of the 1980s that so resembled his earlier work.

2. **Aerodynamic Compressibility:** Compressibility problems were framed as the big barrier to breaking through the speed of sound at 760mph at sea level (660mph at 36,000ft). This term framed the changes of aerodynamic behaviour that began in the transonic region as pressure waves piled up (hence compression or compressibility) in the airflow around and upon the wing and airframe as its speed approached the speed of sound's own pressure speed. With the wings offering differing (lower) pressure upon their lifting surfaces, and the fuselage offering slower localised airflow pressure effects, a whole series of differing factors and values begin to afflict high speed prop and jet aircraft. As airflow effects built up into a series of localised concentrations surges, a shock wave would build up – from the nose, canopy and especially from the wings and the boundary layer effects.

Conventional aircraft shapes with long fuselages and big tails would become locked into an increasing longitudinal stability which pilots would 'fight' at the controls as the centre of gravity of the aircraft moved forwards under such effects. With shaking, buffeting and localised aerodynamic effects on centres of pressure, lift and speed, the behaviour of the airflow at approaching the speed of sound became a real issue (yet one made mythical). Local body and wing surface issues caused the airflow to accelerate or change speed variably – as the speed rose – with a range of effects on the aircraft's trim, control surfaces and handling, this was the 'compressibility' problem. A nose-down pitching effect as speed rose was its most obvious and violent symptom.

Among other solutions, the all-wing delta shape could solve the compressibility issue – perhaps even more effectively than sweeping the wings backwards away from the shock waves that formed at high speeds, as earlier expounded by the German aerodynamicist, Busemann. By careful design of the wing and tail and their combined effects, swept and then swept deltas, cured the problem. So swept and thin aerofoil wing design was the stepping stone to overcoming the sound 'barrier' and the effects of the shock waves and drag that framed it. From Lippisch's works and to swept, deltoid tailless shapes penned by the émigré Russian, M. Gluhareff, for the American's in 1941, the answer to compressibility was well known – yet ignored for several years more until Germany's expert researches confirmed it.

3. **Planform**: German scientists discovered there were several routes to shaping a wing that could achieve high speed and supersonic flight. At high speeds up to just below the sound barrier and just above (Mach 0.70–1.5) the swept-wing worked, but beyond Mach 1.5 the aerodynamic and structural needs of the swept-wing were not ideal. Swept-wings are long, thin and mounted at an extreme angle to the fuselage. This means they are far more difficult to be made strong enough to not suffer from in-flight failures caused by structural issues. Having to build strong, heavy wing spars and mounting frames could soon have an impact on the performance of the aircraft. Beyond Mach 1.5, a wing needed to be stiff and strong, not thin, long and slender. Again it was Lippisch who realised this very early in the 1930s and he made the move to the lower aspect ratio or 'fatter' style of all-wing planform, which led to the in-filled form of delta or triangular wing shape now so familiar on supersonic airframes. Aspect ratio is the ratio of the wingspan to the average width (chord) of the wing in forwards action. A straight-winged glider with its long thin wings has a high aspect ratio, whereas a short stubby-winged aircraft has a low aspect ratio.

Highly swept-wings, especially long thin ones, have problems with low speed lift and spanwise flow at low speeds – which is why we see flaps and leading edge slat devices attached to them in order to restore camber and lift to the swept thin wing at take-off and landing speeds.

If we amalgamate all the problems and the solutions, the answer comes out as the triangular shaped wing – the delta. This has the advantages of sweep-back but not the structural and aerodynamic disadvantages and is very good at reducing transonic and supersonic problems. So the delta had a beneficial swept leading edge, but a shorter span and a much stronger main wing structure that suffered less twist or bending. Of lower aspect ratio and yet with a swept front, the triangular wing planform was found to be the ideal combination of shape and structure at supersonic speeds. As lift induced drag does not rise as quickly beyond Mach 1.0 in comparison to induced drag *below* Mach. 1.0, issues of induced drag related to sweep-back are less vital. With the delta compressibility effects minimised, Lippisch's delta was ideal.

As wings rely on suction from their top lifting surfaces, there are changes in the speed of the air flowing over the wing and slower air under the wing. Herein lies the creation of wing-based lift, action-induced drag and stability changes, and therein lay the secret of the advantages of the delta shaped wing in reducing these problems that so afflicted near-constant width shape (chord) wings.

Lippisch also proved that the low-speed control issues of the delta-wing were far less critical than others thought, providing attention was paid to shaping (curving) the leading edge and the wingtips to avoid violent, speed-related airflow changes and tip-stalling. Lippisch's P.13 delta-wing model with its curved or ogival (not straight) leading edges and tips, seems to constitute proof positive that he was correct – not least as it is an early 1940s iteration of what can only be regarded as a precursor to the wing of the Concorde and the modified wing of the Vulcan and a range of other types. The work on leading edge and top curvature is perhaps the crucial advance as applied to the original straight edged triangle of the delta type – and it was Lippisch's work. The superiority of the thin section, low-aspect ratio delta-wing in reducing the changes in stability that occur at transonic speeds and penetrating the aerodynamic regime of Mach 1.0 became very apparent

Of particular supersonic interest was the German discovery that a short, stubby and almost unswept wing could also penetrated the sound barrier and be efficient beyond Mach 1.5 – providing that it had an ultra-thin aerofoil. This wing shape seemed to be a bizarre contradiction of the benefits of long, thin, swept-wings, or the delta, yet with low aspect ratio, short wings were *also* found to delay compressibility. So it was discovered that there were two aerodynamic routes to supersonics. Short stubby wings were first applied in a supersonic iteration to the A-4 (V-2) series rockets of von Braun in an attempt to cure issues of longitudinal stability, but after 1945 were seen on British, American and other supersonic airframes – notably the Bell X-2. However, the combined aerodynamic and structural benefits of the delta planform would dominate supersonics in the post-war era. The delta was then a combination of swept-wing thinking and shorter wings.

The delta's other main advantage was that a horizontal tailplane could be dispensed with – saving drag and weight. So the delta was the true tailless type by 1945. The delta-wing may be larger than a normal wing, but the drag rise from its large size was more than bettered by the drag reductions that stemmed from the delta's other benefits of no tailplane, thinner aerofoil, a minimal fuselage, lower wing loading, better performance, hidden engines, stiffer structure and simpler control surfaces, all of which created the advantageous aerodynamics of the delta.

4. **Aerofoil**: Making a wing thinner and flatter, or less cambered, means less air has to be 'pushed' out of the way – over or below the wing – although this can reduce the amount of lift a heavily cambered wing section would create. The thickness of the wing is measured by comparing its sectional depth to its width or chord – dividing of the two creates a thickness/chord ratio. Design of the aerofoil was discovered to be critical at transonic and sonic speeds (the DVL's Dr Götheret being a lead researcher in this field).

A series of tests at the DVL, allied to similar work undertaken at NACA, much of which stemmed from the German glider design revolution of 1925–1935, had suggested the very thin and less cambered aerofoils of the

1940s – not least via the Supermarine Spitfire's unique use of thin aerofoils. Via testing at the DVL wind tunnels, German researchers found that slimmer, less cambered aerofoils provided a gateway to supersonic flight. The symmetrical, thin wing section was found to have much lower drag and could be made to trade off drag reduction with loss of lift coefficient.

5. **Wind Tunnels**: The Germans made huge advances in wind tunnel diffuser design and efficiency, and the above listed advances stemmed in greater part from these wind tunnels and subsequent actual flight testing. The effects of the shape and details of the wind tunnel upon the results stemming from the object being tested were known and much work was done to reduce the unwanted influence of tunnel shape effects upon the test model. As speeds increased, the Germans also realised that a subsonic wind tunnel suffered from airflow that ceased to represent the air that would be present in-flight – that is, the test section or model is not in unadulterated free air and is likely to yield inaccurate results irrespective of the scale effects. A convergent-divergent airflow 'nozzle' effect limited the subsonic wind tunnel to approximately Mach 0.089.

In the supersonic wind tunnel the issue of reflected airflow, or shock waves off the test model on to the surfaces of the wind tunnel, was also discovered to be an issue. However, if these values were known, they could be accounted for. If pressure and density were measured, then proper quantifications could be made – sometimes by using an interferometer, which could also find the boundary layer over the wing. At the DVL in Göttingen, subsonic and sonic wind tunnels contributed greatly to wartime German research and were carefully designed to minimise scale and tunnel-section flow effects.

Even in late 1907 – before the Wright's had taken to powered flight, Prandtl had set down thoughts and calculus upon high-speed (or supersonic) airflows. He had even suggested a steam-driven wind tunnel that would provide airflow in excess of Ernst Mach's nomenclature of the ratio of the speed of an object to the set speed of a sound wave – hence Mach 1.0 (Mach having defined the effect at Prague University several decades earlier during studies into sound waves).

The creation of the *Aerodynamishce Versuchsanstalt Göttingen* (AVG) institute and the *Kaiser-Wilhelm Gesellenschaft* (KWG) as overseeing sponsors and mentor-bodies to research were, by 1912, the precursors of German advance in aerodynamics. After the interruption of the First World War, the Göttingen laboratory was instigated and by 1925 was on the cusp of defining the great German glider design advance that was the stepping stone to the advancement of powered flight design trends into the 1930s and the supersonics of the 1940s.

By 1934, Göttingen had become the centre of the source lode of aerodynamic advancement. Adjuncts included that work of a Prandtl associate, Jakob Ackert, who created a supersonic flow wind tunnel at the *Eidenossiche Technische Hochschule* in Zurich and a further tunnel for the aviation-minded Mussolini near Rome. By 1934, the German researcher Carl Wiesenberger had built an intermittent (rather than continuous) flow wind tunnel at Aachen's technical institute. This would reach a Mach 3.3 flow speed (by forced evacuation of air as opposed to induction flow) in 1935. A Wiesenberger associate, Rudolf Herman, would go on to take such learning to Peenemünde where, after years of modifications to the nozzles used in the wind tunnels airflow pattern, airflow of Mach 4.4 and beyond would be achieved as a world first and lead to the study of hypersonics. He would also take his knowledge to Wright Field, USA, by 1946.

In mid-1945, the invading Allies were utterly shocked to find not just a range of wind tunnels across Germany, but that their attainable speeds were far in advance of anything in America or Great Britain.

The principal German high-speed wind tunnels were unique and a gateway to knowledge about supersonics that was way beyond Allied research. From Peenemünde to Volkenrode, Mach numbers of M. 1.0 to M. 5. + were achieved. In May and April 1945, two of these wind tunnels were seized and taken to the United States of America and Great Britain respectively.

Key details of German wind tunnel capability[3]

* **DVL Berlin**

  1939: Circular closed wind tunnel of 9ft diameter with maximum Mach number of 1.0 and a section pressure (atmosphere) of 1.0.

* **AVA Göttingen**

  1938: Rectangular open wind tunnel of 4.3 x 5.1in with maximum Mach number of 3.0 and a section pressure of 1.0.

  1939: Circular open tunnel of 8.5in diameter with maximum Mach number of 1.0 and a section pressure of 1.0.

  1941: Square closed wind tunnel of 2.5 x 2.6ft with maximum Mach number of 1.0 and a section pressure of 1.0.

  1945: Square closed wind tunnel of 8.5 x 8.5in with maximum Mach number of 5.0 and a section pressure of 1.0.

* **LFA Volkenrode**

  1940: Closed square wind tunnel of 16in x16in with maximum Mach number of 3.0 and a section pressure of 1.0.

  1940: Square closed wind tunnel of 10in x10in with maximum Mach number of 5.0 and a section pressure of 0.8 to 1.0.

  1942: Circular closed wind tunnel of 9ft diameter with maximum Mach number of 1.9 and a section pressure of 1.0.

1943: Circular open wind tunnel of 40in diameter with maximum Mach number of 4.0 with a section pressure of 0.1 to 1.0.

1945: Square closed wind tunnel of 37in x 37in with a maximum Mach number of 1.8 with a section pressure of 0.1 to 1.0.

- **Munich**

1945–46: Square closed wind tunnel with a maximum Mach number of 1.0 with a section pressure of 0.1 to 1.0.

- **St Otzal**

1942: Circular closed wind tunnel of 26ft diameter with maximum Mach number of 1.0 with a section pressure of 1.0.

- **Kochel**

1940: Square section open wind tunnel of 16in x 16in diameter with a maximum Mach number of 4.4 (later increased to M5+) with a section pressure of 1.0.

1941: Square section part-open wind tunnel of 7in x7in with maximum Mach number of m3.3 with a section pressure of 1.0.

1941: Square section open wind tunnel of 40in x 40in diameter with a maximum Mach number of 1.0.

6. **The 'Critical' Mach Number**: Another major German wartime discovery centred on the Mach number and effects of airflow at certain Mach speeds. This framed the aerodynamic 'compressibility' problem that pilots all encountered when trying to break through the mythical sound 'barrier'. The Mach number at which the speed at some point upon the aerofoil reached the speed of sound could be computed from the measured air pressure distributions. This 'local' effect found upon the wing bore no relation to the drag that was rising across the wing as speed rose as an overall Mach number. So the localised airflow behaviour that reached the speed of sound first was termed as the 'critical' Mach number. It was initially thought to be a limiting speed at which the wing would work, but opinion was changed to the view that if no adverse aerodynamic effects were seen above the critical Mach number, the wing could still work until the two Mach values interacted at a higher speed. Another development was the realisation that the critical Mach number was not a limiting moment. This led to the view that, although a wing section could be designed to have a minimum excess local aerofoil speed as a critical Mach number, the differences between such a wing and a wing designed *without* such consideration, were surprisingly small.

7. **Powerplants and The Jet Conundrum**: Another key component of high speed flight was the creation of power and its effect as delivered thrust. If Whittle 'invented' the first true, viable jet engine, we can and must cite early aviation's first thoughts concerning compressive thrust. Of De Louvre's

idea for an oil or hydrocarbon derived fuel being ignited or forced in a 'tube' or 'pipe' and the consequent propulsive effect, we can add the works of J. Butler and E. Edwards who had similar propulsive force ideas using other mediums – even steam. Add in the jet-tube ideas of Nicholas de Telescheff, and the later fan compression effect jet tube ideas of Henri Coanda, and the early thoughts circa 1900 can only be cited as precursors to Whittle and others.

As Whittle was fighting the British establishment and its reluctant attitude and behaviours in regards to his new idea of an engine without a propeller, minds in Germany were receiving a more accepting endorsement. Whittle had been harbouring his idea for years, but in Germany, the Walter company and its rocket thrust type motor and the true 'turbine' works of von Ohain might be said to be further ahead in development terms, not least as he produced a 1,000lb thrust jet engine in 1939 (the HeS 3B) that was fitted to the Heinkel 173. On 27 August 1939, at Marienehe airfield, the He 178 became the first true jet turbine aircraft to fly – piloted by E. Warsitz. The British and Whittle would not fly their jet until 1941. The year 1938 also saw the French Leduc ramjet non-turbine design being postulated, but it would be the Germans who saw the idea through to actual flight.

As early as 1935, the Munich based *Bayerischen Motoren Werke* AG – better known as BMW – had begun to build small jet 'fan' turbine-type engines. In Dessau, at *Junkers Motorenwerke* – as in Jumo – and with Hugo Junkers by now dead, they were soon to build functioning jet turbines. Willi Messerschmitt favoured BMW's lead in turbine blade and combustion chamber designs, but, ironically, latterly had to re-engine his Me 262 with Jumo engines as the BMW engines were unsuitably sized. Heinkel teamed up with Hirth and both that concern and Focke-Wulf soon developed ideas, not just for turbine-cycle jets, but non-turbine ram-air driven athodyd-type powerplants. Heinkel's He 011 jet engine may have yielded up interesting blade, turbine and combustion chamber ideas.

One of the Fedden Missions other remits was to inspect advanced German jet engine developments. This was done at BMW, Junkers and at Heinkel. The BMW 003 jet engine works at Eisenach and other locations were visited and top engineers interrogated – notably BMW's Dr Bruckmann. Bi-fuel engines and reusable rockets were a key area of interest for the Fedden teams, as were jet-prop turbine developments and advanced fan blade designs and metallurgical studies.

The BIOS report on BMW's engine expertise clearly stated that: 'The target contains an important rocket motor testing station. There is no doubt that the target is one of the outstanding German stations for stationary tests on rocket motors. Stations of comparable importance seem to have been only at Peenemünde and Berlin'.[4]

Fedden himself, as a director of the Bristol Company, was an engine expert and had known BMW's main piston-engine four-stroke cycle designer Dr Amann before the war – BMW Frazer-Nash and Bristol had had an engineering relationship. A British 'Frazer-Nash-BMW' car had been marketed based on BMW 328 underpinnings.

Work on the development of the jet engine and rocket motors formed the key motive power advances that carried the wings and shapes that the experts researched in Germany's wind tunnels. This was in advance of Britain's efforts in sheds with a frustrated Frank Whittle.

A significant component of the engine development equation was to ensure efficient conversion of kinetic energy to pressure at supersonic speeds. Just as with the wing compressibility and drag effects, these new speeds could seriously affect how a jet engine might work. Feeding the correct airflow to the engine was a vital parameter and one that bad fuselage and wing design could negatively affect. Somehow, supersonic air entering the jet engine had to be slowed down to create the best pressure required for the thermodynamic combustion cycle. Again, studying these requirements in supersonic wind tunnels would lead to advances in knowledge within German science; von Ohain's works in the early 1930s were a clear pointer to the realisation of a jet 'turbine'. Another Göttingen University luminary, von Ohain, and the Heinkel company, designed the first operational turbojet engine.

At Göttingen, Dr Oswatisch was a leading figure in such research. He suggested that the jet engine intake shock wave could be dispersed into a series of lesser shock waves that would beneficially tune the local airstream into the engine duct. These oblique angled shock waves across the compression of the air would create a much more efficient air supply. He designed an orifice duct for the jet engine's air supply that solved the intake speed issue of the airflow into the turbine. A series of shock wave diffusers were designed and built into the intake duct to bring the airstream down to a speed that was ideal for the engine to breathe.

In the development of rocket power, two main themes were apparent – the type of fuel (liquid) to be used and the effects of the rocket exhaust on speed and direction. A great deal of work went into perfecting these issues.[5]

For the jet engine, a crucial design consideration was where on or in the airframe the jet engine was to be mounted – because airflow and air supply to the fan blades and compressor section was vital. Avoidance of internal stalling was crucial. Should the engines be buried in the wing roots, or even in the fuselage, or should they be 'stuck on to' the wings or body via struts or pylons?

These are all obvious questions for today's student or practitioner of aircraft design but, in 1940, they were unknown fields, dark arts, that few designers had explored. The early explorers of these techniques were men steeped in the high speed flows and high speed wind tunnels of wartime Germany. A French engineer named Leduc created his athodyd in 1938.

However, Bramo, BMW, Messerschmitt, Heinkel, Hirth, Junkers and Focke-Wulf were among the first to suggest jet engines, significantly, engines that were podded and mounted on short pylons, away from the fuselage and wings. This was of huge engineering significance – Focke-Wulf drew up the world's first rear-engined, pylon-mounted jet and ramjet configuration. This was before Vickers in Britain strapped a small early jet onto the back of a test and development Wellington after the end of the war. The Heinkel and Skoda works applied the athodyd ideas of Dr Sanger to ramjet or athodyd propulsive effect to wartime engine design. The V-1 type of flying bomb used an Argus-type engine, which was an early use of a gulping or pulsating breathing mechanism of the non-compressor athodyd.

A key stepping stone to creating these designs came from the development of the aerodynamic duct or intake – the first jet intakes – and from this work came the first aerothermodynamic ramjet types devoid of turbine blades and compressors, relying on tuned combustion to concentrate thrust alone. Wartime work in Germany, and late wartime studies in Britain by (Sir) Stanley Hooker of Rolls-Royce and Mr E. Relf of the then newly established Cranfield College of Aeronautics, had led the studies of jet aerodynamic inlets and at Cranfield – a new form of powerplant – the combustive effect ramjet that was the athodyd.

This airflow-ram-type engine and its intake requirements is one where a propulsive duct or airflow controlling duct determines how the engine

Fw 283.

'breathes'. German research into supersonic airflows had revealed that very high speed airflow into the new jet engines could badly affect their function and another concept evolved (it would be the British Rolls-Royce studies for the supersonic Olympus engine as applied to Concorde that would finally solve the supersonic jet intake airflow issues).

8. **Athodyds**[6]

In 1943, Dornier used an early athodyd or ramjet idea and Focke-Wulf and Heinkel took up the reins of study with Focke-Wulf of Bremen, building a 9ft long, 4.5ft diameter bi-fuel athodyd rocket engine. Designed by a team led by Hans Multhopp, the Fw Ta 283 airframe was the rear-mounted twin-engined machine as illustrated – being the world's first known iteration of pylon-mounted, rear-engined, jet powerplant configuration. Such a concept would be copied by British, French and American designers soon after 1945 across the military and civil markets to date.

The athodyd or ramjet research led to the idea of a supersonic speed capable engine that had no turbine intakes blades and no compressor, but relied on ducted, shaped, combustion and expansion to create thrust. This was the forward-facing duct in which air is compressed in a divergent stream; solely by forward motion – a ramming or ram effect when fuel can then be injected in a highly pressurised region to produce expansion and jet type reaction. Some experts, like S. Hooker, were said to be sceptical of such a powerplant, others, like E. Relf, thought it was the future. By 1946, a British athodyd research theme was under the lead of Sir Benjamin Lockspeiser, Director-General of Scientific Research. At the end of 1946, having studied the German research, the US Navy began athodyd research – notably for missile powerplants.

Today, this athodyd-cycle, non-turbine concept provides the foundation of thinking for sub-orbital flight propulsion.

In the less esoteric field of revolving turbine cycle compressor jet engines, BMW of Munich and Walter of Kiel would respectively dominate the field – with BMW making a larger diameter fan-bladed core than those employed by Junkers of Dessau. Yet BMW would also work to combine the turbine-cycle jet with a rocket type thrust in the BMW 003R combined engine unit. It comprised a normal gas-flowed jet turbine of 2,400lb (max) thrust with a BMW 718 rocket fuelled by nitric acid weighing 180lbs and delivering 2,750lbs of thrust for three minutes. An Me 262H (*Heimatschutzer*) was thus equipped as a jet/rocket machine and climbed to 28,000ft in two minutes with an endurance of sixty minutes at 30,000ft. By using rocket thrust to climb, the jet turbine and its normal fuel load could then provide normal high level flight and range.

The Walter company designed rocket-powered types such as the Walter HWK 507 powered Me 163B – using the famed T-Stoff (hydrogen peroxide) and C-Stoff (hydrazine hydrate and methanol) fuel formulas that represented devastating advances in airframe and powerplant designs and left the Allies speechless. By August 1945, several specimens of the HWK 509 were in Britain and in America, where they were intensively studied – as was the Me 163 Lippisch-designed, swept-wing airframe that went with the rocket motor. In America, at Wright Field, Lippisch himself was on hand to explain all.

Although a Messerschmitt-led project, the Me 262 and others such as Heinkel-Hirth and Arado would also use the BMW bi-fuel configuration to power their machines in the He 162 and Ar 234. In 1944, at Focke-Wulf, chief designer Kurt Tank had considered a design for a bi-fuel fighter of twin-boom tail design not dissimilar to the D.H. Vampire but stopped work to progress the Hans Multhopp influenced, T-tailed TA 183 advanced swept-wing fighter. The Vampire was an early British jet design of remarkable aerodynamic quality that grew from the equally remarkable D.H. Mosquito. Early jet engines, even of Rolls-Royce design, were sensitive to airflow and inlet design and in the D.H. Vampire the de Havilland team under Messrs Wimpenny and Newman as chief designer and chief aerodynamicist respectively, provided an advanced solution to the problem – albeit devoid of a swept-wing. The Vampire was, by 1946, the leading example of British output – but by that date, de Havilland had had access to German swept-wing data and the DH 108 – looking like a Messerschmitt/Horten hybrid with a D.H. Vampire fuselage section thrown in, was in the design process. Meanwhile, rocket power was all the rage.

Pure rocket types of Germany's advanced design bureaus fell into three distinct themes – normal non-expendable airframes like the Me 163, 262 and P.1104, semi-expendable types such as the *Natter*, and special purpose, small airframes used for specific combat duties such as the Arado miniature rocket fighter that was air-launched.

Given that the He 178 experimental gas or jet turbine type first flew on 27 August 1938, it is obvious that the five years of rapid and funded development left the Germans far ahead in terms of jet and rocket power knowledge. For the last two years of the war, rapid development in widely scattered sites and even underground factories heralded a new age in propulsion – much of which was seized by the Allies in April-June 1945. In the summer of 1944, German jet turbine types went into active combat service in the form of the Me 262 and the Arado 234 – both with Junkers Jumo engines. The Jumo was an eight-stage axial flow compressor type with a single stage turbine spinning at nearly 9,000rpm. Thrust was of 1,980lbs. The Jumo had replaced the Heinkel-Hirth and BMW units originally designed for the Me 262, which were shorter cored, greater in diameter and a two-stage turbine. This was a more advanced design yet was larger and slower to be built and produced. All early German jets seemed to be designed around ease of access for maintenance and removal rather than pure efficiency in terms of weight, speed and combustion chamber design that Rolls-Royce had focused upon by 1946 in the Nene and the Goblin.[7]

We can surely add that the heavy bombing of Germany from 1944 must have impacted the design and production of advanced jet engines and Hitler's last gasp orders to make such 'wonder weapons' would have put the emphasis on speed of build, using whatever came to hand, rather than the continuance of exquisite engineering and metallurgical practice. Despite this, the combination of advanced jet turbine engine design and the Me 262's swept-wing of thin section aerofoil and chamfered fuselage contours represent a true example of just how far German science had advanced.[8]

Much of the above described aerodynamic and powerplant works were applied to aircraft, rockets and guided missiles. The key advances were the swept-wing, the delta planform, the all-wing and the tailless figuration, and the jet and rocket engine technology. This knowledge, seized by the Allies under Operation Paperclip, the Fedden Mission and other projects, was the core of the advance that German aerospace science gave to the world post-1945. When Colonel Harold E. Watson and his men raced into Lechfeld airfield on 26 April 1945 to seize the Me 262s, an Me 163, an Arado 234 and all their secrets, the history of jet aviation was changed in a few minutes.

Chapter Eight

Aerospace

The New Frontier

The year 1927 had seen the Germans create the *Verein für Raumschiffahrt* (VfR) as the Society for Space Travel. Based in Berlin at their own rocket flying field, or Raketenflugplatz, amateur groups of 'experts' worked on developing viable rocket-powered aerial devices. Early members of the group included Hermann Oberth, Walter Hohmann, Rudolf Nebel, Klaus Riedel and an 18-year-old young aristocrat with a title and family resources behind him and his ideas of space flight – his name was Wernher von Braun. By 1931, before the Nazis took power, the group had launched a liquid fuel-powered rocket to a height of 3,300ft (1,006mtrs). Despite the economic crisis sweeping the world, by 1932, von Braun and Nebel had demonstrated the potential of the rocket to the German Army. The Army knew that whilst powered aircraft manufacture was still illegal, there were no constraints on rocket study. Hitler took power just a few months later and, with appropriate injection of funds, so was established the German rocket research base at Kummersdorf. From there it was but a world war and mass carnage as a step to the moon.

The British were also toying with thoughts of interplanetary space travel and founded their own society for the study of such a subject in 1933. The Americans had also founded the American Interplanetary Society or Rocket Society in 1930.

The stepping stone to space lay in the key that the delta-wing's realisation and development had been the study of finite lift theories: the development of ellipsoid wings and from there, all-wings, then swept-wings and thence delta-wings. From swept and delta forms, came speed, and from speed there was a link to ballistics and rockets that would lead to space flight. These steps were, in the main, taken by German aerodynamicists for the reasons previously outlined. Even NASA itself, today admits that the Americans were just 'pupils of the wartime Germans'.[1]

However, Dr Robert H. Goddard's astronautical obsession and knowledge, later framed by his rocket research work circa 1941 in the New Mexico desert, should not be ignored. His predictions of high speed flight and travel between the earth and the moon were all accurate and his ideas for using control surfaces in the rocket efflux were indeed advanced. It seems Goddard perhaps toned down his research papers about space travel in order not to be rejected as an eccentric or fantasist amongst the minds of perceived wisdom that ruled the day in the period 1915–1935. Of undoubted significance, Goddard's works were eclipsed by the giant scale of von Braun's devices and the thousands of A–series (V–1, V–2) that the Peenemünde team created as viable weapons. The A–4 or V–2 production and (mobile) launch programme was moved south to the Harz Mountains base after Peenemünde was flattened by RAF bombers.

Goddard died in 1945, just as Operation Paperclip's treasures were being realised, he may have predicted rocket flight in his work *'A Method of Achieving Extreme Altitudes'*, but it was the Germans who achieved it and had a hand in every viable missile system and rocket flight since.

Like the Americans, the Russians too had had a space flight pioneer. His name was Konstantin Eduardovich Tsiolkovsky. Born in 1857, Tsiolkovsky was an early pioneer of rocket power and had an obsession with space travel. He was the pioneer of liquid propellants and power. Crucially, he laid the groundwork about the difference between power and thrust and the effects upon thrust of exhaust ejector or efflux effects – vital arbiters in rocket design. Like the later von Braun, Tsiolkovsky drew sketches of space stations and *Skylab* type constructions. The first Soviet rocket to use a liquid oxidant combustive propellant was the GIRD-X, designed by M.K. Tikhonravov and S.P. Korolev (the man who later built Soviet spacecraft), which, on 25 November 1933, flew to just over 16,000ft (4,900mtr). Tsiolkovsky also thought of vectored thrust control effects and control surfaces; he also suggested an auto–stabilisation idea and pondered on separate sections of booster rockets that would release from the main rocket airframe. Such works laid the foundations of Russian space science before the von Braun effect post-1945.[2]

French space and rocket travel was overlooked in the post-1945 rush for war-prize material and more recently the French have refined their expertise in the field. However, it is to France that we look for another astronautic pioneer in Robert Esnault-Pelterie, who designed monoplane aircraft and then studied the possibilities of rocket power and space flight. When Esnault-Pelterie presented his work to the French Physical Society in 1912, he was another man whose vision would be laughed at by the powers of perceived wisdom. Yet by 1928 and the presentation of his paper, *'The Exploration by Rockets of the Upper Atmosphere and the Possibility of Interplanetary Travel'*, Esnault-Pelterie's thoughts had become more palatable to the learned men and their societies. A fan of Jules Verne, Esnault-Pelterie also predicted nuclear fusion and its power source.[3]

If Alexander Lippisch provided the key, and Fritz von Opel the money for late-1920s rocket-powered flight experiments in Germany, then Hermann Oberth, of what was Transylvania, can be said to be Central Europe's early pioneer of rocket thought. His 1923 paper, *'Die Raket zu den Planetenraumen'* (The Rocket in Interplanetary Space), defined in detail the problems and possibilities of space travel. The reader will by now expect that the perceptions of the then moment, the learned men, would dismiss Oberth's thoughts, and indeed they did. Yet, in the Second World War, Oberth was streamed into Peenemünde at a late stage in the A-series A4 (V-2) rocket project. Its size and scale amazed even Oberth.

In Sweden, Sixten Sason was the man who would pen the aerodynamic design of Saab's first car in 1947 – the UrSaab or 92.001 prototype that looked like a flying saucer rather than a car. Yet, as early as 1941, Sason had designed a *Projekt X* cranked-wing delta shape aircraft with pressurised cockpit, drooped nose viewing and, of note, rocket power amongst its advanced design features. This design was another forgotten piece of genius from a northern European mind.[4]

Despite the precursors of the rocket or space flight thinkers, it was from the German wartime studies of the developing types of wing planforms, aerofoils and lift behaviours that came the step into transonics and then supersonics. Advanced wing design led to a high speed fascination that lay in tandem with rocket flight. Swept-wing knowledge was soon transferred to the design and actuation of the wings and fins attached to von Braun's rockets. From supersonics came rocket flight, missile design and control, leading to unmanned and then manned flight in space. The pathway was clear and, after the machinations of early aviation and the monoplane to biplane retardation that was then followed by the second genesis of the monoplane and its own stepping stone to the swept-wing and jet age, the proponents of the pathway were, principally (with some exceptions) of German origin.

It was in the Kummersdorf and the Peenemünde research that the details and the failings and success of supersonic developments were first framed – these advances stemming directly via a streamed line of design discovery from the early-1930s works of men like Lippisch.

From 1940 to 1945, the science of high speed airflow and supersonic flight control for aircraft, ballistic missiles and rockets, were defined. Principal issues in studying supersonic flows revolved around the design and function of the (often small) wind tunnels themselves. Solving these issues – as the Germans did – would open the doors to missile and rocket technology and to hypersonics. The crucial effects of airframe friction, the boundary layer and gaseous rocket flows, were all investigated in Germany during the war. It would be the 1950s before high speed American-designed and built wind tunnels would reach the hypersonic parameters. Meanwhile, the history books were loath to record that the first ever research into shock waves was by Ernst Mach in 1887 when he photographed such waves seen over a bullet in flight and that one of Prandtl's students, T. Meyer, used Schlieren apparatus to visualise supersonic flow in a nozzle in 1908. From there it was but only a few short years to the practice of interferometer and shadowgraphs.[5]

By 1944, German experts would be using a Mach 4.4 wind tunnel and investigating hypersonic skimming. Seizing this knowledge, Allied scientists steeped in the modern era of aerospace via German work on high-speed airflow focused on the issues of lift, control, and flight behaviour in terms of drag and stability, as well as powerplants and systems. The wind tunnels to define these issues required huge amounts of power and were not always measured in inches – that Mach 4.4 tunnel at Peenemünde was 40ft in diameter. Yet the Peenemünde experts also touched hypersonics – beyond Mach 5.00. As early as January 1944, changes to the functioning of the main Mach 4.4 wind tunnel saw its flow speed leap to Mach 5.18, which truly was hypersonic. NASA's lead scientists were clever men and also working on high speed airflows, but their significant steps in creating supersonic and hypersonic wind tunnels came in 1947 – after they had had access to German research. This is not to say that the men of NASA would not have got there, it is just that the Germans got there long before NASA and the reason why does not lie solely in the issue of funding.

Commentators have framed the case that America, of its own merits, was further ahead than the British or anyone else in high speed flight research after 1946, yet the obvious launching point of the stepping stone the Americans took having occurred after it secured the Nazi research, often fails to be illuminated.

Von Braun was *not* the first rocket man, nor the first successful rocketeer, yet he was the man who brought all the strands together, added knowledge that only Germans had shaped from the paradox of the *Treaty of Versailles*, and then in wartime taken the steps that built a viable sub-orbital rocket craft that would then give rise to orbital and interplanetary space flight and exploration. Without von Braun, the A-series weapons, the Saturn series and Apollo programme would not have come to fruition as and when it did. The first 1920s suggestions of rocket power for an airframe came from Lippisch with his Opel-sponsored studies and from an Austrian, M. Valier, who had suggested in 1927 that a Junkers airframe could be rocket (as opposed to piston) powered.

Von Braun had it all: looks, charm, brains, appreciation of art and culture, without doubt a bit of polymath, and he came from noble lineage with family support. Not to have achieved something would have been surprising.

Under von Braun's charismatic leadership a team of over 500 ex-German rocketeers got to work in America, at the US taxpayers' expense to the tune of billions of dollars.

Eugene Sanger and Early Thoughts

Before Peenemünde and its rockets, early research into high speed flight – latterly defined as hypersonic flight – was conducted in the mid-1930s by Eugene Sanger, a scientist of Austrian lineage. Sanger had become interested in the concept of the antipode – the shortest route around the globe's sphere to a destination – otherwise cited in normal sub-troposphere flight as a 'great circle' route. But Sanger's ideas were of sub-orbital flight. As early as 1928, his doctoral thesis had been focused upon rocket-powered flight, although he was guided by his tutors to more conventional thoughts concerning wing design. Once again a great mind was being constrained by the perceived wisdom and conditioning of those who 'knew everything' and refused to believe man would reach out into space. By 1934, Sanger had written a book about rocket flight and proposed a fuel mix of liquid oxygen and a petroleum based combustant. Speeds of Mach 10.00 were suggested by Sanger.

Soon, ably assisted by his intellectual, mathematician wife, Sanger created a design for a machine that would touch the sky beyond the troposphere. He called it the *Silbervogel* – Silverbird – and its form was remarkably prescient with a lifting body fuselage, and sharp, short, broad chord wings. Only the small tail surfaces exposed a lack of knowledge about high speed airflow effects. Sanger's silver machine would, he claimed, reach Mach 13.00 and have an exhaust tube velocity of 3,700 metres per second. It was not a pulse jet or ramjet, but a boost-glide machine that would achieve a terminal powered velocity – then glide along until a descent profile was required. As early as 1934, Sanger had claimed his Silverbird would reach Mach 3.5, traversing 5,000km (downrange) and losing only 20km in altitude amid its descent ratio.

After a period at the DVL, Sanger moved on to a new variant of his Silverbird ideas – a true atmospheric surface skimmer type of machine. By 'bouncing' off the atmosphere in a series of prescribed manoeuvres and lift coefficients, the craft could be economically ranged to fly around the world. Ignored by Hitler and the Air Ministry, despite working at the DVL as a rocket specialist, Sanger had little to do with Peenemünde and rocket science, but his ideas were suggested as having a military application. Was this the true beginning of hypersonic-boost-glide or skimming flight?[6]

Eventually Sanger designed a defining form for his hypersonic surface skimmer – smaller wings, a flat-bottomed lifting body fuselage, smaller refined control surfaces, work on the engine intake orifice, and a configuration that would be mirrored by British and American designs for such vehicles more than sixty years later. Of significance, the Nazi regime patented Sanger's idea under the title 'Gliding Bodies for Flight Velocities Above Mach 5.00'. Officially published by the Reich, the details of Sanger's idea were circulated among the elite of German aerodynamics – Prandtl, Heinkel, Georgii, Messerschmitt, von Braun and Kurt Tank. Via such dissemination, the details were part of the material scooped up under Operation Paperclip. From there came new data in the creation of the art of hypersonics. The Russians, however, missed out, and Stalin devised a bizarre plot to kidnap Sanger, his mathematician wife, and assistant Bredt, from their temporary residence in Paris. It came to nothing but its reality underlines just how vital the securing of advanced design was to those outside of Germany. Soon afterwards, the Soviets' own chief rocket designer G. Tokaty-Tokayev defected to Great Britain.[7]

Tangentially, the French began their supersonics research on early test airframe flights in 1953 via the Sud Ouest S.O. 9000 Trident. For the French too had secured some degree of German knowledge in early 1945. Sanger's presence in Paris can only have been a benefit.

The eminent Sanger was appointed the first president of the new International Federation of Astronautics in 1951 and he died in 1964. His work surely touched the design of the North American X-15 rocket-powered high speed research machine. Perhaps Sanger's greatest legacy was his work to show that small-wings, as applied to rocket-powered bodies, could enhance lift and range potential, notably as a skipping or skimming flight low orbit device. The realities of such research were manifested in the American 1960s *Dyna-Soar* programme, and more recent ideas such as BAE's hypersonic skimmer, and various American and German pulse-cycle low orbit transport machines of lifting body design concept as the flying flat-iron with small-wings and cargo and passenger potential as well as military application.

In the X-15 liquid-fuelled rocket machine with over 60,000lbs (27,215kgs) of thrust – air-launched, 22ft (6.70m) span with a trapezoidal wing shape having forward sweep to the trailing edge – demonstrated an amalgam of German, British and American findings. Having achieved Mach 3.00 and 314,750ft (95,936m) in 1964 and going on to Mach 6.72 (adjusted for height at 4,534mph (7,297km/h) by 1967, the X-15 defined the outcome of wartime supersonics research.

1945–1950 British Supersonic Design Amid a Denial of Reality

German research into swept-wings was evident from late 1930 and Lippisch's initial test models were flown at the Wasserkuppe in the winter snows. By 1938, Lippisch had shared much of his work on swept and delta-wing planforms and airflow analysis – not least via NACA publishing its memorandums and from Alexander Lippisch himself presenting a lecture at the RAES on 15 December 1938 – where Beverley Shenstone acted as his host and interpreter.[8]

Of significance, Lippisch's 1935 work, *'Verfaren zur Bestimmung der Auftriebsverteilung langs Spannweite'* (Method for the Determination of the Spanwise Flow) – latterly published as NACA Technical Memorandum No.778, can only have been a notable step forwards in assessing wing behaviours. During the war, the work of Lippisch and others manifested in Göring's advanced devices. The Me 163 and Me 262 both announced the success of swept-wing research prior to 1945. The Germans had realised that the swept-wing was the key to transonic and supersonic flight. Seizure of the highly advanced Messerschmitt P.1101 swept-wing jet fighter really was the key to a host of 1950s jet fighter designs that stemmed from Allied aircraft manufacturers. In America, Bell would use its secrets in their X-5.

From early advances in glider wing design via the Göttingen research group and the Rhon Rositten Gessellschaft design bureau and Lippisch's office at the Ursinus House, Wasserkuppe, German aerodynamicists had unveiled the secret to high-speed flight. Willi Messerschmitt would of course be charged with turning such research into the swept-wing aircraft that would, in a post-conflict area, form the basis of American and British supersonic research via their own iterations of swept-wing and all-wing airframes. In 1935, a Lippisch contemporary, Dr Adolf Busemann, had presented a paper on drag reduction through use of swept-wings. In 1946, Busemann went to America under Operation Paperclip and worked at NACA (Langley). By 1951 he was a professor at the University of Colorado.

In Britain such early research was also somewhat ignored, as were some aspects of the work of the established aerodynamicist and author of '*The Elements of Aerofoil and Airscrew Theory*' (published in 1926), Hermann Glauert, who had proposed similar studies of high speed flight. During the Second World War, the lack of further research into swept, high-speed wing planforms in Great Britain seems to have led to a curious blind alley (perpetuated on both sides of the Atlantic). Yet curiously, despite wartime constraints on time, money and material, the British established not just the Brabazon committees, but significantly, a tailless design investigation under the Tailless Advisory Committee that was suggested in 1942 and formally convened in 1944. Despite this group, supersonic research focused on bullets, their shape and adding wings to such a form.

The British, and the men at the National Physical Laboratory (NPL), seemed to have decided that if a bullet or cannon shell could achieve transonic velocity and if an aircraft was to do the same, then it should be of similar shape to a bullet. The study of ballistics soon led to the belief that all you had to do was stick wings on a bullet-shaped body, and had not the V-2 rockets landing on London proved that bullet-shaped projectiles could go supersonic? It must have a been a massive shock for the learned men of London (and Long Beach) to have set their eyes upon the swept-wing styles of the war-prize machines, from Horten all-wing jets to the Me P.1101. Before then, the British designs for supersonic wings would follow the Spitfire's lead and be very thin aerofoil section wings, with sharp leading edges. The study of a swept-wing to be used on any potential British supersonic aircraft seems to have been either never considered – or dismissed.

At the end of the war, as the thousands of German experts were 'lifted' and shipped to Cherbourg and Calais, with some routing onwards to London, the British had in their hands many leading names of highly advanced knowledge – men like, Alexander Lippisch, Martin Winter, Hans Multhopp, and Reimar and Walter Horten. Yet they were allowed to drift away or be 'poached' by the Americans. The British seized a large number of German airframes, yet ignored the creators of those airframes. Meanwhile, the Americans and the Russians seized as many of the actual brains (as opposed to the product of the brains) as they could. Under Operation Paperclip, America offered German designers new facilities, new homes, and new lives. Even the Russians built new research facilities for the thousands of German scientists, experts and engineers that they scooped up in Prague, Berlin, and on the road from Vienna. In America and Russia, these German experts set to work again and provided their respective hosts with the massive advances of 1950s aerospace science. Britain did not, or could not, afford to house Germany's experts, nor absorb them into Britain's dishevelled research buildings – often wooden huts or crumbling brick sheds lacking funding or adequate heating.

As *Pedantica* wrote from Cambridge to *Flight* on 7 March 1952, the obvious questions were why did Britain not encourage the continuation of German science by its experts – unhindered – even if it was in Germany, but under suitable controls? Prototypes could have been allowed to be built and then shipped back to Farnborough or Boscombe Down for test flying. Having received a great shock (at the advanced nature of German science), British industry should have invested in such scientists and continued the stream of ideas.

Under British control, German design teams were split up and their facilities destroyed. Locked into their own mindset, the British scientific establishment seemed remarkably disinterested in these German men and their secrets. Apart from a few months of interrogation, and being made to provide some drawings (which were then rated 'Top Secret' and could not be viewed by their authors!), such men were allowed to drift away back to Germany, or, more interestingly, to be snapped up by the Americans and to be spirited away to vast research complexes in the USA, where they would, over the next decades, secure the future of aerospace for America. There, every single piece of war-prize information was copied, microfilmed and disseminated across the American industry. Knowledge transfer was grasped and acted upon, centres of excellence were created, but back in London, despite gathering all the war-prize aircraft together under one roof at RAE Farnborough, the British ignored the data, only noting some of it as useful. They issued dismissive research reports and, incredibly, still refused to believe in the advances of the German designers.

In 1945, British transonic and supersonic knowledge was derived from wind-tunnel data and was very limited in its scope – the Royal Aircraft Establishment's first high speed wind tunnel having been completed as late as 1942 after a five-year cogitation. Speed above Mach 0.80 was beyond the scope of this tunnel, or any British research. Of aerodynamic compressibility and of the swept-wing's delaying shock values, of stall behaviour or control surface effects, there was little known in Britain until research funding began to manifest in late 1943 and transferred to early outcomes in 1944.

It would be the late 1940s and early 1950s before British 'names' began publishing papers and articles espousing the benefits of high speed aerodynamic researches – playing down the German origins. It seems that, in their denial and belief that British was best, the British handed the Americans the keys to the secrets of Nazi technology that had studied and solved the major issues of high speed, delta, and all-wing flight.

There had been one bright spot in the gloom however. In late 1943, enter the Miles Company and the route to its later M.52 aircraft. The Miles Company had made wooden sports aircraft, yet was tasked with taking Britain through the sound barrier in an all-metal craft. It seems a strange plan, but there were experts on hand and the NPL, who would assist under the cloak of secrecy.

Having researched and designed an all-wing device in 1938, F.G. Miles moved away from the all-wing during the war and focused on his idea for an unswept, ultra-thin aerofoil that would break through the aerodynamic compressibility issues of the sound barrier – the M.52.

The men of the Miles Company put much far-sighted research into their supersonic machine, but it was a rocket-shaped fuselage, to be powered by an early jet, and sporting the addenda of straight, unswept but thin wings. These small, short, biconvex wings were limited in span so they lay inside the nose shock wave buffet zone. Of interest, the thin wings were clipped and of asymmetric minor/major chord axis ellipsoid planform with a forward swept trailing edge, designed to enhance control response. However, the fuselage was a tubby, long barrel, and there was no wing fillet. The tailplanes were, however, swept. Low speed handling of the razor sharp, super-critical wing in the landing configuration would surely have been very interesting indeed – a 170kt runway threshold speed had been calculated, which was very high. The spectre of tip stalling and lateral oscillation cannot have been a minor concern.

This design and its planform lacked swept-wing transonic research and followed the short, low aspect ratio thin wing 'blade' research route to transonic drag reduction. Yet hidden within its design, there lay a key – that of the all-moving tailplane which Miles had evolved. But the Miles – that was fitted with two differing power developments, ultimately with a ducted fan-effect Power Jets

Ltd jet turbine and an afterburner – would rely on sheer brute force of power to try to push its way through the sound barrier; which by 1946 had become the mythical portal to the future.

The year 1946 would be a defining moment; for just as the German swept-wing, rocket power, and all-wing research was being dismissed in Britain and devoured in America (and to some extent in Europe and Russia), the British Director General of Scientific Research at the Ministry of Aircraft Production, Sir Benjamin Lockspeiser, told F.G. Miles that the M.52 supersonic experiment was over – cancelled. The national debt and the lure of rocket research had led the new British Labour Government to cancel an airframe as it was near-complete, this was the first, but not the last such occasion a British Government would take such short-sighted decisions, the cancellation of the Vickers V.1000 being the ultimate example of governmental stupidity in which – Sir George Edwards noted – Britain handed the future of large civil airframe design and manufacture to America.

In an act of irony, F.G. Miles tried to save the situation by suggesting a cheaper method of achieving high speed flight with the M.52 was to equip it with an 'off the shelf' German rocket engine – of which many were simply lying about. Use of a German gyro stabilisation control was also mooted.[9]

Upon its death, the M.52 was announced as a research programme that had now been completed. Supersonic flight would – according to the clueless new government – be explored using rockets and pilotless radio-controlled devices. One thing was for sure, the British in their ivory tower of learning were hardly likely to admit that German research had left them standing – a fact rather underlined by the fact that, by 1947, the RAE had drawn up a swept-wing, T-tailed supersonic research airframe that had 55° of sweep and a revolutionary T-tail; both courtesy of the men who had studied such things in Germany circa 1937–1945, Martin Winter and Hans Multhopp. Multhopp would soon leave RAE Farnborough to become an American and pioneer research into lifting bodies and designs that led to the Space Shuttle itself.

The M.52 was clearly a journey up a contentious route. Even Barnes Wallis would, by 1946, be heading a Vickers-Armstrong research unit that would embrace German swept-wing and all-wing technology and lead him to the variable geometry 'swing-wing' concept. But Wallis and Vickers would (under government guidance) spend five years exploring the blind alley of radio-controlled, pilotless, air-launched test models of rocket-propelled transonic design.

Meanwhile, across the Atlantic, the Americans were also racing to the sound barrier via their own rocket-powered straight-winged device that would initially be unable to break through the compressibility and control reversal issues of transonic flight – notably to be launched from an airborne carrier aircraft in the same manner as had been proposed for the M.52.

The key to the successful supersonic flight of the straight-winged, unswept Bell X-1 on 14 October 1947 was the adoption of an all-moving tailplane – an idea first seen on the M.52 and handed over to the Americans by the British Government, which ordered the Miles company to put everything it knew from M.52 – *all* the technical data – into crates and ship it straight to the USA for American boffins to dissect. Shortly afterwards, and against military advice, the same Attlee-led British Government shipped 'gifts' of Rolls-Royce 'Nene' jet engine technology to the Soviet Union, where they provided the Soviet industry with a massive technical leap forwards and the key to jet-powered flight via their own incarnation of the Ta 183 jet airframe and Messerschmitt P.1101 designs in the form of the 'copy' that was the MiG-15. In a few short years, MiG-15s and MiG-17s of German design provenance, and with Rolls-Royce derived jet engines, would be shooting down British and American aircraft. The irony was less than amusing.

The Bell X-1 is fact, and it adopted an all-moving tailplane and 'officially' broke the sound barrier using the unswept, thin wing theory. The X-1 was air-launched and thus avoided the take-off configuration issues that could have afflicted such a wing choice. The M.52 was fact, but also a fiction at the hands of those other than its creators. The period 1945–1950 seems to have been a self-inflicted British hiatus in supersonic design. The British would catch up of course, but they would do it using delta-wings, all-wings and swept-wings, whose provenance was not of Britain, but of Germany. In a strange paradox, British supersonic research was curtailed, yet swept-wing and all-wing research was finally embraced. There did, of course, follow a reversal of policy about supersonics, but the lost years of British supersonics research are a salutary lesson in egoism.

The Americans, circa 1944, had originally thought of straight-winged, stubby, rocket-powered sledges to take them past the sound barrier. There were, briefly, two schools of design though – swept-winged and straight stub-winged. The Americans and the British were turning out straight-winged, unswept, jet fighters, whilst the Russians were seizing upon the advantages of their swept-wing discoveries courtesy of German research. Yet, once the Americans grasped the swept-wing benefits from their own securing of German secrets, the straight-winged aircraft suddenly sprouted swept-wings. Only one more step was needed to embrace the delta and then the art of supersonics.

The swept-wing Me 262 might have become the first aircraft in the world to break the sound barrier of supersonic flight. It may even have achieved this over Germany in a 70 degree dive from above 30,000ft in early 1943, or during British testing in 1945. How likely is the claim? Theoretically, it was possible, but in terms of controls and aerodynamic compressibility, were the Me 262's wings and variable incidence tailplane the key or the problem? We will never know if the Me 262 managed supersonic flight, but some say it did indeed touch the sound barrier. But if it did, it did not, for history – as written by the victors – says that the supersonic honour of breaking the barrier went of course to Colonel Charles Yeager as an American in an American designed and built machine on 14 October 1947.

In aerodynamic terms, the evidence is against the Me 262 having broken the sound barrier – though Messerschmitt test pilot G. Lindner told his British interrogators in 1945 that he had touched 600mph, or above Mach 0.86. Given the number of pilots killed in high speed dives in Me 262s, the breakthrough is unlikely to have occurred. But what of the all-wing and rocket-powered Me 163? In aerodynamic terms, the evidence might be in favour of it having achieved supersonic flight in 1944. Yet in Allied flight testing by Captain Eric Brown, it demonstrated nose tuck-under at high Mach numbers. Of note, a Heinkel 280 (V7) – a more orthodox airframe and planform, and with its engines specifically removed as part of a flight test programme – achieved 578mph as a glider in a near-vertical dive in 1943. We might safely observe that just as the Germans achieved supersonic near-orbital flight, so too did they achieve near-supersonic flight. Many think that G. de Havilland may have broken the sound barrier in the Lippisch-inspired DH 108, but de Havilland did not live to confirm the fact.

The annals of history say that Captain Charles K. Yeager, in his Bell X-1, first broke the sound barrier – despite its blunt, straight wings and old-fashioned shape. But what if a 60 degree swept delta-winged device, with an advanced shape that had been born in one of Germany's unique high-speed wind tunnels, had tried to attempt the sound barrier using either a German rocket motor or a BMW turbo jet – or even a re-engineered Rolls-Royce 'Nene'?

Incredibly, just such an airframe, designed by the advanced DFS, had been seized by the Russians and taken back to the Soviet Union in mid-1945. If any airframe was likely to have beaten Yeager and the Bell X-1 to the sound barrier, this DFS design would have been the machine to do it. Unsurprisingly, that is just the claim the Soviet Union made in April 1947 – nearly six months before Yeager went supersonic. But can we conjecture that the top German glider design body, which had become the home of powered, high-speed flight design and testing, provided a different history? One thing is obvious; the DFS delta design was far more likely to exceed Mach 1 than the tubby old Bell X-1, so the aerodynamic evidence favours the DFS design realised under Siegfried Gunter, who was in the Soviet Union at the time.[10] As it stands however, history gives Yeager the nod; despite the fact that only brute propulsive force got his stubby, straight-winged device past Mach 1.0, he did do it.

From the early 1950s, across the Atlantic, Alexander Lippisch had taught Convair and the US industry how to build and fly very successful delta-wing fighters and bombers alongside swept-wing icons such as the F-86 Sabre – itself re-winged from straight to swept-wings – to meet the MiG-15 over Korea and save the day after early losses using previous designs against the amazing Russian machines.

The Americans would not waste what they would learn.

Chapter Nine

The Rush to Seize the Science

The Operations Game

In April 1945, teams of Allied experts in high speed cars and on motorbikes, supported by DC-3, Lancaster and other aircraft, convoys of trucks, and supporting military staff, were dispatched deep into the still-gasping remains of the Third Reich in order to secure the future of science as war-prize technology. Yet many months beforehand, towards the end of 1944, small, select teams of American aviation experts had crossed the Rhine with the American Army and begun the trawl through Germany in search of its scientific secrets.

In early May 1945, as the ground war in Germany began to end and Hitler paced towards his suicide, long before Victory in Europe Day (VE day), the search for science really got going under a series of preordained groups.[1] They were pre-planned because the Americans and the British knew as early as 1942 that there would be 'war prize' science treasure to seize. Of interest, these groups represented the first real, State organised Anglo-American-European exercise aimed at managing the future sharing of potential assets and policy. It can be no coincidence that the leaders of Paperclip's managers – the Office of Strategic Studies (OSS) and its offspring the Central Intelligence Agency (CIA) – would become the lead names in the American Committee for a United Europe (ACUE), which was founded as early as late 1947 with Rockefeller funding. The aim of the ACUE seems to have been the dismantling of German political and industrial power in order to create a unified European trading and political block – not least as a bulwark to the Soviet Union. From the ACUE came noteworthy links to the founding fathers of the European Union and the Bilderberger Group.[2]

The late Prince Bernhard of the House of Orange, prior to his marriage into the Dutch royal family and his founding role in the Bilderberger group, not only had links to I.G. Farben and had links to his native Germany's National Socialist political movement, but had also been an operational intelligence officer for the Allies during the Second World War, with a specific focus on aeronautical technology, as a pilot, his favoured field. Prince Bernhard, questioned by the author, stated that the joint works of the aerospace research groups of Operation Paperclip and its affiliates and offshoots, were indeed the foundations of the American advance in post-war aviation. On the joint efforts being the catalyst for creating a wider geo-strategical and industrial mechanism or movement, he would not be drawn, but simply made a wry smile and a look straight in the eye, that conveyed its own message. Prince Bernhard noted the close links between Dutch, British and other European airlines and air forces to the American industrial machine, and the fleet equipment procured by those airlines and air forces from American concerns post 1945 (the prince's own, later alleged links to the Lockheed F-104 procurement by the Royal Netherlands Air Force were not discussed).[3]

To have such a figure openly accept that what went on under Paperclip (and by default the corporate and geopolitical implications inherent), was indeed a harvesting of science that became the foundations of a future, provides a small vignette of the importance of what happened in the race across Germany in the spring and summer of 1945. That the Americans (and to a lesser extent the British) were, in 1945, ready to hit the German ground running in the search for material gain and technological advancement, proves the point. They did it through the following mechanisms:[4, 5, 6]

- **US Army Air Force Technical Intelligence Service (Air Tech/Intel)**: This was the early iteration of an intelligence asset mechanism to be deployed into Germany. Its task was fully operational in 1944. Thanks to having monitored German technology during the war, and surveyed crashed German aircraft that had contained new science and new ideas, the US Army Air Force Technical Intelligence Service (Air Tech/Intel) had a good idea of the advanced materials that would be there for the grabbing when tactical or strategic intelligence became something else. By the summer of 1944, just a few weeks after D-Day, intelligence men at Wright Field had begun to create and then deploy a science and technology gathering mechanism. Weekly bulletins of findings were issued.

    The British had been busy too – with experts inspecting crashed German aircraft for evidence of new science and techniques – not just of electronics or aerodynamics, but also of advanced metallurgy, magnesium, alloy and extrusion processes that were unknown to the British.

    Sweeping Germany clean and making a point of removing what they wanted from the impending segregation of the Russian zone or sector, the Americans grabbed what they could and destroyed what they left behind – notably at Peenemünde. This led to an interesting situation where the Americans seized dozens of completed V-2 rockets and hundreds of semi-completed V-2s and many of tons of spares. Conversely, the Russians only managed to secure one or two completed V-2s and the parts to build perhaps ten to fifteen more. This meant that the Russians were much more careful of their hoard, only risking firing and flight testing of their V-2s after long and exhaustive preparations and study in the post-war period.[7]

Experts by the hundreds were scooped up from German aeronautical and academic research sites, entire aircraft company factories were looted and thousands of tons of research documents driven off to Antwerp, Calais and Cherbourg, for shipping back to the United States. A vast armada of large, Atlantic-capable ships queued up in these ports awaiting the treasures that the Americans secured. DC-3 aircraft shuttled seized experts back to Paris and London for onward shipment across the Atlantic and to new lives. Some, like von Braun, were escaping from the onward march of the Russians, and were keen to meet the Americans, others hid out in rural locations. 'Mr Delta' – Alexander Lippisch – managed to escape from Austria (then under Soviet potential threat) and place himself and his family into western hands. And von Braun was at risk from both sides, he, like many German scientists with access to weapons technology, had been made to become a member of the SS, and as such would have been a target of the Russians. He might also have been on a Führer -led target list to murder such experts and deny their knowledge to the Allies.

Near the Nordhausen/Mittelwerk site of rocket and weapons construction, von Braun and his team buried their research paperwork in an old mine working. The Mittelwerk site, packed with technology, was to become the focus for a 'race' to secure the trove of rocketry secrets. Von Braun's separate hiding site in an old mine working nearby would be found and swept clean in under ten days by the Americans before the Soviets forces took over the sector under the a terms agreed by the Allies. President Roosevelt's untimely death and the Truman presidency had little effect on the race for science.

From 1945 onwards, the thousands of documents and reports collated under the CIOS, FIAT and BIOS programmes, charted the mining of all Germany's scientific expertise – not just in aerospace. The gain in electronics, electromagnetics, physics, metallurgy, electronics and a vast array of subjects, truly was worth every penny in future gold. The defining control arms of the race to plunder Germany of her science were:

- **OSS**: Office of Strategic Studies – the forerunner of the Central Intelligence agency (CIA). Run by W. Donovan, W. Bedell Smith (the CIA's first director) and Allen Dulles (latterly CIA director).
- **JIOA**: Joint Intelligence Objectives Agency (JIOA) search teams, under the Office of Strategic Studies.
- **OTS**: Office of Technical Services, directed in 1945–1947 by John C. Green. OTS gathered 1,800 reports of German scientific research running to thousands of pages. By 1948, two million individual indexed documents had been recorded

by the teams of several hundred researchers of the Office of Technical Services at Wright Field.

- **CIOS**: A Combined Intelligence Priorities Objectives Sub-Committee (CIOPS) was the first official American iteration and sanction of ideas that had been brewing for many months to secure German science. CIOPS became the Combined Intelligence Objectives Sub-Committee CIOS.
- **BIOS**: British Intelligence Objectives Subcommittee. The British version of CIOS, from CIOS/BIOS came the budgets and the authorities to act, and act fast – using whatever men or material were required to be commandeered. CIOS/BIOS was also behind the fact of leading German weapons designers being held in London from early 1945 onwards – including Dornberger, von Braun, Messerschmitt, Lippisch and the Hortens.
- **BIPS/BIOS/BIGS**: The British Interrogation of German Scientists Groups. Entitled by these acronyms, they all had diverse yet related remits. An Enemy Personnel Exploitation Section operated within this set.
- **CSDIC**: A Combined Services Detailed Interrogation Centre was behind the interrogation of prisoners and scientists up to 1947 at locations in Belgium, Germany, and beyond. The last CSDIC facility at Bad Nenndorf was closed in the summer of 1947.
- **FIAT**: The Field Information Agency: Technical – this was most active between 1945–1948 and the aim was to secure German technology under the guise of 'the advancement and improvement of production and standards of living' under a United Nations remit that cited the 'proper' exploitation of Nazi technology. Badged under a Field Intelligence Agencies/Technical umbrella, 500 operatives formed teams that were placed directly into the offices of German industry. Up to 1948 they mined information and IP.
- **Technical Industrial Intelligence Branch**: Latterly the TIIC, the Technical Industrial Intelligence Committee, was created as an agency of the Joint Chiefs of Staff, but transferred to the Department of Commerce in January in 1946. The TIIB sent over 400 investigators into Germany.
- **TIIC: Technical Industrial Intelligence Committee**: This was the search group mechanism, composed of 380 civilians representing seventeen American industries – that is with direct links to major American manufacturing concerns. Then came teams of the Washington D.C. based Office of the Publication Board.

As late as 1947, large Allied ships were sailing up German rivers, their holds and decks packed with airframes, jet engines, gliders and crates of paperwork en route to Britain, Canada and America. From Operation Alsos, to Operation Overcast, to Operation Paperclip and beyond, the Allies knew what advances lay in the 'flugzeugbau' and barns, factories, forests, caves and mines of a defeated Germany.

Many German experts lived 'on-the-run', desperate to escape Russian revenge. Some had even been contacted and 'persuaded' into Allied hands long beforehand. The Russians invoked Operation Osoaviakhim to seize technology. Approximately six months *after* the Americans first began an unofficial, unstated race across Germany to seize technology, the British Fedden Mission arrived about 12 June 1945 to see what they could find in the ruins of the Reich.[8]

The records say that not until 26 April 1946 did official presidential sanction for the transporting of German technology and experts back to America actually kick in as a directive of the Joint Chiefs of Staff (D: 1067/14) to preserve such records and material.

If Paperclip was the over-arching name, Operation Alsos and the joint CIOS Anglo-American Operation Epsilon were significant in scooping up physicists. Under Operation Epsilon, nine leading members of Germany's nuclear fusion team were taken to London and detained at taxpayers' expense. Having initially been taken to holding centres at Antwerp, (and in the case of the rocketeers, Cuxhaven) many experts – notably the nine nuclear/uranium experts – arrived in secret in Britain via the Special Operation Executive and airfield at Tempsford. From there, Hall Farm, near Godmanchester, Cambridgeshire, and addresses in north and south London, such as locations at, 6, Hall Road, St Johns Wood, were the centre points of the interrogation of German scientists and experts (especially from May to August 1945). These, as well as the Kensington Palace Gardens and Wimbledon locations, were home to Germans, including those collected under Operation Matchbox – the programme to rescue German scientists from the Russian-occupied zone of Germany. The SOE, MI6 and MI19 were the lead British players and even built a London holding point that became known as a 'Cage', where German prisoners of war and latterly seized scientists, were accommodated and interrogated (latterly subject to allegations of torture being practised). Other 'Cages' were located around Great Britain, notably in Wales and the north.[9]

Oranienburg

Having discovered that the Heinkel and Horten all-wing airframes were being tested at Oranienburg and that the core of Germany's nuclear fusion team were also present there, working on rare materials, the Americans decided to deny the advancing Russians (into whose zone Oranienburg would fall) access to its secrets and bombed the site to obliteration on 15 March 1945 with nearly 2,000 tonnes of bombs. This effectively denied the Russians the chance to seize any of Oranienburg's nuclear research secrets – or anything else. The mission was clearly carried out against Russian interests – not principally against the German war machine.

Even Germany's relationship with its Japanese ally was to be inspected. Experts from Heinkel had been present in Japan and much knowledge transfer had taken place between the two powers. From elliptical wings to all-wing and rocket secrets, Japan and Germany had shared much – and anti-radar technology had found its way to Tokyo too.

And what if German experts were to flee to Nazi-friendly nations in Asia, Africa or South America? Attempts to deny such experts travel to these destinations were slow to gain pace under a 'Safehaven' project label.

The key operating mechanisms for seizing science were framed by the 'Operations' projects. All well-funded and supplied, their lead components were:

- **Operation Paperclip**: Paperclip was only signed off as an entity by President Truman in July 1945, and its 'official' act of transporting German scientists to the USA is cited as having begun in 1946. However, prior to Operation Paperclip, a veritable rash of 'Operations' had set the process. Of significance, thirty-two Allied intelligence groups worked at securing German science.
- **Operation Alsos**: An American-led project to secure German atomic secrets, and to secure top expert, W. Heisenberg, also framed by projects entitled Operation Big, Operation Epsilon and Operation Crossbow.
- **Operation Backfire**: Based out of Cuxhaven on the Baltic coast, a British project to bring together ex-Peenemünde experts and materials to test V-2 technology in Germany secured a successful launch during October 1945. Senior Allied figures observed the event.
- **Operation Lusty** (Luftwaffe Special Technology): From late March 1945, American and British experts in the military services collaborated to find and seize advanced Luftwaffe airframes; and design and research paperwork that went with them and their technology. Many of the experts came from Wright Field and were trained in the Air Technical Intelligence unit (ATI) to form the nucleus of an exploitation department. One of the teams was led by Lieutenant Colonel H.E. Watson and raced across Europe searching for advanced jet and non jet-powered technology. It was Watson's team who secured the Me 262s from Lechfeld near Augsburg and routed them to Paris and then to Cherbourg. Other war prize material was shipped from Antwerp and Hamburg. Operation Lusty secured over 16,000 items and by 1948 this load of advanced design materials was distributed from Wright Field to Davis-Monthan Field, and the US Naval School at Patuxent River.

- **Operation Overcast:** Forerunner in mid-1945 of the official 1946 implementation of Operation Paperclip requirements to secure and transport German experts already interviewed or held, back to the USA.
- **Operation Surgeon:** A British project to deny the transit of German technology into Soviet hands.
- **Operation Harass:** An American project to secure potentially useful Germans from the Russian zone. It was active up to late 1947.
- **Operation Osoaviakhim:** Russian equivalent of Operation Paperclip.
- **Project 63:** A programme designed to assist the passage of German engineering experts into American aviation for major brand names including: Lockheed, Martin Marietta, North American Aviation, and others.
- **Special Mission V-2:** As early as April 1945, this project raced towards the Nordhausen Mittelwerk V-2 facility in order to successfully recover over one hundred V-2s in various states of completion within what would soon, according to the *Treaty of Yalta*, become the Soviet Zone. Nearly 350 rail freight wagons were needed to transport the V-2 treasures westwards to safety. From this act stemmed the American space programme.
- **The Osenberg List:** Originally a Nazi Government project of the Third Reich to find, recall, and secure top German technologists and engineering experts from active duty and place them in the safety of a special unit that could focus on Hitler's later directives to secure 'wonder-weapons' to beat the Soviet Union. A list of those men required for return from normal duties was drawn up by the *Wehrforschungsgemeinschaft* – German military research work group. The list was created by W. Osenberg and fell into the hands of Allied agents in March 1945. From this list were gleaned Dornberger, von Braun and many of Peenemünde's expert technicians. Of interest, Dornberger was held in a de facto incommunicado state by the British for more than a year before he arrived in America as part of Operation Paperclip.
- **Apple Pie:** A project to capture senior German military men who had had special responsibility for the commissioning and construction of military technology and advanced hardware. The securing of SS General Hans Kammler, procurer of Peenemünde, was the responsibility of this plan.
- **Ashcan/Dustbin:** An American-British project focusing upon military intelligence that was first based in Paris and then transferred to Germany.
- **Eclipse:** A team tasked with destroying V-1 and V-2 armaments, but which was not used due to all such devices being seized and made safe by Allied forces.

So keen were the Americans to get to the German science first, that their technical experts had crossed the Rhine with the front-line troops in late 1944. Some American experts were captured when von Rundstedt launched his counteroffensive. The American race across Germany to seize its science was planned, structured, and given an unlimited budget. Aircraft, ships, trucks, fast cars, motorbikes, *anything* that could be used to find, seize and secure, advanced aircraft, rockets and jet engines. The Russians were quick off the mark too.

The Fedden Mission[10]

The complacent British Government would take months to put together a small team as the Fedden Mission. In one farcical scene, having discovered that the Americans had carted off a jet-powered Horten Ho 229 all-wing jet fighter from Gotha-Friedrichroda in April 1945, the British simply burnt the next similar Horten device that they found. Meanwhile, the Americans then managed to get an example of the Horten Ho 6/V2 into Northrop's Californian facility for evaluation, within weeks of seizing it.

To quote Sir Roy Fedden from *Flight*, 29 November 1945: 'My own mission received every possible co-operation, but in general the limitations of manpower and transport, and the intensity of our own war effort, had prevented us making such thorough use of the opportunities presented by the enemy collapse'.

Fedden's mission (supported in concept by Sir Stafford Cripps) came under the overview of a plan cooked up in the Air Ministry as Operation Surgeon – in which German experts were to be hand-picked and brought back to Britain. Fedden intended to visit fifty-two locations in Germany, but in the end, visited thirty-one. Fedden took with him a senior RAE aeronautical scientist in the form of Professor Dr W.J. Duncan, and a range of specialists that included, W.J. Stern of the Allied group, J. King a metallurgical specialist of the RAE, and a translator plus supporting crew. By the mission's third day, they had got to the *Luftfahrtforschunstalt fur Aerodinamische* (LFA) and its treasure of high-speed Mach 4+ wind tunnels at Volkenrode. However, the LFA and many of its resources had been carted off almost in their entirety by the Americans as they raced to beat the Russians to the science. The wind tunnels would be the last things to be seized – or 'saved' as some might see it. Of note, the high-speed airflow interferometer was not in evidence – yet later cited in American research.

Under the BIOS and Fedden Mission remit, the British Party No.1264, scoured German aviation company offices to seize material, interview 'target' subjects and glean as much as they could. The team contained leading British figures including representatives from Short Brothers: Sir John S. Buchanan, CBE, as technical director and Air Vice-Marshal R.G. Parry as liaison officer, as well as Mr H.L. Piper (test pilot), Mr W. Swallow (chief production engineer) and Mr D. Keith-Lucas, chief aerodynamicist assistant.

Fedden, once back in London, went on to evidence just how advanced German high-speed wind tunnels were and that they created data that was not available *anywhere* outside Germany. Fedden implored the British establishment not to ignore the advanced German knowledge. He boldly stated that the British should use the best technology in the world – which was, he said – *German* technology. Fedden recommended making use of the captured German scientists and their science in Germany, not by shipping them home in the manner that the Russians or Americans were then doing. Decades later, Fedden's correctness of view was reinforced by Derek Wood's opinion in his book, *Project Cancelled*.[11]

So here was the admission from an unimpeachable source (Fedden) that the future of the best aeronautical research lay in German science, yet despite his work the British establishment took little advantage of what was on offer. Instead, individual British aircraft companies and research bodies made as much use as they could of what they had been told, or had found, but government policy was to sidestep it all. Yet back in industry, even de Havilland is said to have managed to have a man inside Messerschmitt's advanced swept-wing Oberammergau drawing office before Fedden's team arrived. Of note, the American intelligence objectives team had been sifting through Messerschmitt's research for nearly six weeks before the British arrived.[12]

Fedden left a small number of his team in Germany after he went back to London to try and persuade the civil servants that their certainties were wrong. Fedden even cited the German jet engine testing facilities as being far beyond anything Britain's men-in-sheds had. As a former top engineer and director for the Bristol Company, Fedden knew about engines and had a pre-war business relationship with BMW's engine designers – so he knew where to look and how to assess what he saw. Fedden was neither a fool – nor a man likely to get carried away by the potential of unproven technology.

The British Fedden Mission and other operations did, however, secure a range of notable figures from German aeronautical design during their sweep of part of Germany. At one stage in April 1945, a holding camp near Wiesbaden contained the Horten brothers, Alexander Lippisch, Willi Messerschmitt, Kurt Tank, Hans Multhopp, Ernst Heinkel, Woldemar Voigt, Richard Vogt and other notables. Several of these men would end up in a 'safe' house in London for many weeks and at the RAE Farnborough, where they would be made to draw what they knew, only then to be banned from any access on the grounds of secrecy. In late 1945, there was a brief period of internments, interrogation and then a strange interlude where they were allowed to return to Germany or progress into the warm welcome of American hands. Fewer than fifty German aeronautical experts were retained in Britain whilst the Americans and the Russians are estimated to have scooped up thousands of them.

Within months at Farnborough, the RAE made a big show of exhibiting the advanced German airframes and material it had got hold off via various strands of the effort, but the British Government and many of the learned men, turned their noses up at creating a policy around the German science. The Americans and Russians (and the French) had no such qualms and, having grabbed all they could, they jumped ahead. All-wing men and rocket men were seized, not just at Peenemünde on the Baltic, but at research facilities like Adlershof and Oranienburg outside Berlin. In a design bureau in Mariendorf, advanced gyro and navigation instruments that gave the advance over the rest of the world were seized – later to appear in the Apollo series. At Lechfeld airfield in Bavaria, the entire retinue of Me 262 operations was seized.

From early forays in late 1944, by the spring of 1945, American intelligence experts were pouring into Germany under the various arms of the American administration in the form of the US Army Ordnance division; the US Army 104th; the Technical Industrial Intelligence Committee; USAAF; experts from Wright Field and the US Navy. Even Charles Lindbergh got a free pass to rush to Germany and be an 'expert' to assess the science. The Canadians, including members of the National Research Council and all-wing research groups, were also touring Germany looking for science and interrogating men.

Men like Colonel Harold E. Watson, USAAF (Air/Tech/Intel); Major Robert Staver (US Army Ord); Major Calvin Corey (US Army Ord); the US Army's top rocket ordnance man, Colonel Gervais Trichel; Colonel Holgar N. Toftoy; Major William Bromley; Maj General Hugh Knerr and many others, led the rush to grab what America knew it wanted. The focus was on all-wing, swept-wing, and rocket/missile technology.[13]

The Lechfeld hoard and other treasures of technology were collected under the 'Luftwaffe Special Technology' project entitled, Operation Lusty: this alone collected over 16,000 items weighing 6,200tons that yielded nearly 3,000 items of specific interest for study. Large teams of analysts and translators worked for more than two years to assess and understand the scientific treasure trove. Of great significance, the Volkenrode hoard yielded to the Allies the world's only wind tunnel capable of Mach 4.4 (modified in January 1945 to Mach 5.18), 40ft wide and built as part of the Nazi rocket research. It was dismantled, driven across Germany and shipped to the US Navy's Ordnance Laboratory in White Oak, Maryland. Another high-speed wind tunnel was seized by the British and taken to the Royal Aircraft Establishment (RAE) at Farnborough. Also seized was the single design prototype example of the Lippisch (Lp) delta-wing Lp.DM-1 and the plans for its variant the Lp.DM-2, which had a smaller tail fin. These designs were whisked off to the USA and, after testing by NACA, which verified Lippisch's delta claims, became the basis of the delta-wing fashion that manifested in the early 1950s.

They were the true stepping stone to a whole raft of military and civil airframes – including Concorde itself.

The Russians Advance

The Russians were also early participants in the race to seize the science and scientists of the Reich. Even the advanced and unusual thinking of Viktor Schauberger was pursued despite his lack of 'establishment' credentials – his home was stripped bare to its bones as Russian forces searched for his drawings and plans. But it was not the Russians who captured Schauberger, it was the Americans. Schauberger was held for one year by the Americans in strange internment and he was reputedly manipulated into disclosing his works. Freed soon after, Schauberger was dead within days, but his technology was soon under study thousands of miles away across the Atlantic.

Boris Chertok was the Russian who led the Soviet teams to the technology that would later be translated into space travel reality by Sergei Korolev as the enigmatic leader of the Soviet space program. Korolev had begun his flying career as a glider pilot flying B.I. Cheranovsky's all-wing gliders in the 1930s. Strangely, it was the British Intelligence services who had liaised with their Russian counterparts about German rocket sites in Poland and along the Baltic coast. From that lead, the Russians devised a plan to secure what they could of jet engines, swept-wings and rockets. As late as April 1945, the Russians, led by a General Petrov and including Chertok, flew into Germany and began the hunt for advanced technology. Once secure in their agreed sector, the Russians would gather up part-built rockets, spares, technicians, scientists and create a local centre for rocket research evaluation, prior to moving it back to the Soviet Union.

Although the Russians seized many thousands of middle-ranking and lower-ranked researchers, they failed to capture more than a few dozen really top ranking experts in aeronautics and rocketry. However, a leading von Braun associate in the form of Helmut Grottrup did join the Russians and his knowledge of telemetry and missile guidance was to prove invaluable. A small number of senior German airframe men also chose to go east rather than to America. This included men who had worked for Junkers in Dessau, and for Focke-Wulf and Kurt Tank, as well as the renowned Heinkel designer Siegfried Gunter, whom the British had turned down as a potential designer. The Soviet forces also overran the *Henschel Flugzeugbau* factory in Schonefeld, Berlin. There, the Red Army seized several jet prototypes, including the P.132 single jet airframe and many drawings for missiles and a twin-jet, all-wing aircraft. Henschel also yielded, to the Red Army forces, a cranked wing design known as Project 135. However, it was the earlier-arriving

US forces that had seized Henschel's design for a 75mm anti-tank gun that the company had fitted to aircraft in the war.[14]

Even a former head of the DVL, Professor Bock, was in the Soviet zone. So were Hans Wocke, Wilhelm Benz and Bruno Baade. Like the Peenemünde rocketeers, these airframe and aerodynamics men were, between 1954 and 1958, allowed to return from their isolation in the Soviet Union to what had become East Germany (DDR). It was not freedom, but at least it was not the snows of Stalingrad or beyond. By that time, the experts had been milked for all that their knowledge was worth and the Soviet response in the Cold War framed for decades to come. Heinkel's man, Siegfried Gunter, is widely believed to have penned the core design culture for Soviet-era fighter-bomber design.

From the DFS, the Russians secured much data on swept-wings and supersonic flight. Some of the futuristic DFS wind tunnel prototypes were shipped to Moscow and with their T-tails, swept planforms and in some cases, delta shapes, they were the basis of the Soviet fighters and bombers that shook the west in the late 1950s and early 1960s. The DFS 346 and the DFS 480 series provide ample evidence of designs that were re-engineered into Soviet successes. The Russians got to Mittlewerk on 14 July 1945; The US had scoured Mittlewerk but had left things behind – carelessly.

The Americans had filled more than 300 rail freight wagons and over fifty air cargo transport flights with V-2 components and plans – and up to 100 actual V-2s. Soon, 104 ex-Nazi rocket scientists would reside at Fort Bliss, Texas. Although the Americans had secured rockets, nozzles, guidance systems, instruments and launch devices, they had left some material behind. This included at least one vital gyro device and many V-2 body panels – with the vital aerodynamic features in place. The Russian team grabbed all of this and enough parts to build several V-2s. The combustion chamber and nozzle and adjustable vane designs were crucial to von Braun's efforts and they were crucial to Russian efforts too, as several examples of these key parts of the V-2 were found in a wood in 1946.

Mittlewerk/Nordhausen had produced A-4/V-2 series rockets, which in final form pumped out just under 30 tonnes of thrust at 29 tonnes – the same thrust that Concorde's four Bristol Olympus jets would deliver twenty-five years later.

Hans Kammler – Reality or Conspiracy Theory?

What of the enigma of Hans Kammler – the Nazi's leading beast of slave labour who supplied, airframe and rocket construction programmes and built concentration camps? Did he really commit suicide in Czechoslovakia in 1945? Is this why he and his 'war crimes' were absent from the Nuremburg Trial? Or as 'theorists' and a recent German television documentary suggests, did he live? Did America spirit Hans Kammler away to a new rocket, or an anti-gravity or disc technology, research reincarnation, under an assumed name and cleansed record?

Is it possible, as an unknown-known?

Kammler was a sort of operations manager within the Nazi hierarchy. As such, he would have been on the list of the 'Apple Pie' project to seize such people. In fact, he might have been the number one target – he had after all been instrumental in building concentration camps and had deployed 60,000 slave labourers in Poland at the site of the Nazi 'Bell' project. Project Apple Pie had the core remit of seeking out the movers and shakers amid the Reich's military operational hierarchy.

Rising to the rank of general, Kammler had overseen the logistics of the Warsaw massacre and Albert Speer's architectural excess, as well as organising the secret factories across Germany that housed advanced science. The development of von Ohain's jet engine technology was managed by Kammler, as was von Braun and his team of over 500 experts and technicians at Peenemünde. So Kammler truly did have his hands on the levers of power. At the end of the Second World War Kammler was reputedly ordered to seize sixty-two of Germany's leading aerospace scientists and murder them at the command of Adolf Hitler. So great was the scientist's knowledge that Hitler preferred them dead, rather than Red – or American. Those who dismiss the anti-gravity disc flight story as a fantasy must ask, what was it that those sixty-two German academics died for? Yet did it really happen? What were those scientists' names?

The fact is Kammler took no action against von Braun, his team, or his knowledge: we might have expected Kammler to machine gun the entire team on the Führer's order or upon his own behest if the alleged evidence of his personality was anything to go by. Why did Kammler allow von Braun and 500 experts to escape? Was it because Kammler had done a deal with the American forces – rocket secrets and rocket men in return for a new life?

Upon the afternoon of 17 April 1945, Kammler disappeared and, say theorists, he did it along with the sole remaining example of Germany's giant, long-range Junkers JU 390 air transporter.

Beforehand, Hans Kammler had been involved in one of the greatest scientific achievements of the twentieth century, for he was the logistical provider behind the research and facilities that informed the alleged flying disc technology of Germany. These were translated from the Prague University-based 'disc' and anti-gravity works and the 'bell' shaped lifting body research of Viktor Schauberger. Kammler was also the operations man behind the German uranium and nuclear fusion facilities, these works being the foundations of the German atomic research.[15]

Kammler's fate remains a divisive and disturbing enigma in a debate of risky provenance.

Chapter Ten

Outcomes

From Re-Engineered Enigmas to Blatant Copies

After seizure of the war prize material in 1945, aviation was heavily influenced by the knowledge taken from a recumbent Germany. It might be suggested that it was only after this date that American, Russian, French, or British aviation was influenced by the advanced secrets found and looted from Germany's wind tunnels and design bureaus. However, there is a riddle in the air, because, much to the horror of the 'British is best' school of thought, it is now evident that critical aspects of the highly advanced aerodynamics inherent in the design and shaping of British aircraft starting as far back as the Supermarine Spitfire, stemmed from Germany and, in the case of the Spitfire, from the hand of a Canadian who had been trained in Germany by Junkers, Lippisch and others.

This means that the first British airframe to contain some degree of German technology was a pre-war airframe – the Spitfire. By 1937, British gliders aped German glider design, but after 1946, British and American aircraft design did more than mimic German trends, it represented them in what can only be called a blatant arrogance.

Supermarine Spitfire – Partly of German Science?

Some have suggested that the Spitfire aped or 'copied' the wing design of the Heinkel He 70. This is a gross error of fact and science, because the Spitfire's deliberately distorted, forwards–swept, two–part asymmetric elliptical wing planform shape and design is very different indeed from the He 70's single aerofoil, simple symmetrical ellipse. Differences in planform and aerofoil technology offer distance between the two designs. Still the falsehoods of an He 70 derived German link to the Spitfire are made. Yet the irony is that, although such claims are factually wrong, there was indeed a German link to the science of the Spitfire. It is a link that has only recently been fully researched in the form of a book[1] and an RAeS paper.[2]

The bile and ire with which such evidence is claim of a link to German design, have been met after being published and have revealed that, eighty years on, British pride still smarts with any suggestion that German science could have informed

British practice. Those who react with such anger and certainty in the face of multi-referenced evidence, only reveal the limitations of their abilities and the weakness of their certainties. For without in any way undermining or attacking the work of R.J. Mitchell, the facts are that advanced aerodynamic design stemming directly from the thoughts of Prandtl, Junkers, and Lippisch, contributed to the design of the Spitfire alongside R.J. Mitchell's own genius that stemmed from his Schneider Trophy winning experiences. And of the Spitfire's ultra-thin aerofoils – two sections uniquely blended together – these stemmed from a Supermarine visit to NACA in June 1934, just a few months prior to the selection of the Spitfire's aerofoil(s) choice from the new NACA series – themselves informed by German practice.

An unrealised reality is that, because the Spitfire's aerodynamicist (Shenstone) had learned his skills under Junkers and Lippisch – indeed assisting Lippisch with the realisation of the delta-wing, a great deal of all-wing and delta-wing design features went into the Spitfire's wing. The aerodynamic techniques of the elliptical lift pattern and then the all-wing lift behaviours and the delta techniques were the groundwork for the Spitfire's modified ellipse and double, blended aerofoil with its resultant handling prowess. A Spitfire, when flown by an experienced pilot with gliding or aerobatic skills, could outfly anything in 1940. Even Walter Horten, as an Me Bf 109 fighter pilot with Adolf Galland, had had no answer to an expertly flown Spitfire. Galland, of course, is famously quoted to have praised the Spitfire's handling and dogfight capabilities – asking Göring for Spitfires. Walter Horten knew that no contemporary Luftwaffe fighter could match a Spitfire flown by an expert and that jet or all-wing design was the only possible answer to deal with the fighter.

War and an Irony – the Spitfire Wing Planform

Legend has it that the Supermarine Spitfire's elliptical wing was (a) *solely* the design of Reginald J. Mitchell and, (b) that it was in some sense 'cribbed' or 'derived' from the earlier elliptical wing planforms of Ernst Heinkel and the Gunter Brothers, as seen in the Heinkel He 70. Neither claim, however often repeated and reprinted, is correct.

Yes, R.J. Mitchell was aware of the ellipse before B.S. Shenstone worked for him. Yes, Mitchell had previously experimented with basic ellipsoid wing planforms. But, as confirmed by many who were witness and who are referenced in the relevant literature, it was B.S. Shenstone who suggested not just the ellipse, but also the forensic modifications, the thin aerofoils and wing fillet for the Spitfire's wing. Thus claims about Shenstone's role in the Spitfire's design are not unsubstantiated; they are also proven across numerous comments, references and views, even of Mitchell's employees and his own son. The plain fact is that nobody else in the world except Shenstone had just trained in Germany with Junkers and Lippisch at the gateway of the swept-wing and delta-wing, and investigated the leap from elliptical lift patterns to modifications to lift behaviours and span loadings.

So the first British (or Allied) aircraft to benefit from early aviation's monoplane research and from early German sailplane, all-wing and delta-wing research was the Supermarine Spitfire of 1936 – *prior* to war. The Spitfire was British, but its significant technological advance lay in a wing created by a Canadian from British, German and other research. Long before Operation Paperclip, there were pieces of German science embodied in the Spitfire's wing – but to repeat the point because the falsehood has become so fashionable, not, repeat not, the elements so often mistakenly ascribed as Heinkel He 70 simple planform influence, where even 'experts' have repeated the falsehood. It has also become paradoxically fashionable, on the one hand, to state that any suggested German influence upon the Spitfire is wrong or even traitorous to the British reputation and that of R.J. Mitchell, and on the other hand, contrarily, to suggest that actually, the Spitfire's elliptical wing was 'copied' from the Heinkel He 70. This bizarre internally inconsistent situation is now acted out not just in print, but across the World Wide Web.

R. J. Mitchell conceived the concept and the context of the Spitfire, but his 'dream team' of experts created the actual item (as he always admitted, yet which others forget). They did this through an amalgamation and aggregation of experience across numerous works – notably the Supermarine S-Series Schneider Trophy float plane racers, the Supermarine flying boat designs and the abortive Type 224 gull-winged, pre-Spitfire prototype: from these were extrapolated knowledge that was then conjoined with advanced German wing research that had been not just studied, but contributed to by B.S. Shenstone.

Therefore, inside Supermarine was a young man with unique work experience in his CV, he was Beverley Shenstone; the Canadian, who in 1934 was in his mid-twenties and, despite his youth, he had qualified as Canada's first Masters Degree in Aeronautics, he was an RCAF trained pilot on Avro 504s and became the first Canadian to earn his 'C' badge at the Wasserkuppe gliding centre in Germany. Shenstone also spent three years studying in Germany with Junkers and Lippisch from 1929–1931, an event that was a deliberate act arranged by several men (notably Professor J. Parkin and Air Vice-Marshal E. Stedman RCAF) who had direct links to the Canadian and British Intelligence services.

Via various strings being pulled through RCAF and RAF liaison with the Air Ministry in London, young Shenstone was placed directly into the heart of the world's leading aerodynamics crucible in Germany. There he trained under Hugo Junkers and Alexander Lippisch. He also had access to (and met) Ludwig

Prandtl and his research work. Shenstone also got his hands dirty working on the production floor of the Junkers factory and learned to work with alloys and structural elements. He also helped not just calculate the mathematics for Lippisch's all-wing and delta-type early planform designs, he helped build and fly the test models. Shenstone had also been building boats and designing test hulls since he was boy. So here was a theoretician, yet one who had worked in metal fabrications, was a qualified power and sailplane pilot, a yachtsman and a man who had experience in Professor Parkin's advanced new wind tunnel at the University of Toronto and who had spent time enmeshed in the advanced German glider and all-wing design school centre – the Göttingen crucible that the aeronautics world flocked to circa 1930.

Shenstone had also been one of the first non-Germans to study wing fillets and their benefits. This happened when Junkers were trying to solve interference drag issues with their ribbed-skin airframes and took place before the likes of von Kármán published upon the subject. The German, H. Muttray, was also evident with his expanding research notes on the best way to refine the wing fillet theory. Such knowledge went into Shenstone's brain and re-emerged as the large and forensically tuned wing fillet that was added to the Spitfire's design – the Spitfire being the only 1930s fighter to boast a wing fillet – of relevance the Messerschmitt Bf 109 lacked one.

By 1932, Shenstone had authored several papers stemming from his German studies. Of relevance, one such paper was a discussion about methods of determining spanwise flow and the needs and effects to obtain desired lateral stability at high angles of incidences. This was timed just after he had returned to England in late May 1931 and had had his path to employment with R.J. Mitchell assisted by at least one luminary of British aeronautics in the form of Air Commodore Sir John Adrian Chamier. Chamier was a Vickers director, and a figure of the British Intelligence service. Soon employed by R.J. Mitchell at Supermarine in Woolston, Southampton, Shenstone was the man who, within four years, had shaped the Spitfire's ellipsoid wing, its wing fillet and many of its aerodynamic design features. The distinctive modified double ellipse planform of the Spitfire wing was calculated, designed and shaped by Shenstone (with mathematical assistance from the forgotten name of Professor R.C. Howland), its structure and shape was designed by the likes of Messrs Clifton Faddy, Fenner, Fear, Mansbridge, Shirvall, J. Smith and H. Smith – all the Supermarine design and draughting 'dream team' under R.J. Mitchell.

Key to the Spitfire's performance in level, turning, and stalling flight, was its unique wing shape and blending of ultra-thin aerofoil sections. Above all, the modified double-ellipse offered advanced lift characteristics and turning ability, yet at low wing loading and with remarkable performance from the ailerons near or at the stall. The whole aerofoil also worked in the transonic speed environment and at the slow-speed end of the scale – with no need for leading edge devices – nor a wing 'fence' to control spanwise flow. This had never been done before and was a major, yet often unrecognised, advance in aerodynamics.

Previous elliptical wings – as seen on the Heinkel 70 and Bäumer Sausewind – were symmetrical single ellipse planforms, being devoid of advanced modifications in planform let alone in twin-aerofoil section tuning, or aileron or wing root forensics. Contrary to often repeated inaccurate claims, the Spitfire's double ellipse wing had nothing to do with the Heinkel wing, indeed the Spitfire had differing planform, differing aerofoil(s), differing wing loading, differing structure, and a totally different aerodynamic drag and flow and resultant performances.

The proof that the original He 70A design (or the one-off 1936 Rolls-Royce engined He 70G) did *not* influence the Spitfire is unchallengeable. In the first place, the He 70 had its first flight on 1 December 1932, was in Lufthansa service by March 1933 and was seen at the Paris Air Show of 1933 – not 'first seen' at the Paris Air Show of 1934 as some commentators have claimed when trying to confabulate a 'last minute' 1934-dated He70 design, linkage, to the Spitfire being penned at that time (late-1934). The He 70 had visited Croydon airport several times, notably on 17 June 1934, long before the 1934 Paris Air Show where the He 70 made its second 'show' appearance. So the He 70, contrary to the claims of many – notably K. Agnew in 1993 in *The Journal of Design History*[3] – was not some kind of design 'revolution' that appeared in 1934 as the Spitfire was being designed. The He 70 had been around since 1932 and had little or no relevance to the late 1934–1935 design and build process of the Spitfire. The elliptical wing of the He 70 was very primitive indeed in comparison to the modified, mathematically unique form of the double, asymmetric ellipse of the Spitfire. It was the Spitfire's modified ellipse that inspired others, even Barnes Wallis, to pursue later elliptical planforms.

Of great significance to the conspiracy theory or 'copyist' claims about the He 70 and the Spitfire, the aerodynamically unique Rolls-Royce Kestrel-engined He 70 was built – from January 1936 – at Rostock, *after* the first Spitfire airframe-in-the-metal was completed in December 1935 at Eastleigh and, having made its first flight on 26 March 1936, entered Great Britain and was granted a CAA flight permit after 6 April 1936 – three weeks *after* the Spitfire's first flight on 5 March 1936. Therefore no aerodynamic, planform or structural knowledge transfer could have taken place between the Rolls-Royce He 70 and the Spitfire – as is so often falsely claimed. Of note, the Rolls-Royce He 70 of Kestrel/Merlin engine lineage was uniquely aerodynamically different in fuselage and engine cowling design from its German-engined predecessors, so much so that as a suggested Spitfire influence it is another falsehood.

Similarly, no last-minute late-1934 'cribbing' or 'copying' of the He 70 design by Supermarine took place after supposedly seeing the aircraft for the first time a few weeks earlier at the 1934 Paris Air Show, as so many have claimed. That is simply because the He70 did *not* appear for the first time at the 1934 Paris Air show and was thus neither a shock, nor any kind of design revolution or influence at the time; or in the manner some claim that it was.

Only in total airframe (wing and fuselage) smoothness criteria did the He 70 influence the Spitfire – as Shenstone always stated, and of note, the Heinkel only achieved this with many hundreds of kilos of hand-applied filler and paint, and by only having its skinning attached to longitudinal stringers in the body, not as was normal, also in the vertical stringers. This technique was 'a cheat' as it reduced the effects of skin 'panting' or aero-elastic movement which would have proved a disaster for the smooth, filled skin surface. Owing to the loss of strength by the skinning not being attached in the vertical axis, it required massive over-gauge strengthening in the chassis – as the Heinkel's monocoque was so denuded in skin strength.

So the whole 'Spitfire-copied the He 70' storyline is a myth. Yet the irony is that there was some level of German science to be found in part of Shenstone's ideas that he brought to Mitchell's Spitfire wing – Prandtl, Junkers, Muttray and Lippisch being the ancestors of such knowledge.

The principal point of the Spitfire wing design is that the forward, or front of the wing, is formed from a semi-ellipse having a small minor axis which was merged into a common major axis to blend into a rearward semi-ellipse of large minor axis. Add to this the front D-nosed spar, the Spitfire wing form advanced almost unheard of mathematically derived shaping work in the use of two ultra-thin blended aerofoils, and a tip-stall delaying forward sweep at the trailing edge that gave superb aileron performance. Issues of sink and source, skewness and kurtosis were investigated across the entire aerofoil blend. Adding the large wing fillet and underwing vorticity channels aided the Spitfire wing's incredible combat winning handling performance. Lift distribution, elliptical lift patterns, induced drag and curvilinear lift circulation, were all enhanced far beyond any attempt ever tried. The small tail fin and tailplane also played a major role, and the RAE experts were aghast at the small scale of these vital features. Experts also told Mitchell that the blended double aerofoil section wing was too thin, but they were wrong. The true work of design genius resulted in the Spitfire's amazing wing behaviours and turning circle.

Thus it was that the benefits of the ellipse as a modified ellipse (allied to other applied features), gave the Spitfire its better turn radius, lower drag coefficient, lower wing loading, better lift pattern, retained wing energy, and better stall behaviour than any other aircraft of the time, British, German or anything else.

As an example of this factor, consider that the high speed, low wing loading and low drag of the Supermarine Spitfire came not just from its asymmetric and conjoined elliptical planform, but also from its unique use of two, ultra-thin aerofoil sections and the manner in which they were joined together along the wing and to the fuselage. In comparison, the single aerofoil section of the thick-winged Hawker Hurricane explained its much slower speed, lower wing energy and turning performance, and a loss of 50mph in speed comparison.

Intriguingly, the highly efficient, small, sharp wing of the competing Messerschmitt Bf 109 had a very good coefficient of lift, but to achieve this it relied upon leading edge devices that incurred weight, stability and drag penalties. The Messerschmitt wing had higher induced drag and higher tip drag than the Spitfire – and therefore effectively 'lost' a degree of aspect ratio. It also had a much higher wing loading than its main competitor and a far higher coefficient of profile and induced drags. The Messerschmitt had no wing to fuselage fillet, which according to research[4] cost it a lot in terms of drag and speed. Both the Hurricane and the Me Bf 109 had higher stall speeds and suffered wing drop and spin earlier than the Spitfire, due to the latter's better trailing edge and aileron design. The Me Bf 109 required leading edge devices and ultimately a wing fence.

Comparison of Coefficients of Drag[5]

Spitfire P/1: C_D 0.0197 C_{Do} 0.0187 C_{Di} 0.0010 Wing loading 22lb/sqft
Hawker P/1: C_D 0.0237 C_{Do} 0.00225 C_{Di} 0.0012 Wing loading 24lb/sqft
Messerschmitt Bf109/B*: C_D 0.0265 C_{Do} 0.0258 C_{Di} 0.0019 Wing loading 32lb/sqft

Note* Figures are quoted for early variant prototype airframes. Due to the Me Bf 109 having had an engine-type change from prototype stage to production airframe, with resultant increases in cross sectional area and drag, any comparison of the Me 109 prototype to the two British airframes at prototype stage must be avoided in order to reduce unfair comparisons. The British pair in production retained their original prototype engines and forms, whereas the German type did not.

Note: The early Spitfire prototype was C_D 0.01702. It would be nearly a decade before any other airframe used later knowledge to approach this figure in the form of the P-51 Mustang C_D 0.0.1698. Some Me Bf 109 variants have been cited with C_D 0.030 and above.

How?

But how did a young man like Shenstone, know how to create this advance? Where and how did he learn to create this national icon – the Spitfire – whose aerodynamic advantages won the Battle of Britain and altered the fate of the world and history itself? The answer lies in the all-wing and the delta-wing designs of the German glider design revolution – techniques that Shenstone had trained in when he was in Germany immediately prior to his being recruited via senior figures in national security to work for the Supermarine company – itself part of the defining Vickers company.

Beverley Shenstone had studied at Junkers, questioned Prandtl and Betz, listened to von Kármán, worked with Lippisch and immersed himself in the advanced wing design world of Germany's freethinkers of aerodynamics. Then he visited NACA and its new aerofoil research. Shenstone had helped Junkers solve the problem of its corrugated wing and fuselage skin surfaces causing interference drag, he had studied wing fillet design, above all he had worked with Lippisch on his groundbreaking swept-wing, all-wing and delta-wing design work (Lippisch credited Shenstone's contribution in his autobiography). Shenstone built models with the Lippisch team, experimented with smoke tests on wings and had been part of a forensic study into the differing lift patterns of the delta-shaped wing planform. Add in their close study on trailing edge design, leading edge smoothness and camber and spanwise flow, and the young Shenstone (still in his twenties) was probably one of the most advanced and experienced aerodynamic young thinkers of 1930–1935. Unlike other cited 'stars' of aerodynamics, Shenstone could also fly gliders and powered aircraft and design and helm yachts, and he had worked on building airframes.

After a summertime visit to the Wasserkuppe in 1930, Shenstone briefly went back to Junkers, and then returned to Lippisch to spend hours with him during the winter of the Wasserkuppe. There, the Lippisch team of Groenhoff, Hubert, Jacobs, Kramer, Voepel, Wagner and Wegemeyer, gathered in the wooden buildings and, heated by stoves, these young men threw themselves into creating, calculating, and testing the first values for swept-wing and delta-wing design. Yet it was only by studying smoke trails of wing vortices that physical proof of calculus could be confirmed or be denied. One large model they built was so big at a 12ft span that it had to be removed from the building via an upper floor window. It was here that the unusual (rearwards pitching displacement) stalling behaviour of the delta planform was discovered and the importance of trailing edge design and control surface shape and location researched for the first time. The very successful flights of Lippisch's first full-size machines, and a demonstration at Berlin, soon confirmed that he had cracked the secret of swept-wing and delta-wing planforms. This issue of the tail or tailless configuration was one which Lippisch would ponder for several years to come. In 1930, he had just seen his paper *'Recent Tests of Tailless Aircraft'* published in the journal *L' Aerophile.*

Through such unique learning, Shenstone, upon arrival in Britain, was also uniquely equipped to contribute to the world's most advanced monoplane fighter that was the Spitfire. Adding Shenstone's expertise to Mitchell's high-speed flight, Schneider Trophy-gained knowledge and the freethinking of the Supermarine team (backed by Vickers and major figures of political power) could only lead to an advanced outcome. Any reader in doubt of such claim simply needs to compare the Rolls-Royce Merlin powered Spitfire with its identically powered, Hawker Hurricane rival, and ask why two machines designed to meet the same specification and perform an identical role, were so different in terms of aerodynamics, structure, and resultant performance?

Shenstone's appearance at Vickers-Supermarine was no accident, or act of fate, it was arranged via those to whom Shenstone had been sending back notes on his discoveries in Germany, after they had placed him into the heart of advanced German design in 1929. Buried deep inside Shenstone's personal archives, and only recently found, are documents confirming such facts. One letter to him in 1938 from a very senior leading luminary of British aircraft design clearly states: 'If the Germans had known what you were up to, you would have been shot.'[6] Even after the war, correspondence to Shenstone from the top names in British aviation refer to his activities in Germany and his intelligence gathering, not just in terms of design, but also in his attempts to warn the British Government of the danger that was building. As expanded in the book, *Secrets of the Spitfire*,[7] and a the subsequent RAeS Journal paper by Dr J.D. Ackroyd[8], there is now no doubt that the Spitfire wing design, however much an R.J. Mitchell, Schneider series experience derived device, benefited from some degree of German science that was transferred via Shenstone and his unique studies in Germany 1929–1931.

So the Supermarine Spitfire was the *first* British aircraft to use aspects of advanced German science in its design.

As for the likes of the DH 108, Avro 'Vulcan', Handley Page HP 80 'Victor', the Aerospatiale/BAC 'Concorde' and a host of others, including the Hawker P.1067 'Hunter' (whose shape is very similar to that of the Me P.1101/2 series), these were the next re-engineered, re-branded iterations of advanced German science that shaped the history of modern aviation. Before that happened a war had to be won, and the Spitfire helped make that happen and it did so using an amalgamation of British and German knowledge – just like a host of airframes post-1945 – Concorde included.

April 1945: The Treasures Are Yielded Up

If the Spitfire's heritage was less 'pure' than the English portrayed, this was as nothing compared to post-war aircraft of British and American branding. From early 1945, the world of aircraft design changed. In the Lippisch-derived delta-wing designs of the 1950s and 1960s, we can see the true roots of modern aerodynamic design.

The American General Dynamics Corporation's, Convair B-58 Hustler can be cited as the 1950s most elegant iteration of 'pure' delta-wing and is of note for its pylon-slung engine mountings, which defied the usual buried, or grouped, engine layout usually assigned to the delta planform. The pylon-mounted, 'podded' and 'buried' engines that defined American and British airframes from 1947 to date were conceived and tested in the early 1940s by Focke-Wulf, Arado and Heinkel designers, notably, Hans Multhopp, Rudinger Kosin and Wilhelm Benz respectively. Neither should we forget that the world's first patent for an all-wing aircraft came from Junkers, as did the design for the world's first four-engined, jet-powered, swept-wing bomber in the form of the Ju 287.

From Arado 234 to Handley Page Victor and Beyond

On 27 February 1945, a key war-prize, in the form of the Arado 234 four-jet aircraft that was in service with the Luftwaffe, was forced down by Allied fighters in the last days of German resistance to Allied victory. The Arado was captured just beyond Allied lines near Segelsdorf, but within twenty-four hours had been seized by the Americans.[9] The German army had fought hard to stop the aircraft being captured, but failed. Immediately, US Army technicians carefully took the Arado 234 apart in the field and loaded it on to trucks.[10] The convoy was escorted under guard across a Germany that was still fighting, and went through France and to the Normandy port of Cherbourg. Hours later, the Arado was being inspected in British expert hands. In that moment was set yet another defining moment in post-war western aircraft design and in the forthcoming Cold War.

Designed to be a twin-jet and four-jet fighter-bomber with wide adaptability in its airframe, the Arado 234 was an advanced, working, large jet aircraft – larger than anything the British or Americans had created – it made the Gloster Meteor look like a pterodactyl. Contained within the Arado 234 series and its Blume and Kosin design, there lay real success in advancing the art of the jet-powered airframe beyond the prototype stage. Although its wing was not heavily swept back, it was, in fact, highly advanced and a gateway to the crescent wing planform's successful realisation. The 234's planform and layout offered the key to a jet fighter-bomber configuration, and to high altitude reconnaissance aircraft design, by blending speed, lift, payload, drag and armament parameters into a defining form that would be copied for decades.

Eight weeks after the seizing of the Arado 234 by the Americans, the British had stormed the Arado factory in Warnemünde, near Berlin, and seized many design drawings, wind tunnel data (notably crescent wing data), and prototype parts – all of which were quickly consigned to Britain and its RAE at Farnborough, then to be naively handed on to the Americans. Less than eight weeks later, the Russians seized the sector of Berlin that the Arado works had lain within, but they got little metal from the Arado works for, on this occasion, the Americans and the British had got there first.

Within seven years of this defining moment of seizure of science, a range of British and American jet-powered airframes began to be announced. Ultimately, the HP 80 Victor, with its Blume and Kosin-derived form and crescent wing, also using a Multhopp T-tail, and wing root-buried engines, would manifest as a Cold War nuclear bomber warrior. Beside the Victor, a range of large, twin and four-engined jet airframes, that closely aped the Arado 234, would appear in the colours of industry and of the USAF and RAF. These would include the English Electric Canberra, the Curtiss XP-87, the Martin XB-48, the Consolidated Vultee XB-4 and the Ilyushin IL-16. The Arado 234 design was also aped by the Canadian Avro four-engined jet airliner. Arado was also working on a series of all-wing delta designs of Siegfried Gunter design. Encapsulated within this episode of Arado design, we can see the true facts of seized science and denied provenance.

Cold War Warriors: V-Force

Boeing may have used German swept-wing research to turn out the B-52 and the consequent 707 and its derivatives, but it was the nuclear bomb-carrying British V-Force that defined German knowledge transfer. The aforementioned HP Victor handled like a fighter, flew fast due to its sleek form, and had range due its crescent wing and semi all-wing effect. With its Multhopp T-tail and advanced wing concealing buried engines, the Victor was the encapsulation of German advanced aerodynamics applied by British design. British commentators admitted that the works of Kosin, Lippisch and Horten had proved of assistance – a classic piece of British understatement!

The Avro Vulcan took that a step further. The British said the Vulcan was designed by Chadwick (it was), but the furthest they went to crediting Lippisch for the aircraft's form was to state forms of words that said Avro had been 'inspired' by German wartime research and that such research was 'advantageous'. The reality was, of course, that the Vulcan was a Lippisch wing that was refined into a British bomber, with its all-wing planform delta-wing giving a low wing loading, low drag and a huge capacity for fuel and armament. Above all, came the benefit of amazing handling, the Vulcan wiped the floor with every other bomber and made the B-52's flight behaviours look weak. The 'flying-wing' Vulcan was just that, and it could climb vertically, turn tightly with an energised wing, and even perform incredible rolls and wing-overs. The Vulcan could lose 20,000ft in 90 seconds, recover in 1,500ft using its wing energy, and then climb away almost straight upwards.

The Vulcan was, and remains, an incredible machine and as we acknowledge Avro's and Chadwick's engineering skills, we also have to note that the Vulcan was the leading embodiment of German aerodynamics (non-rocket) research acquired in 1945. The Vulcan was Lippisch's greatest legacy.

The delta-wing was soon realised as perhaps the ideal solution to issues of structural strength, handling, and speed – and the Avro 707 and Fairey F.D. 1/2 proved the point before the Avro 698 'Vulcan' made its mark. American delta thinking soon saw podded engines on pylons dangling from their clean, thin delta designs – which solved some structural and engine issues, but created 'dirty' pylon and 'pod' related airflow near the previously clean delta.

The tamer airframe in the V-Bomber fleet was the excellent Vickers Valiant. This too, featured German high-speed wing and engine location research outcomes, notably of Arado, Messerschmitt, and Heinkel design motifs. A Vickers design, with British engines just like the Avro and Handley Page machines, yet steeped in the lore of German wind tunnel studies into high-speed flow in the same adjunct manner that, in recent MiG and Sukhoi airframes, we can surely see the legacy of Heinkel and Gunter 1940s design work on delta-wing and all-wing design.

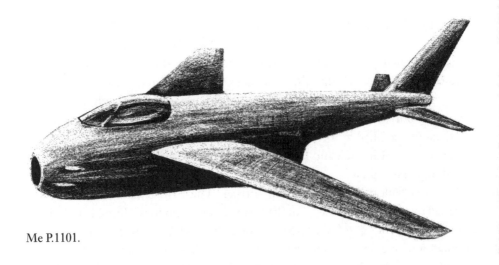

Me P.1101.

Voigt and a Swing-Wing

Who invented variable wing-sweep? Barnes Wallis? Maybe not, for Voigt's Messerschmitt Me. P.1101 prototype must be the basis, not just of a swept and variable wing idea, but also of a sharply swept, ducted engine, single-seat fighter design. The fact the American 'copy' that was the Bell X-5 seemed identical was of no accident, for the Me P.1101 was also seized and shipped back to America. Intriguingly, much of Voigt's Messerschmitt P.1101 research fell into French hands, who, unlike the British, had no need, nor compunction, to hand it to the Americans, and refused to do so. The Me P.1101 was not without problems, it was far too heavy for a glider designer like Willi Messerschmitt to countenance and the 40° wing sweep, with proposed variable or 'swing-wing' mechanism, defied solution in the ill-funded dog days of a war about to end. Yet, with its internally-mounted wing geometry gearing design, the P.1101 would signal the successful 1960s use of such. So, the P.1101 would be no last-ditch wonder weapon, and was not suited to rough-and-ready construction and short airframe life. Yet within the Me P.1101 lay many future design trends; the P.1101 still looks like a 1980s airframe.

Strangely, yet somewhat unsurprisingly, the Bell Aircraft Corporation's chief designer, Robert Woods, just happened to find himself standing in a barn in Oberammergau, in early 1946, staring at the Me P.1101. It was, of course, an expensive and difficult journey from the USA to the hills of southern Germany, but someone had to do it.[11] The consequent Bell X-5 was, even to the most pro-American observer, an alleged blatant copy. Other 1950s American swept-wing fighters look like crosses between the Me P.1101 and the Multhopp Ta 183. In doing so they would take on the MiG-15s that were also blatant copies of German design.

Although ultimately unsuccessful in terms of being directly copied, the effect of the Me P.1101 would also lead to its designer, W. Voigt, finding himself at Wright Field, Dayton, Ohio, in 1946 – thence to a career in the US aerospace industry. And the P.1101 was not to be Messerschmitt's final fling in design terms either, because the ultimate route that Messerschmitt advanced design was to take, followed the all-wing path. From the P.1101 came the P.1102 as a tailless all-wing idea (with vertical fin) and a series of jet-powered all-wing airframe proposals designed to meet the Reich's last final struggles for a weapon to strike fear into American hearts.

Messerschmitt had not been an avid follower of the all-wing and his thoughts on tailless design included a vertical fin or 'tail', but not a drag inducing horizontal stabiliser tail unit. Yet, as a glider designer prior to his powered-designs, Messerschmitt had kept a close eye on the Hortens and Lippisch. Ultimately, the

P.1111/12 design proposals of early 1945 were advanced all-wing ideas and again, looks like an early iteration of a later British idea, the DH 108, and the American Northrop X-4. Of significance, here too, in the P.1112, we saw the annular, wing root/leading edge/engine air intake concept for the first time – later seen in the de Havilland Comet, Vickers V.1000 and Valiant, and in production in the Handley Page Victor – as well as a host of American machines.

Of the world's first swept-winged jet fighter Me 262 (and the even more aerodynamic Me 262 HG), we can say that this airframe taught others more about wings and high-speed flight than can be easily grasped. The Me 262s stepping stone was a monumental moment of learning for the Allies that seized it and its technology. Overnight, straight-winged jets from de Havilland, Gloster, Lockheed and others, were utterly redundant, thrown upon the dustbin of design. The Vampire might not have been rendered useless, but we can say it was of restricted ability no matter how much it was loved. De Havilland soon designed the DH 101 and the key DH 108 and then the DH 110 Vixen. Glosters, Lockheed, North American et al, all went swept-winged 'overnight'. For the British, the Hawker P.1067 Hunter became their swept-winged dream machine, despite its 'borrowed' technology.

Crescent-Shaped Planforms – The Often Forgotten Advance[12]

The idea of a swept-back, crescent-shaped wing was seen in the works of early pioneers, not least Weiss and Handley Page, but a reverse crescent- shaped planform wing – one where the sweep reduced towards the wingtips – was shaped in Germany and applied by the Arado company and its chief designer, Walter Blume, deputy Hans Rebeski, and the aerodynamicist Rudiger Kosin. Kosin had studied forward-sweep and varying back-sweep. Arado proposed a crescent-winged two, and then four-engined bomber with a sweepback angle of 37° on the inboard wing and two cranks to 29° and 25° towards the outboard wing section.

The benefits of the compromise of a crescent wing was the reduction in wing sweep near the wingtips and that it moved the load on the wingtips forwards of the axis of the wing and improved airflow near the tips, rather than degrading it. This also reduced unfavourable behaviour near the stall and at high Mach numbers, yet retained the advantages of sweep more generally. Tip-stalling and spinning risks at low speed were thus reduced and a better-handling machine created. The wing might have to be a bit stronger and the wingtips thinner to ensure good airflow, but the crescent wing would be lighter in construction than a delta-wing and did provide another solution to how long, thin, highly swept-wings could be made to work and to do so safely across the speed graph – not just at high velocity and high altitude cruise. Of interest, the 'kinks' in the varying sweep of the crescent wing do not seem to produce significant localised airflow disturbances.

There is little surprise to be found in the claims by the British Handley Page company who built the superb Victor bomber with its crescent wing, that it says it started investigating the crescent wing in 1946. Yet it omits to mention that just a few months earlier, in April 1945, the British had scooped up many drawings and research data on crescent wing design from the Arado company and its aerodynamicist Kosin, in Berlin – when the Arado factory was seized by British troops and accompanying experts. By 1946, Handley Page were looking at that data, and by 1951 were proposing a crescent-winged bomber – which became the 'Victor' – also using a T-tail and wing-root buried engines.

What of straighter, less swept, or even unswept-wings, surely they could not offer the aerodynamic advantages of the swept-wing? Science soon revealed that after the benefits of a swept-wing at supersonic speed, an (almost) unswept, short, low aspect ratio wing planform could, with very thin aerofoil (as thin as 3 or 4 per cent thickness/chord ratio), also offer lower supersonic drag. Such 'stub' wings stemmed in part from the short stub wing learning as applied to von Braun's rockets. At Mach 1.5, the lowest drag came from a highly swept-wing, but the next lowest drag, could, said the experts, come from a small, unswept-wing that, instead of delaying compressibility, just 'fought' through it into the supersonic airflow advantage.

It was at approach and landing speeds that such highly swept and, also unswept but thin aerofoil section wings, became problematic – unless dangerously high, thrust and fuel-hungry landing speeds were to be used. All sorts of lift generating – yet ultimately drag and weight inducing – flaps and slats might be used. But surely the advantages of a moderately swept all-wing could solve all these conflicting themes?

In terms of the powerplant revolution, the likes of *Flight*, and Mr Keith-Lucas,[13] also postulated on two themes of great note, given the date of 1952. The first was Keith-Lucas' suggestion that swivelling engine thrust/exhaust might be used to assist landing and the second was what type of airframe might be able to house an atomic reactor powerplant? An atomic-powered aircraft would require a large deep receptacle to house the reactor – was the answer the deep-hulled flying boat with all its internal room for a massive atomic engine? Or was the more likely receptacle for an atomic powerplant the deep wing box of a massive all-wing machine?

Multhopp Ta 183, T-Tail Revolution and Lightning Legacy

The work of Ta 183 designer Hans Multhopp also directly touched British aviation, because in June 1945 he was detained in London and then at RAE

Farnborough (along with Martin Winter) and there, made to set down on paper his advanced aerodynamic thoughts. Multhopp had escaped the Russian overrunning of the Focke-Wulf works and brought his ideas to Farnborough. He was then set amongst a group of ex-Göttingen scientists and returned to Germany for a brief period. By early 1946, Multhopp had been singled out and was one of very few ex-German designers sought by the British – hence his time at the RAE Farnborough in 1946–1947. Multhopp and Winter worked well together and drew up a design for a supersonic aircraft – one that did not have the barrel fuselage and unswept-wing of the Bell X-1, which, at this time, would blast its way through the sound barrier using brute force and ignorance.

The Multhopp/Winter idea featured highly swept (up to 60°) wings of thin section and turbojet power. With a prone pilot configuration, thin fuselage and minimal undercarriage, the machines were estimated to be able to achieve over 800mph/1,285km/h.[14] The design had the Multhopp T-tail too – this had emerged as Multhopp shaped the stunning Ta 183 swept-wing fighter at the Focke-Wulf design offices. The Ta 183 was arguably the most advanced and most influential non all-wing design to come out of Germany and the Second World War.

The Multhopp/Winter supersonic design for the RAE – of summer 1945 origin – could have secured a glittering supersonic future, but it did not. The only rational explanation is that the British were embarrassed and ashamed that the two men could turn out something so spectacular. Cash-strapped Britain was also unable, and unwilling, to further the design. Amazingly, Multhopp and Winter were, as 'aliens', then denied access to their own (by now 'secret') design drawings at the RAE and put under a form of house arrest before being 'dropped' by the British. During this time, Multhopp's design works came to the attention of British aircraft experts and it comes as no shock that the prototype design for the English Electric P.1 'Lightning' bears very close similarity to the Multhopp/Winter RAE design for a supersonic swept-wing interceptor. The fact that the much vaunted Lightning fighter, which posed as the sharp edge of British design, was in fact a

Fw TA 183.

German-derived device, should by now come as no surprise. Multhopp and Winter were, by late 1949, poised to join the American Martin Aircraft Company, which went from building the massive 'Mars' flying boats to swept-winged fighters like Multhopp's Martin XB-51 and then to missile systems, very quickly indeed.

Another Multhopp design signature was his decision to suggest two rear-mounted podded engines on pylons in the swept-wing Focke-Wulf Ta 283 design – a machine powered by a ramjet athodyd gas turbine technology.

Of de Havilland Speed

Surely the DH 110 Vixen looks, for all the world, a near copy of the Focke-Wulf F.6 'Flitzer', and provides the reader with further evidence of just how significant the German research, and its seizure, was to Great Britain. Having had a man inside the ruins of Messerschmitt's Bavarian advanced design office at the time of the Fedden Mission, de Havilland soon transferred all its 'findings' into building a reputation for very fast, swept-wing excellence.

Those sceptical about the influence of the swept-wing and all-wing after the Second World War should not forget that de Havilland's advance into its famous high-speed handling wings came directly from the company having access to German wing technology and the immediate manifestation of the DH 108. The fact that the original DH Comet airliner designs were as straight-winged as the DH Vampire and then suddenly turned into a swept back, all-wing proposal of obvious Horten and Lippisch lineage cannot be denied. Curiously, the Comet 1 prototype's leading edge slats were removed and subsequent events may have indicated the unwise nature of such a decision.

That the Trident used a T-tail that was too stubby and too small to avoid deep-stall issues and rear-mounted podded engines, allied to a swept-wing, can only be of relevance to research used. Much of this was observed by Boeing and transferred into the excellent 727 with its much better wing aerofoil and consequent runway performance – allied to a taller, larger T-tail and tailplane that made it less likely to suffer a deep-stall.

For America, we can only stare at the Bell X-5 and notice its direct resemblance to Voigt's Messerschmitt Me P.1101 design that was 'lifted' by American forces from Oberammergau in 1946. Of the all-wing Northrop X-4 – well, it is identical to the Me. P.1111. Of the effect of the Me 262 and its more advanced variant the Me 262 HG-3, we can see its effects in varying degrees in the features of so many aircraft. And how close was the McDonnell Douglas F-4 Phantom to the Heinkel P.1080?

Was the first 'big twin' airframe and aerodynamic concept a Boeing, Airbus or Hawker Siddeley airliner? Of course not, for it was the Junkers Type 140/150 twin-engined jet designed by Professor B. Baade and realised as a full-sized airframe by him and ex-German designers in the Soviet Union by 1948. This swept-winged, wide-bodied military airframe, with its wing/pylon-mounted engines, was the first 'big-twin' and the first design to successfully introduce the concept. It went on to influence Soviet and Western airliner design.

Saunders Roe and a Supreme Irony

After de Havilland had strapped an Me 163-inspired swept-wing on to a Vampire, a British portal to high speed fighter design was opened, albeit using seized German research. It soon became clear that a new type of high-speed, high-altitude fighter airframe would be needed to counter the threat of Soviet incursion in the upper flight levels. By 1950, as the Cold War festered, European nations needed a quick response airframe. Ultimately, this would be in the forms of the English Electric P.1 Lightning and the ill-fated Lockheed F-104 Starfighter. Before those two airframes were delivered, a stillborn British fighter would briefly shine upon the world's design stage, only to be consigned to history by the idiotic decisions of politicians and the machinations of the American war machine.

Enter the Saunders-Roe SR.53. This was a bi-fuelled, jet/rocket-powered British iteration of the Me 163, and an offshoot of the DH 108 research. Designed under the lead of Maurice Brennan at Saunders-Roe in Southampton, the SR.53 looked like a reinvented Me 163, with the addition of a Multhopp T-tail atop its stubby empennage (this was the first British swept-wing and T-tailed airframe). Short swept wings and a climb rate of 43,000 ft/min under catalyst effect rocket power, gave this bi-fuelled machine supreme abilities. It was developed into the rocket and jet-powered SR.177 as a production proposal for British and European air forces, using a Gyron jet engine and a Spectre liquid oxygen rocket motor for rapid climb to combat intercept altitude. The handling was superb, the performance brilliant, but the British needed foreign investment to build the SR.177 and they were bankrupt. American money was intended to support the SR.177 as a new pan-European defence fighter, but that money never came, firstly, because of the British-created Suez Crisis and then because Lockheed foisted its F-104 Starfighter upon European air forces despite its design, payload, and performance weaknesses.

The SR.177, which had RAF and RN support, was killed off, despite the fact that the new Luftwaffe had been very interested in this new British iteration of a German Second World War design concept. So died SR.53 and SR.177 as potentially world-beating, export currency earning airframes, that could have been Cold War warriors in a strange reversal of fate to defend German and European borders against the Soviets using a British design born from Nazi research. And of the eventual Lockheed Starfighter and its German variant – the F104G? That such an American-designed device killed hundreds of pilots in non-combat flight upon the ethos and incompetence of its stubby, high wing loading design, was an irony that must have hurt. The SR.177 would have been a better bet, but it died at the hands of politics and Lockheed's alleged 'sales' practice that tainted the hands of many on both sides of the Atlantic.

The All-Wing Men

Leading the field of seized treasures of German technology came the all-wing, delta and swept/discoid low aspect ratio wing designers, who stepped into new areas of research that lay outside the constraints of perceived wisdom. From them came some of the most remarkable aircraft designs ever seen, and yet in their conceits, the victorious Allies would embrace some designers and their designs, yet apparently dismiss others. The passage of time has revealed that that dismissal may not have been as clear-cut as we were led to believe.

Of spanwise flow, lift distribution and coefficients, drag, control surfaces, leading edge flow, yaw control stability authority, wake turbulence control and engine configuration, all was contained within the German all-wing and delta studies. Seven decades on, those works underpin 'modern' all-wing and blended-wing aerodynamics.

The names of the leading all-wing research and design enthusiasts and developers in Germany were:

(Pre-Second World War)
Hugo Junkers
August Kupper
Alexander Lippisch

(Pre-Second World War and Onwards)
Reimar and Walter Horten

(Second World War)
Heinrich Hertel Siegfried Gunter
Ernst Zindel

From their works, and more specifically from the works of Lippisch and the Hortens, the all-wing came of age over fifty years after the early pioneers explored its advantages and Lilienthal had set minds thinking.

As detailed earlier in this book, the Horten all-wing work and the Lippisch delta-wing work were the core of the papers, plans, models, prototypes and full-size airframes that were seized and carted away by the Allies. Add in the related works of Messerschmitt, Heinkel, Gothaer and others, and the vast treasure trove of aerodynamics seems utterly incredible. Yet, while the world knows about von Braun and the American moon landing outcomes, fewer people know just what technology, or great importance, was framed by German aviation up to early 1945.

Of significance, the Horten Ho series of swept-wing, jet-powered all-wing airframes, notably the Ho 8; Ho 9; Ho 229, Ho 13 and Ho 18, demonstrated aerodynamic and structural details that have, without any doubt, informed later all-wing American practice, notably in the forms of the Lockheed F-117 'Stealth' fighter and the Northrop Grumman B-2 all-wing bomber. Reimar Horten's advanced airflow calculus and features to create a stable all-wing were, and remain, groundbreaking reference points. Recent all-wing outcomes include drones and civil airliner proposals as 'blended wings'. Without denying Northrop his due credit, the American all-wing airframe renaissance can only refer to the Horten research. One look at the wing sweep angles, aerofoils, the planform designs, the sculpted central body details and the design and location of control surfaces and trailing edge devices reveals that the effect of Reimar and Walter Horten was, despite the CIOS Wilkinson Report, far more pervasive than previously admitted.

Of Lippisch's influence, a wider audience exists, but with his advanced aerodynamics discoveries of not just swept-wing, but delta-wing behaviours and of methods to step into the supersonic flow environment, we can recognise truly world-class work and effect. Not content with a 'straight' leading edge to his deltas, such as the defining Lp DM.1 and DM.2, Lippisch also worked on the curved leading edge and drooped type tip area that were added to the Vulcan and to Concorde by their own respective aerodynamicists as refinements to the delta concept. Of the Fairey Delta 1 and 2, of the Avro 707, of the DH 108, even of the early Comet airliner proposals, the influence of Lippisch are as clear as they are in the shapes of similar American 'X'-type prototypes and later series production airframes.

Siegfried Gunter's time in the Soviet Union resulted in a range of swept-wing, and all-wing delta-type airframes with twin tail fins that echoed Heinkel and Gothaer iterations of Lippisch and Horten thoughts – just as with the American Grumman F-14 fighter – can the almost all-wing MiG-29 be anything other than German influenced? French access to seized Junkers, Heinkel and other research documents (if not actual airframes) can only be cited in terms of post-war French designs such as those of Fouga and Dassault.

From the Hortens, from Lippisch, and from the unique high-speed wind tunnels of the DFS and other German establishments, came the major advance in aerodynamics knowledge which was stolen and then in no small degree, shamelessly repackaged as the product of brilliant minds in America, Britain, France and Russia during the Cold War and the 'golden' years of Western aerospace technology. As proven by the thousands of tonnes of seized material, as framed by the CIOS Reports, the sheer weight of German knowledge carted off from April 1945 onwards, frames modern aviation knowledge.

A Vast War Prize

The key aerodynamic, airframe and engineering features designed in Germany and manifesting in post-Second World War Allied aircraft design and production – as collected under Operation Paperclip et al make an astounding list:

- High-speed airflow and supersonics
- Swept-wings (rear and forwards sweep)
- Delta shaped wings
- Crescent wings
- Variable sweep wings
- Pivoting (oblique)wings
- Cranked wings
- Thin aerofoils
- Airbrakes
- Leading edge devices
- T-tail
- V tailplanes
- 'Lifting-body' design effects and features
- Pylon-mounted engines
- Wing pylons, fuselage stub wings and pylons, rear-mounted configurations
- Ducted engines
- Wing-root mounted engines
- Advanced control surfaces and elevons
- All-wing design developments
- Disc aerofoil developments
- Advanced undercarriage design
- Advanced glazing
- De-icing technology
- Metallurgical/alloy construction and methods for airframes
- Research into high altitude flight effects upon human body
- Jet and rocket engine design and development, notably fan blades and nozzles
- Vertical take-off and landing (VTOL)

- Helicopters
- Contra-rotating props
- Rockets and missiles
- Composites
- Anti-radar airframe materials technology

Careful analysis of the shapes, airframe details and aerodynamic features of a vast range of post-war Allied aircraft reveals massive similarities between many of them and the remarkable stable of German airframes and knowledge that the Allies had grabbed.

The Post-War Aircraft Influenced by German Aircraft Design:

Derivative, non-German Airframes	Cited Influencing German Designs
Aerospatiale/BAC Concorde	Lippisch delta-wing design
Avro 707	Lippisch delta-wing design
Avro 698 Vulcan	Lippisch delta-wing design
Bell X-5	Me P.1101
Boeing B-29	Arado 234 series designs
Boeing B-47/B-52	Swept-wing and pylon engine research
Boeing 707	Swept-wing and pylon-engine research
Boeing 727	Multhopp T-tail and pylon engine designs
Boeing 737	Me 262 wing/flap/engine
Boeing Supersonic Delta	Lippisch delta-wing design
Boeing blended-wing designs	Horten all-wing design
Chance Vought A4/Corsair/F-8 Crusader	Me. 'Zerstorer' PII
Consolidated/Convair XF-92	Lippisch Lp. DM-1/DM-2
Curtiss XP-55	Henschel HS.P75
Curtiss XP-87	Arado 234
Convair B-46	Lippisch delta-wing design
Convair B-58 'Hustler'	Lippisch delta-wing design
Convair XB-53	German forward sweep research by Vogt; Blohm and Voss P.209/Junkers Ju 287 V3
Convair XFY-1 VTOL	Focke-Wulf 'Triebflugel' and Heinkel L2.
Dassault Mirage	Horten IAe 34 and IAe 48
Dassault Mystere IV-A	Focke-Wulf Ta 183 design
de Havilland DH 101	Lippisch P series and Messerschmitt
de Havilland DH 108	Lippisch P series and Voigt P.1111
de Havilland Vampire	Focke-Wulf F.5
de Havilland DH 110 Vixen	Focke-Wulf F.6 'Flitzer'
de Havilland Comet	Horten all-wing influence on prototype
de Havilland DH 121/HS Trident	Messerschmitt swept-wing research and Multhopp T-tail

Derivative, non-German Airframes	Cited Influencing German Designs
Douglas Skyrocket	DFS 346 and Messerschmitt designs
English Electric P.1. 'Lightning'	Multhopp and Winter design for RAE 1945
Fairey Delta 1	Lippisch Lp.12/13
Fairey Delta 2	Lippisch Lp.12/13
Fouga C.170 R 'Magister'	Heinkel P.1079A
Fouga Gemeaux	Blohm and Voss designs
Gloster G.A. Javelin	He P.1080
Handley Page P.8 'Victor'	Arado 234 V16 and Ju287; DFS 346
Ilyushin II-16, II-26, II-28	Arado 234 series and Me 264 V-jet
Lockheed F-104 'Starfighter'	DFS 346
Lockheed F-117	Horten all-wing design; Ho 9; Ho 13A
Lockheed XFV-1 VTOL	Focke-Wulf' 'Triebflugel'
Lockheed C-141 Starlifter and C-5 Galaxy	Multhopp T-tail and Junkers research
Martin Matador	DFS 346
Martin X-24B	Multhopp lifting body research
Martin XB-48	Arado 234
Martin XB-51	Multhopp design and Arado 234 series
McDonnell Douglas F-4 Phantom	Heinkel P.1080
McDonnell Douglas F-101 Voodoo	Me 262 HG-3
MiG-15/17	Focke-Wulf Ta 183 Multhopp design
MiG-21	Heinkel/Gunter/Lippisch design
MiG-29	S. Gunter Heinkel, Horten, Lippisch works
NASA AD-1 pivoting sweep	Vogt design oblique wing and forward sweep. Blohm and Voss PV209
North American F-86 Sabre/F-100 Super Sabre	Focke-Wulf Ta 183 and He P.1078A
North American XB-70 Valkyrie	Lippisch delta design
Northrop Grumman B-2	Horten all-wing design; Ho 9, Ho 229, Ho 18 A/B
Northrop Grumman F-14 S	Heinkel/Gunter/Horten/Lippisch works
Northrop X-4	Messerschmitt Me. P1111/P.1112
Republic P-86 Thunderjet	Focke-Wulf Ta 183 and He P.1078A
Ryan X-13 VertiJet	Lippisch DM.1/DM.2; P.12/13
Saab J-29	Focke-Wulf Ta 183 and Me P.1101
Saunders-Roe SR.53	DFS 346
SFECMAS Gerfaut	Lippisch Lp 12/ 13
Vickers Supermarine S.508	Heinkel He.P1079A; Me P.1110/2; Me 262 and Me 262 HG
Vickers Valiant	Me P. 1107/P.1108
Vickers V-1000	Me P. 1108/AB
Vickers VC10/SVC10	Multhopp T-tail, swept-wing research, rear-mounted pylon engine research

The post-war advance in helicopter design also stemmed from German helicopter research and the works of F. Doblhoff, which included jet-driven rotors – this concept was later evolved by the Allies. Production of German helicopters, prior to 1945, came from Flettner and Focke-Achgelis. Focke-Achgelis fitted high-powered BMW engines to their later helicopters. A 'backpack' man-carried rotor lift design came from Nagler-Rolz. Much of the German helicopter technology found its way to Wright Field and there the Flettner 282 helicopter was flight tested.

From the hundreds of thousands of pages of seized documents and from seized airframes and their designers, a vast hoard of research was grabbed for future use by the Allies. The above summary frames the picture of how billions of pounds and years of research work were saved. From the seized German aerospace works, came the vast leap into the technology of the Cold War and the industrial might of the British and, more sustainably, the American aviation industry for the next seven decades.

The Ultimate Irony of Stolen Science

The ultimate irony must lie in the fact that, during the Korean and Vietnam wars, respectively, Germany's advanced 'wonder weapons' – its technology – were actually tested in combat by the airframes that the Americans, and the Russian-supplied Chinese and Vietnamese had built using that very Germany technology, which they then all deployed in Asia.

MiG-15 and 17s, that were almost direct copies of Multhopp's Ta 183, were pitched into dogfights with American P-86 Thunderjets and F-86 Sabres/F-100 Super Sabres that were also close copies of the Ta 183 and other German swept-wing research. Add in the delta-winged USAF fighters, the F-4 Phantom – itself a close version of the Heinkel P.1080 – helicopters and T-tailed transports, and you have a sky full of German design-originated, yet American and Russian-built airframes, all with not a Luftwaffe marking in sight.

In the 1956 Suez crisis, France's close 'copy' version of Multhopp's Ta 183, the Dassault Mystere IVA, was also deployed in anger. If the Cold War had erupted, the same scenario of ex-German science being deployed by the western powers, would have taken place over Europe – and also using Lippisch and Koisin-inspired British V-bombers of Vulcan, Victor and Valiant, and Canberras, as well as American Convair deltas and Arado and Messerschmitt-inspired Martin and Boeing machines. All would also have been arrayed against German-derived MiG and Sukhoi delta types from the USSR. Only Northrop's flying wings would have been absent.

The success of the German-derived airframes as Chinese and Vietnamese operated MiGs and the success of the American operated fighters in turn, surely proves that if the Allies had come up against these airframes in their original German guise in 1945, the course of the Second World War may well have been interrupted. Therein lies the proof of the story and the proof of the concepts.

Chapter Eleven

The British and the All-Wing

Beyond the amazing John W. Dunne and a tailless, swept all-wing monoplane

When box kites and biplanes were the order of the day, and few had read of Lanchester or Junkers, John W. Dunne designed a stunning aerodynamic treatise amid an all-wing tailless lodestone for aerodynamics. Sadly, he was ordered, by his backer, the Army Balloon Service (forerunner to the RNAS, RFC and the RAF itself) to abandon his original monoplane idea and build a biplane. Yet still he managed to cheat orthodoxy and think outside the wretched box kite cage.

Colonel J.W. Dunne[1] was a polymath thinker, the author of several books – two being entitled *An Experiment With Time*, and *Nothing Dies*. He was a pioneer of aerodynamic thinking and a man who realised that straight 'plank' type wings attached to a heavy or complex tail fin and horizontal stabiliser wings had many disadvantages. We do not really know where Dunne's inspiration came from, but he was a true original thinker of all-wing and tailless configurations. Was Dunne a visionary of druidic proportions amid his future vision?

Dunne wanted to be rid of the tail, yet also realised that removing its fulcrum, or 'moment arm' effect, would create major issues. Dunne decided to sharply sweepback his wing planform designs and by doing so created an in-built longitudinal 'lever arm', or fulcrum effect, by the fact of the rearwards swept part of the wing being angled back from the front of the wing layout. Thus, the wingtip control surfaces were set well behind the centre of mass – thereby creating a balancing and actuating effect. Dunne's ideas created wingtip flaps that were rudders, elevators and ailerons at the same time – he suggested a linked, geared, synchronised control stick action to each opposing effect from port or starboard panel – rather like an elevon or a roll control spoiler, or damper as we see today. Dunne did this in 1910.

Dunne's early experiments were based on a monoplane of V-shape, but he was soon persuaded to create V-shaped biplanes as tailless types of the earliest form.

The then, Lieutenant Dunne's, early swept-winged tailless devices were built as early as 1908 and his successful D.5 flew in 1910, but it would be 1913 before he framed his ideas in a 1913 RAeS paper *The Theory of the Dunne Aeroplane*.

Dunne was aware of Ahlborn's research into the *Zanonia Macropcarpa* seed and its own tailless effect, but expounded his own aerodynamic reasoning. Dunne's focus was to create an automatically self-stabilising aircraft that was without a vertical 'tail' that might 'flick' the machine when stalled or over-controlled. Initially based at Farnborough, he then secreted himself away at Blair Atholl, in Scotland, to test his machines away from public scrutiny under government edict. There, with official sanction and some funding, he built a series of gliders and then powered, V-shaped, tailless craft.

Dunne would, however, achieve profile in 1913, when his Blair Atholl Syndicate project was latterly based at Eastchurch, Isle of Sheppey, on England's south coast. There, he fitted his D.8 airframe with a powerful Gnome engine of over 50hp and flew the English Channel in the all-wing's first sea crossing as the first long distance flight of a swept-wing, tailless aircraft. It was a defining moment in aerodynamics, yet one ignored at the altar of Bleriot's (monoplane) traverse of the Channel and thence at the hand of the biplanists. Licence building of Dunne aircraft in America was also suggested.

Dunne's main realisation, his code of thinking, was to rid aircraft design of the need for a large tail fin and rudder and build in automatic stability – a self-righting aircraft. Writing in an early 1911 edition of *Flight*,[2] Dunne expounded on how the tailless all-wing type must be shown to demonstrate that good turning performance, with correctly gauged and applied banking (a precursor to the glider piloting needs of hand and foot co-ordinated turn and bank effect) without any side-slipping losses, could be created and executed without the need for some large vertical, multi-ruddered collection of tail-mounted surfaces. Was Dunne effectively framing the tailless scenario of today against the wisdom of the two or three control surfaced orthodoxy of the Wright-derived biplane era? It seems he was, and for that we can cite him as a true pioneer of low drag, all-wing tailless configuration.

By 1911, Dunne had also invoked a downturn at the wingtips – creating an early anhedral effect. The wingtips were turned down and carried a control surface upon them. This was applied to a Dunne monoplane design – devoid of the biplane layout which made fitting a vertical panel so easy – between the wings vertically stacked configuration. This delivered a vertical surface aft of the c.g – to greater effect. Wing twist washout (with wingtips flying at a negative angle of incidence), flaps and ailerons, all applied to a V-shaped, highly swept all-wing and tailless machines (as mono and biplane in the Edwardian pre First World War era) seems an amazing advance while surrounded by flying planks of biplanes and triple controlled, triple ruddered devices.

Dunne's designs were automatically stable – the true all-wing and tailless 'grail' of effect. Of course they were in biplane form, beset with bracing and wires, but the aerodynamic and configuration step had been taken. If the Wright-type configuration was inherently unstable – requiring trained piloting skills, Dunne's ideas could have provided aircraft that were much easier and safer to fly. Yet Dunne was denied the chance to persevere with this experimentation, as his financiers sought the safer enclave of the biplane and its ease of design, construction and sale. If only Dunne's ideas had not been smothered by the biplane orthodoxy, aviation might have taken its great step forwards to the all-wing and tailless earlier. Instead, despite Lippisch, the Hortens, Northrop, and others, Dunne had developed automatic stability in the airframe and a two-functioned control mechanism that was far easier than the three-cycle orthodoxy; John William Dunne also used tricycle undercarriages decades before they became de rigueur. Dunne also had the brilliant idea of mounting his aircraft's engine radiator end on, parallel to the airflow and not as traditionally placed, head-on into the airflow as a barrier. By mounting the radiator longitudinally, or in-line, Dunne greatly reduced frontal area and drag, and made the radiator flow-path function in a lateral stream of clean smoother flow, with no loss of cooling effect and all the benefits of removing the 'barn door' ram airflow action.[3]

If we see Dunne's thoughts and constructions in a total package, he becomes the British hero of all-wing, swept and tailless thinking, circa 1910. It is an incredible, yet ignored, legacy.

As Lippisch and the Germans would soon practice, Dunne evolved his advanced ideas through building models and testing them in flight. He may not have researched the scale effect as Lippisch did, but Dunne followed an intellectual research psychology of his own – one that was a correct and latterly applied route to advancement. Dunne applied early knowledge about tails and wings to a tailless configuration of swept-wing shape. He bypassed early rules about tail size and what was called 'longitudinal dihedral'. Dunne also conceived his early form of washout – which was a reversed, or opposite application of twist in comparison with what was then practice – Dunne's application being that the wing's leading edge (not its trailing edge) was depressed towards the tips, as opposed to raising the trailing edge towards the tips. Dunne also seemed to have devised a way of not losing too much lift coefficient at low speeds through drag increases. He did this by thinking about aerofoil camber, creating variable incidence and camber sections for his wing designs.[3]

Dunne's work inspired others – few realise that (Sir) Richard Fairey's work with Dunne, in 1911, would pave the way for his own swept-wing and delta-wing studies, culminating in the Fairey FD.1. Fairey was lead engineer on Dunne's all-wing project at Eastchurch and built four tailless types – one being a monoplane. Other members of the Fairey/Dunne group included later Fairey company men such as V. Nicholl, M. Wright, and F. Dawson. By 1913, Richard Fairey had moved to the nearby Short Brothers.[4]

Another (albeit later) follower of Dunne's lead was F.G. Miles – who gave a nod to the Dunne school of thinking in his 1938 iteration of a flying wing type – the X2 all-wing airliner proposal. Sir Frederick Handley Page began as a monoplane enthusiast and his first designs were monoplanes, and of note, *with* highly swept rearwards crescent-shaped wings (that aped Weiss ideas). Handley Page's *Bluebird*, of May 1910, showed Dunne influence in its highly swept monoplane planform and the HP5 of 1911 derived stability from its crescent-shaped swept-wing. But Handley Page would soon become enmeshed in the commercial realities of biplane orthodoxy – right up to 1930 when it produced its braced HP42 behemoth. It would take German wing research to get Handley Page back to the crescent wing in its post-war Victor.

Another Dunne enthusiast was Geoffrey Hill, who, by 1924, had built his first iteration of the all-wing type and went on with his Pterodactyl series. At the same time as Dunne's work, Jose Weiss, Alsace-born, but living in Sussex, England, created a series of swept-wing and tailless models and full-scale glider types that were of advanced shape – albeit bird form inspired. By 1909, a Weiss machine piloted by F. Gordon England, flew successfully in public and would influence F. Handley Page.

Geoffrey T.R. Hill – Visionary

In Britain, a few visionaries persevered with the all-wing and tailless route and we can surely state that Geoffrey Hill was the true British visionary of the concepts. It was as early as 1923, in a post-Dunne context, that G.T.R. Hill (later to become Professor) began investigation of all-wing and tailless flight.

Hill wanted to explore stability and low drag contexts. Like many, he had noted that in nature and its flying species, the vertical tail surface is noticeable by its absence – birds and insects being (vertically) tailless in such context. So were borne a series of Hill-designed *Pterodactyls* (after the prehistoric reptilians) that became all-wing, swept, tailless devices.

Hill was concerned about the risks of stalling aircraft, particularly to young inexperienced pilots, and from his own biplane experiences he was motivated to try and create safer, more stable airframes. By using carefully designed wing forms and 'elevon' combined controls surfaces, (but it seems not finally deciding on a canard) Hill conceived a super-stable, anti-stall machine. Hill studied the aero-isoclinic wing that retained its shape despite in-flight loads and therefore did not suffer from adverse aerodynamic loading effects upon its stability and handling.

By 1934, Geoffrey Hill had designed a series of all-wing machines under the auspices of the RAE, and the RAF. Hill had experimented with 'flaps', wingtip rudder panels and combined 'elevon' effect controls surfaces. These led him to create the Pterodactyl Mk.V, which was both stable, yet capable of aerobatic flight manoeuvres. The British Westland company manufactured Hill's machines and in 1923, the 'Dreadnought', an all-wing of M. Woyevodsky design that stalled and crashed on its test flight, and which ultimately incorporated a form of a variable sweepback mechanism and a 'drop' or slat effect upon the swept leading edge. These were significant exploratory events in the late 1930s, yet were essentially ignored by the establishment.

G.T.R. Hill, who had designed the Pterodactyl, spent much time in Canada, not least working with Professor John Parkin's Canadian all-wing research group. This group had been established by Parkin as a direct result of the information passed to him on a regular basis by Hill's former student Beverley Shenstone, during the time he was studying in Germany under Junkers and Lippisch prior to being recruited by Supermarine in 1931. Shenstone was Canada's first ever holder of a Masters Degree in aeronautical design and an RCAF qualified power and Wasserkuppe-trained glider pilot. He also knew both Hill and Kronfeld. G.T.R. Hill focused on control surfaces design and effect in the flying wing, and after the problems with the General Aircraft Company's all-wing prototype, which tended to rear up and fall over backwards at the stall (in a fashion shared with the Delta planform), Hill designed and flew several all-wing test airframes. It was one of these that would kill the renowned glider flying expert Robert Kronfeld. Hill also built an experimental all-wing for the Canadian National Research Council group and the device flew until 1950.

After Operation Paperclip and the Fedden Mission, German knowledge of all-wing machines immediately began to inform British practice. A rash of all-wing projects appeared and de Havilland were keen to promote the high speed advantages of the concept. Yet there had been British interest in the all-wing in the 1930s – stemming from a few people who still believed in Dunne's ideas. After Dunne, in the late 1930s, the British began to grasp the advantages of the all-wing concept – principally of lower drag, greater structural efficiency and weight saving, as well as shorter runway requirements. Some bizarre ideas were touted and small British aviation companies experimented with their own 'takes' on the all-wing idea. In the main, British 1930s all-wing devices were of thick aerofoil section and lacking advanced knowledge on control surface design and lift pattern behaviours.

F.G. Miles and his 1936 All-wing Research Craft

F.G. Miles had designed a large airline transport sized all-wing prototype, the Miles X2, in 1936, which was seen as a drawing in *Flight* in 1938.[5] Miles had become a fan of the all-wing and realised that large craft of this design offered many advantages as transport class airframes. The X2 had a low aspect ratio, a deep wing thickness/chord section and a moderated wing taper. With its great inherent strength and removal of interference drag, the X2 was a safe and aerodynamically 'clean' type that boasted retractable undercarriage, and engines accessible in flight. F.G. Miles devised two operational wing loadings for his airliner of the future – 20lbs/sq.ft and 35lbs/sq.ft – the weight of fuel load carried for the Atlantic Ocean capable variant explaining the higher figure.

In early 1938, several British aero-engineers created exquisite test models of all-wing and tailless ideas. The Westland Company, which had produced the Westland-Hill Pterodactyl, collaborated with a Mr W.P.H. Goodsir in the design of a cranked swept-winged tailless design of front-engined propeller powerplant configuration. Known as the Goodsir Tractor Pterodactyl, the design had a 47° wing-sweep outboard of an unswept inboard wing section and a trailing edge sweepback of 27°. A 4 ½° wing twist, or washout, was employed at the wingtips, which featured small vertical surfaces of elliptical form. Flight tests of the model achieved 49 seconds duration and the design showed excellent stability and a flat glide angle. Although only built as a model, the excellence of the design can only have persuaded Westland to assist the designer and we can surely cite Goodsir's device as landmark in British pre-war tailless thinking.

Burnelli and the von Reitzenstein Cunliffe-Owen prototype

Alongside F.G. Miles' all-wing enthusiasm of 1938, at Southampton in the same year, Cunliffe-Owen Aircraft Ltd announced plans for its flying-wing airliner. Designed by Messrs Fisher and Cooper, this was the Clipper – a craft stemming from a Burnelli UB-14 all-wing design licence, under supervision of Vincent J. Burnelli, yet with a redesigned structure. The company intended to produce the Burnelli UB-14 lifting fuselage as the Cunliffe-Owen OA-Mk1. The resulting, single airframe was known as the *Clyde Clipper*. The machine had a twin-boom tail that emerged from a large, very thick wing centre section that suggested an almost flying-wing configuration. With seating for sixteen to twenty passengers and with the single salon main cabin occupying the wing box centre section, the engines were mounted ahead of the cabin and the flight crew positioned between the engines. One such Cunliffe-Owen aircraft was built and pressed into RAF service in the Second World War and then was given to the Free French forces, with the machine being used by De Gaulle as his personal transport.

Cunliffe-Owen's interest in the flying wing concept stemmed from numerous sources, not least Supermarine, whose base was close to the Cunliffe-Owen factory in Southampton. The Cunliffe-Owen family also had close links with the Wills lineage via the (earlier) marriage of Mary Cunliffe-Owen to Henry H. Wills. Cunliffe-Owen had close links with the Science Museum in London and the Department of Science and Arts under Henry Cole. Cunliffe-Owen had been formed in 1937 (as a subsidiary of the British American Tobacco Company at Eastleigh, near Southampton) to build the Burnelli Flying Wing aircraft under licence, and was named Cunliffe-Owen Aircraft Limited in May 1938 by Hugo von Reitzenstein Cunliffe-Owen. The Cunliffe-Owen company was based in the hangar next to the Supermarine hangar at Southampton Airport. Coincidentally, the Cunliffe-Owen story had links to one of Germany's noble houses – that of the von Reitzenstein, via the marriage of Sir Francis P. Cunliffe-Owen to Jenny von Reitzenstein, the daughter of Baron Frhr Fritz von Reitzenstein of Prussia.

Yet, as 1939 faded, such links would become politically inappropriate and once close-friendships between British and German (not Nazi) families and designers would cease. However, by 1946, and having feasted upon German wing design research, the British seemed to abandon supersonic research, but threw themselves into an all-wing and tailless design episode of great productivity. Yet it was a period that was allowed to die quietly and a return or retardation to orthodoxy manifested – in a vein that hinted at the Edwardian biplane era and its refusal of aerodynamic knowledge.

In 1945, Armstrong Whitworth announced its design for a prototype all-wing device as a test bed glider that was a study for a future powered all-wing of derived design. This aircraft was conceived in wartime and made the most of what was known about the Hill, Northrop, Lippisch and Horten design works.

1946 – Avid All-Wing Aerodynamicists

Over at Handley Page, the company's German émigré, Gustav Lachmann, designed an all-wing type with a small vestigial empennage. It did, however, sport wingtip vertical surfaces as rudders. Driven by two pusher props, Lachmann equipped the wing with his patented slots (or slats) and the first prototype was ready in 1939 – although greatly overweight. A short 'hop' flight took place in 1942 after a weight reduction programme and, by 1943, thirty hours of flight testing had been performed. With the death of all-wing enthusiasm in Britain in the early 1950s, the Lachmann Handley Page all-wing was quietly destroyed in 1953. The tailless HP.80 concept of 1948 would, via seized Arado research findings, become the crescent-winged and T-tailed HP.80 Victor nuclear bomber of the Cold War.

The British had set up an official Tailless Advisory Committee in 1944 as a joint Ministry of Supply/Society of British Aircraft Constructors body. So there was official support for the all-wing before the end of the war – as a direct result of the British and Americans becoming aware of the advanced German all-wing experiments.

Sir Henry Tizard, as scientific adviser to the Air Staff during the war, had defined the need of a long range, high lift, and low wing loading bomber as Specification B35/46. He called for research, all-wing research that would later manifest itself as the British 'V–Bomber' fleet across Avro, Vickers–Armstrong, and Handley Page manifestations of advanced aerodynamics. Within the British Air Ministry, and the Brabazon Committee, there were devoted believers in the aerodynamic purity and potential of massive all-wing airliners and transports. Of note amongst these names could be found Sir Roy Fedden of Bristol's and Beverley Shenstone, who would, circa 1943–1947, somewhat curiously slip from Wright Field to direct employment by the Canadian Government, then to Avro – developing 'disc' science with Lippisch in post-war Canada, only to move on to the tamer world of airline engineering operations at the new British European Airways in 1947.

Avro's Lippisch-derived B35/46 response was to become the Vulcan and in its early forms it had no vertical tail fin, but instead, wingtip rudders and this reflected the themes of Roy Chadwick and Eric Priestly (then Avro Chief Aerodynamicist). From such all-wing planforms, Avro's moved to the delta. George Edwards and his team at Vickers, in Weybridge, also studied thin, highly swept-wings, but in their V-bomber iteration, suggested a sleek, yet conventional outcome – the Valiant – yet it had eerie shades of Arado to its form.

Godfrey Lee, who was Handley Page's research engineer, had visited the high-speed supersonic wind tunnel of the Volkenrode, *Aerodynamishce Versuchsanstalt* (AVA) Göttingen as early as September 1945. Lee was also a co-investigator on the flawed and controversial CIOS/ RAE report on the Hortens. From the British visit to Göttingen, and other findings, came the practice of creating wing sweep angles at optimum degrees of sweep; 35°, 47°, 53°, 57°, and 60° respectively (related to span position and chord). From such came the DH 108, the Vulcan and ultimately Concorde itself. Even the flying boat builders, Shorts and Saunders-Roe, created swept-wing and deltoid flying prototypes. From Hawker to de Havilland, from Bristol (Aircraft) to Vickers and even the diminutive Miles Ltd, all-wing, swept-wing and delta-wing designs were the focus of the moment. A massive all-wing movement manifested, with even *Flight* stating on 9 January 1947: 'Someday the flying wing will emerge as the accepted form of a passenger airliner.'

Since the discovery of the German swept-wing and all-wing tailless research in summer 1945, British aviation literature was, from 1946 to circa 1955, populated by many articles about such designs and their various merits. Designers were spoilt for choice. The pages of *Flight* magazine were packed with articles and reports from the likes of the RAeS on all things all-wing. Various meetings and events took place in Europe and America to discuss the all-wing. One stunning all-wing proposal came in 1952 from the Third Anglo-American Aeronautical Conference. This cranked, swept, all-wing device that deployed a boundary layer suction-wing, was presented by T.S. Keeble. This design concept, supported by experimental glider flight tests of such a device made by the Australian Aeronautical Research Laboratories, suggested a major reduction in drag coefficient, a significant increase in lift coefficient and a resulting 40 per cent increase in payload/range ratio, and a similar percentage of speed improvement – with no trade-off in range.

An all-wing/tailless movement was established and for a time it looked as if even the de Havilland Comet would use a German-inspired, highly swept, all-wing tailless configuration. But, as with the retardation of 1912 and the backwards move to unswept biplanes (when J.W. Dunne was trying to open others minds), the brief but burgeoning 'flying-wing' interlude was soon to be crushed.

As late as 1952, Mr D. Keith-Lucas, chief designer of Short Brothers Ltd, espoused the advantageous aspects of the all-wing. Keith-Lucas had been one of the men of the CIOS/BIOS teams that scoured Germany in 1945–1946 for advanced aerodynamics knowledge. He soon spoke of the advantages of swept-wing design in a lecture to the British Association entitled, 'The Shape of Wings to Come'. This was published in *Flight* on 26 September 1952. Keith-Lucas aptly framed the separate, respective advantages of the all-wing, crescent-wing, forward swept 'M' and 'W' shaped wings of Vogt derivation, and delta-wing planforms. Each has its supporters, and many felt that the shorter, low aspect ratio, flying triangle of the delta offered the best combination of high speed and high strength. Others preferred the tailless all-wing and some showed interest in the aero-isoclinic wing – a wing in which the wing's angle or incidence to the oncoming airflow remains near constant along the wing's entire span, despite the issues of wing flex and in-flight load related distortion. This solution was achieved by careful and deliberate application of wing crank and clever structural effects. Keith-Lucas also discussed the use of boundary layer control and methods of applying suction to the aerofoil in order to benefit lift – this technique could benefit the thick wing sections used on all-wing or 'flying wing' type machines that often had thick centre sections aerofoil shapes.

Of significance, Keith-Lucas opined[6] that aircraft designers had got so used to the conventional arrangement of aircraft with a straight wing and a long slender fuselage with a large tail that designers of the time were likely to look upon tailless or all-wing design as something freakish or unnatural. Proof then, that a prejudged mindset did indeed exist amongst the learned men.

Clearly, the work of Lilienthal, Penaud and others in all-wing design prior to 1900, must have either been forgotten of become deliberately ignored.

So, in a situation similar to that faced by the early monoplane and all-wing lateral thinkers, here was proof that the establishment 'perceived wisdom' experts were in the majority and that even in 1952 it took someone inside that establishment who had different thoughts, to frame the alternatives. A telling line from the lecture was the statement that: 'We have seen how sweep-back was first introduced as a means of providing longitudinal stability and control on tailless aircraft. The odd part of the story is that nowadays we are concerned by the ill effects of sweep-back on stability, both longitudinal and lateral.'[7] Of great note, Keith-Lucas cited birds as examples of how nature had removed vertical tail fins, reduced the size of horizontal tail surfaces, and informed the ultimate efficiency of the all-wing for bird flight. Bats, said Keith-Lucas, were probably the most manoeuvrable of nature's flying machines – and they were all-wing and tailless.

The issue of nose-up pitch being demanded by a pilot recovering from a steep dive, and the aerodynamic effects of un-commanded nose-up pitch due to wing flex making the wingtips that lay behind the aircraft's centre of gravity, flex and twist and lose lift (and causing further nose-up pitch), before creating instability and loss of control were, suggested Keith-Lucas, vital arbiters of wing design and all-wing/tailless design.

The first British delta-wing planform equipped jet aircraft to fly was on 4 September 1949. The crash of an all-wing craft with legendary expert Robert Kronfeld at the controls in the same year signalled that the all-wing story was not yet resolved and, like the biplane, could be put on hold by other agendas.

Chris Wills Talks of All-Wing Design

The late Christopher Wills was a world championship glider pilot in his own right – and the son of famed world champion glider pilot Phillip Wills. As a young man, Chris had been infected with the gliding ethos and rubbed shoulders with the greats of the sport. A German speaker, Chris could see beyond politics and was close to the German gliding scene and a huge admirer of the Hortens and Lippisch. In a series of interviews with the author, Chris expounded on his views that the all-wing offered the greatest aerodynamic advantage and that the Horten brothers really had achieved something that not even Northrop or Fauvel had managed. Chris was convinced that the Hortens had discovered or invented something new, or different, about wing design and control surfaces. He also provided perspectives on how such technology had been used by British and American powers to further their own designs. Chris's views were clear:[8]

> 'Flying wings, or nurflügels, were once all the rage. In my world of gliding, the aerodynamic advantages of the all-wing configuration were known for a very long time and very exciting they were. I have here in my home a glass-encased Zanonia seed – nature's all-wing device. It truly was an inspiration, and from that seed to the machines of Lippisch and the Hortens seems a huge journey. The effects of the German glider design revolution and their

effect upon British glider design always intrigued me, as did the tale of how the Spitfire got its modified ellipse of a wing, which was such an advance and which stemmed in part from German glider design.

'The all-wing and how it was lost to time and aeronautical fashion, only to re-emerge today is an amazing story. The role of the Germans in all-wing development was critical, and the seizure of such technologies after the war another part of the tale. Beverley Shenstone was in my view "number one" – the top aerodynamicist of his time and a major figure, not just of gliding and man powered flight, but also wing design and the development of the airlines. He followed my father into BEA; Shenstone's time in Germany, especially at the Wasserkuppe and the discoveries he made with Lippisch, were the first steps of the flying triangle and touched the Spitfire's wing design.

'What the Hortens did was amazing and an advance that was perhaps obscured by the contexts of that time: they did not use or have access to wind tunnels, so they developed their ideas by real physical testing. This was contrary to all expertise or established thinking at the time. Yet the flying qualities of their gliders were incredible.

'To me there is no doubt that some agenda, or some prejudice, maybe even sabotage, was manifested upon the Hortens at the end of the war by the Allies. The British Wilkinson report seems incredible now – for all the wrong reasons, and the American modifications to Horten Ho 4A airframes seem even more bizarre if you consider that those that made them ought to have known better. Reimar Horten had achieved lift-to-descent (L/D) ratios of 1:35+ with the Ho 4 and may have bettered 1:37. Yet after the war, when the American's tested their seized Horten airframes, they cited 1:27 for the L/D and criticised the designs – yet failed to mention or realize that the changes to the plastic cockpit bubble and centre fuselage shaping that they had forced upon the HO 4A registered LA-AC. Such modifications had wrecked Reimar's bell-shaped lift distribution pattern and destroyed local flow and lift, as well as destabilised the wing.

'An American Horten owner named Hollis Button had given the Ho 4A airframe to A. Raspet at Mississippi State University after it had been repaired and test flown by R.C. Forbes at RAF Cranfield in the UK. Forbes had discovered the Ho 4A's amazing flying qualities and urged Button to take care of the machine, the fine flying qualities of which he was utterly astounded by. The Mississippi University team changed the cockpit canopy design by fitting a convex curved modified centre section and annihilated the double centre of pressure reflex profile that lay just aft of it – the core of Reimar's wing lift bell-curve theory. This had a disastrous effect upon the aerodynamics and eliminated much lift in the vital centre wing region. Worse, to compensate, the university then flew the Ho 4A with the ailerons set upwards – fully up. This destroyed further lift patterns, created a massive drag wake and made the machine susceptible to spinning. Reimar would have been furious. For the Americans not to notice the wing reflex profile effect at centre-span and to destroy it was bad enough, but then OSTIV gave such findings 'official' reference and, just as with Wilkinson's report, the Mississippi University findings became repeated fact – minus the truth!

'What of the Ho 6? This was said to have an L/D of 1:46 – an incredible figure that was well ahead of the normal gliders of the time in the late 1930s. The Ho 6 that the British found in Germany was said to have been burned by them. All I know is that Reimar Horten had reckoned his all-wings were anything from fifteen per cent to twenty-five per cent more aerodynamically efficient than a conventional airframe, and that he proved it, but via Wilkinson and the Americans, his reputation was destroyed – it seems, possibly by an apparent wilful act.

'If a Horten all-wing was flown by a pilot with no all-wing experiences, or worse, little gliding experience, it was unlikely that the airframe would take kindly to rough handling – and then it would be criticised in the flying report. R.C. "Jock" Forbes, who had flown the Ho 4A for the British in 1949, was a top glider pilot and knew how to fly the Horten; Forbes thought that the Ho 4A was a world-beater.

'The fact was that there had been no successful British flying wing (they had all failed to master the stall and spin issues) and that in the seized Ho 4A the British, and then the Americans, had had their noses wiped in it, seems to have been an annoyance. Critically, the British and American flying wing designs still had handling problems and aerodynamic issues – the Horten machines did not. Was this why the Hortens had to be undermined – as if by policy?

'All I know is that through his wing designs, prone pilot configuration, and advanced control surfaces, Reimar Horten achieved something no one else had – the answer and the advance.

'That Horten gliders are being restored and replicas built now, is exciting. To think that they still fascinate people and that new shapes of the future are following their lead is wonderful. Once there was a big, all-wing movement. Those Horten machines were incredible. Like us, the German flyers were about flight and ultimate gliding, politics was not the point. We all just wanted to fly as efficiently as we could. Back then gliding was an Olympic sport and I cannot understand why it is not now when far more obscure activities have Olympic status.

'I clearly remember my father talking about the Hortens, Kronfeld, Hill, and Shenstone. They all knew each other. I know that my father and Shenstone played a part in taking Horten and other gliders from Germany after the end of the war. The Horten's were also spoken to by British Intelligence in London and Bonn in 1945 and 1946. For reasons that we may never understand, they were obscured and their lead ignored.

'With the recent suggested plans for blended wings – or all-wings by another name – which Boeing and Airbus have announced, the all-wing or nurflügel story seems to have come full circle. That the all-wing knowledge has been around for a hundred years seems like a fitting moment to remember that aviation contains many riddles.

'In 1946, I saw my first German glider when I was thirteen, it was a war-prize Weihe that my father had got hold of. He flew it at the first British post-war glider meeting at Leicester. There was also a beautiful Rhonadler present. It was there that my gliding fascination took off, and it was from those days that I realised that advanced 1930s German sailplane design had not just influenced glider design, but subsequent motor-powered airframe design across the world.

'My gliding, my father's flying, and our connection to the flying wing, all seem like a parallel story to conventional design and thinking. My world championship glider was, of course, a gull-winged German machine.

'In the 1940s, many people thought the flying wing, or all-wing, was the next big step and that giant jet-powered all-wing types would soon be the backbone of the military and the airlines. All-wing gliders seemed just to have been turning the key in the door. Now, the all-wing revolution seems to finally have taken root. The all-wing story was obvious to me and a few of my contemporaries, but apparently forgotten or ignored by a wider audience beyond the world of gliding. To see the B-2 all-wing bomber and to think of the Hortens and all the flying wings marks a moment in aircraft design. Things seem to have come full circle.'

Ultimately, the British were so keen on the all-wing and so interested in the German all-wing that the original ideas for the Comet airliners were of a very Horten-like all-wing machine.

Chapter Twelve

The All-Wing Now?

How ironic that today's American achievements in ballistic missiles and in spaceflight are built upon German science and design. How apt that the new future of hyperspace surface skimmers suggested by the giants of airframe building, all reflect German 1930s science and Sanger's vision. How interesting that the all-wing has been revealed as a 'new' basis of military fighters and bombers and drones, and has now been 'reinvented' by modern science to become something called, in short, the 'blended-wing'. Perhaps it has, or possibly the blended-wing-body – the BWB – is a euphemism for fanfaring what modern man, computational fluid dynamics (CFD) and recent aerodynamics can achieve all on its own, without having to give a nod of acknowledgement to those nasty Germans of 1939–1945. But what about J.K. Northrop? He was American after all. But no, the BWB is, we are assured, 'all-new'.

The first 'flying wings' – or all-wings – were British, French and German. Despite attempts by some men of vision to resurrect the all-wing for the British aviation industry post-1945, a culture of denial was propagated. Neither should we forget that the USAF scrapped a whole squadron of brand new Northrop all-wing bombers upon the whim of so-called perceived wisdom. It would be the year 2000 and beyond before the all-wing would begin its comeback and impending dominance. In the interim period of seventy years, German aerodynamic science and all-wing knowledge would be stolen, masked and finally re-presented as modern American and European technology. From the 1850s era of monoplane ideas, to the 1870s, to 1920s ideas of all-wings, the story of aerodynamics and the deliberate retardation of science by the biplane era, paints a salutary lesson for any genius who seeks to shake off the shackles of convention.

From 1950 to 2010, in the all-wing denial and sudden BWB reinvention, it seems to have happened again. We have to ask why? What strange forces shaped the narrative against the potential of possibility?

What went on in French and German design minds circa 1850–1910 – from Issy-les-Moulineux Paris, and then in the vast gliding halls of Göttingen/ Darmstadt in the early years of the twentieth century, can only have influenced what subsequently occurred in the research offices of institutions such as Farnborough, Wright-Patterson, White Sands, Long Beach, San Diego, Seattle and points east of the 1950s European border of the USSR; No other explanation is feasible.

Yet the observer might well ponder the paradox that, despite all this advanced and often unique science, for the Nazis, it did *not* produce vast numbers of weapons (or even 'wonder weapons') based on this amazing science. Apart from von Braun's rocket missiles landing on London in high numbers, and the last-ditch attempts at getting jet fighters and weird exploding 'Natter' suicide airframes into the air, and the stab at an Amerika Bomber, it might seem odd that the Germans did not build and deploy their amazing devices that were capable of winning the war – or even a negotiated peace. The answer lies not in any fundamental failures in the science, nor the advanced designs, but in the blame for not funding and directing, or using this science in war. Hitler's personality-crazed management of policy was at fault, not the designs concerned.

Thus, responsibility for failure does not rest with the inventors of such potential, but instead with the execution of the plan – that idiot strategy that saw Hitler waste the science by his personal dominance of policy and campaign that was so disastrous, not just for the world, but also in strict military terms, for the pursuance of a war. But for Hitler's stupid decisions, but for his madness and disease, the weapons he ordered to be created, *might*, *could*, have been built and used to far greater effect in that war. An all-wing Amerika Bomber painted with swastikas was only months from dropping a crude nuclear device over New York. Instead, the design for that craft was stolen and reincarnated as an American all-wing bomber over sixty years later. The ultimate irony is that German aerospace science was turned into the Allied weapons that framed the Cold War across ensuing decades, and onwards to today's new all-wing aerospace future.

What of the all-wing's and delta-wing's more recent past? Concorde, the Tu-144, the stillborn Boeing supersonic airliner, the Avro Vulcan and a host of delta and all-wing shapes from Sukhoi, Dassault, Lockheed, Bell, Martin, Convair and others that were all users of the Lippisch delta design? How revealing that every one of them has its roots in the 1930s work of Alexander Martin Lippisch. And now we see the work of the Hortens writ large across America's strategic bomber fleet, its 'Stealth' fighter fleet and the new world of drones, some ironically built by Northrop Grumman.

Within two decades, blended-wing body airliners from Boeing and Airbus will also be all-wing derivatives of the works of others from decades ago. As things stand, unmanned aerial vehicles (UAV), or 'drones', of swept all-wing and delta-wing planforms are being designed using advanced computer power and fabricated in composite materials to explore an all-wing renaissance away from the public gaze – hundreds of millions of dollars are being thrown at such devices.

The gradual lifting of the barriers to the use of the all-wing began in the mid-1970s during the apparent 'invention' of modern aerodynamics using new computing power. Work began back then in 'solving' the issues that apparently beset the all-wing. Quite what Northrop thought, we do not know, but given how far he had got with his all-wings – until the 1950s event of principally politically/financially motivated scrapping of his XB-35 and YB-49 all-wing fleet for the USAF – is another story. Money for space flight existed – after all, the Soviets were up to it – but more money for all-wings (whose technical issues Northrop had not completely solved), well that was another matter for Congress to use as a pawn.

From the 1970s came the works that led to the F-117A and the B-2, the former so closely resembling the planform of the Horten Ho 13A and the latter looking like a hybrid between Ho 9/Ho 229/Ho 18, and Northrop XB-35 or YB-49 devices.

Amid this German all-wing story, the American, J. K. Northrop's opinions and works, should not be ignored. Northrop was an avid all-wing devotee and thought that if a conventional high speed airframe had a drag coefficient of C_D 0.023, the range of drag coefficients for all-wing types vary from C_D 0.010 to C_D 0.0113 – and

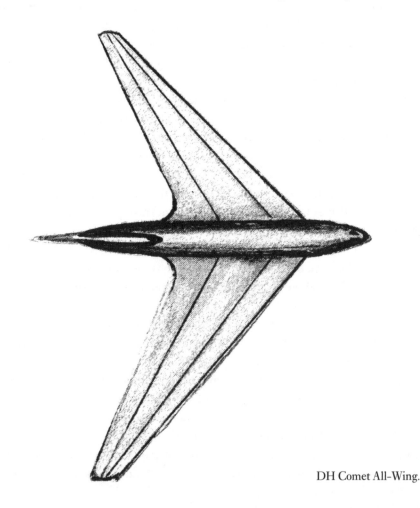

DH Comet All-Wing.

that with development and jet engine power, an all-wing might have forty per cent less drag and save approximately thirty per cent in fuel. He also noted the need for less power to achieve the same speeds as more power-hungry conventionally winged types. Northrop also knew that by spreading the structural loadings and payload throughout the all-wing, that better efficiencies in weight saving and consequent increases in range were obvious. Northrop had to add vertical surfaces to his large all-wings and there remained some stall-related handling issues, but in the main, the public failures of the Northrop USAF were engine related, not aerodynamically related. The fact remains that a fleet of nine operational, giant Northrop flying wings were active and were scrapped in 1950s scenes that framed the excess of power and politicians.

Yet the facts remain that Northrop built an all-wing bomber/transport sized airframe of the manner that Reimar Horten was on the cusp of achieving in 1945. Northrop's, giant prop and jet-powered all-wings were briefly in-flight. The YB-49 exceeded 170ft in wingspan and had huge capabilities.

By the 1980s, the B-2 realised the dreams of Horten and Northrop, but it should be noted that it required a computer to keep it stable in-flight – juggling all its control surfaces constantly to stay within a safe flight envelope – and also required a computer authority co-pilot. The Hortens would not have approved. Maybe the B-2 might even have a gyroscope fitted in its control 'brain' to keep it flying.

In the 1960s and 1970s, the US Government had begun to fund all-wing and lifting body research, leading to a strange range of low-aspect ratio devices that also reflected Second World War German ideas, Chance-Vought's 'Pancake' being the most obvious. Many such projects were based at the NASA 'Armstrong Flight Research Center' and included airframes such as the M2-F1, M2-F-2, M2-F3, X-24 and X-24B.

Blended-Wing: Euphemistic Trick or New Invention?

After the Lockheed F-117A and Northrop Grumman B-2 'Spirit', all-wings were publicly announced, the BWB movement towards establishing the blended wing as the future of high-speed flight began to take serious steps. NASA says it began researching the BWB in 2000, leading to work with Boeing on the Boeing X-48B blended wing airframe proposals. Boeing and NASA stated that a thirty per cent fuel saving would stem from the X-48B's advanced aerodynamic drag reducing features – not much different from J.K. Northrop's predictions in his 1947 Orville Wright lecture! NASA spent the early 2000s putting a scale model of its X-45C through wind tunnel testing in order to research low-speed handling issues and the placement of control surfaces. Reading the works of Reimar Horten may have been cheaper and quicker, but what is a few billion dollars between friends at NASA, Boeing and the USAF.

In a stunning example of how narratives can be set, irrespective of history, *Time* Magazine decided to vote the BWB in the form of the X-45C's derivative – the NASA/Boeing X-48B – the 'Invention of the year' in 2007. The idea of a 'greener' aircraft that had lower drag, longer range, used less fuel and was stronger (it also shielded its engine noise as the all-wing planform does) suddenly ticked all the PR and 'eco' boxes. So the BWB was a new invention, according to the American media. Apparently the BWB was a 'hybrid shape' that took the all-wing and added to it. Of note, the blend of wings and the body create low lift-induced drag and actually create lift. This, we are told, is a new invention.

Boeing had been fortunate that, when it purchased McDonnell Douglas, it found the old Long Beach company had been researching the all-wing for years. Therein were three engineers – R.H. Liebeck, M.A. Page and B.K. Lawdon, who were working on blended-wing body studies for the future, and they became a Boeing research resource.[1] In 1989, the lead scientist at NASA (Langley), Dr Dennis Bushnell, researched how the need for a commercial aircraft that could carry 800 passengers over 7000nm and a speed of Mach 0.85 could be achieved. He looked at the all-wing, or blended-wing body, lifting body concepts and, knowing of the Douglas Company's research in the field, began the NASA focus on the subject.

Boeing's X-48B was to be built of composites – another 'new' efficiency – unless you had seen a Horten Ho 229 at Wright Field in 1945, after it had been shipped via Cherbourg from Friedrichroda, Germany. Similarly, the cranked wing and blended leading edge planform of the Horten Ho 9 can only be seen as a true BWB design, it is so obvious that denial becomes the delusion. Thus, the reader can draw his or her own conclusion as to if today's efficiencies are solely of the BWB. The likelihood of the BWB being a retuned all-wing is more rational. On 20 July 2007, after many years of work on the real thing – the X-48B airframe took to the air at the Dryden Flight test facility, with the 'C' version envisaged to lead to a transport airframe.[2]

Soon, there began a rash of BWB studies at institutions all over the world and students started writing Ph.D. research essays on the new BWB and its benefits – with scant reference, it seems, to the record of past works.

Meanwhile, Northrop Grumman gave us the X-47 'Pegasus' in 2003, Silent Aircraft Initiative designed a proposed BWB airframe, also in 2003, Lockheed/ Martin shaped the RQ-170 tailless device in 2007, Dassault pondered a tailless unmanned aerial vehicle (UAV) and by 2012 EADS Airbus had suggested its own BWB airliner for the future. French researchers, in a national project entitled AVECA, were a coalition of the French ONERA aerodynamics research organisation, and based experts tasked with studying the optimisation of BWB configurations within an Airbus remit. Add in a Chinese tailless idea named 'AVIC 601-S'; BWB research at MIT; the University of Cambridge; Cranfield University and in Russia, and a family of BWB types has begun to emerge.

Of note, BAE Systems 'Demon' project represents an all-wing planform that has no need for conventional control surfaces and looks like a true step change in all-wing or BWB planform.

Of interest, the French research AVECA project has proven the lift-drag ratio advantages of the BWB, but has not fully refined the low-speed wing performance issues of the configuration. It seems that control surfaces and leading edge issues and devices remain the thorn in the side of the BWB, yet with eight decades of research to draw upon it seems strange that the issues have not been solved. As with the early all-wing studies, the trade-off between lift, drag, and control, are all cited as issues. The trade-offs between wing chord, aerofoil types, washout wing twist, spanwise flows and span loadings, lift coefficients and elliptical lift patterns and loadings all seem to present the same issues the likes of Reimar Horten, Alexander Lippisch and Beverley Shenstone solved in the 1930s! And that is without citing Dunne or early experiments by Junkers.

Issues of lift distribution, structural flexings, aero-elasticity and wake drag, should present today's CFD-equipped digital designer with no long-term blockages. But the differing uses and actions of elevons remains a focus of research for BWB designers. Pitch control from symmetrically acting elevons and roll control from asymmetrically acting elevons, are being focused upon by researchers; Yet what of further research into Reimar Horten's 'active' wingtip airflow behaviour and tuned aileron and elevon effects? What of Lippisch's ogee or ogival wing shape related studies and Shenstone's Spitfire-wing trailing edge and aileron works? Are today's young BWB researchers even aware of the aerodynamic flow and effect techniques that were created by these all-wing pioneers?

Burnelli and Others

Vincent Burnelli was an early, 1920s-1930s, American proponent of the 'flying-wing' as a lifting body. His designs were not quite all-wing, in that they had twin-boom tail moment arms extending back to vertical fins. However, like Junkers, he envisaged the engines, crew and payload/passengers, sitting safely within the strength of the main wing box and body. The first Burnelli airframe was the CB-16 of 1929 and over sixty per cent of the structure was the central lifting body wing box form.

As such, we might say Burnelli designed a blended-wing body, but he was certainly not the first to do that.[3] Surely Hugo Junkers heads the list for the creation of a de facto blended wing 'BWB' concept as early as 1910? So for Burnelli it was more of 'lifting body' efficiency. It took him several years to get his early American patent applications through the 1920s process and it would be the 1930s before he decided upon a tailless idea. Of interest, Burnelli sold a licence to the British outfit, Cunliffe-Owen Ltd, and in 1937 that company built a British iteration of a modified Burnelli design in its own Cunliffe-Owen *Clyde Clipper* flying wing, at Eastleigh, Southampton, very close to the Supermarine works.

At the same time, the industrial designer, Norman Bel Geddes, returned from his studies of design, architecture and aviation in France, and although shadowed by other American industrial design legends such as Henry Dreyfuss, Walter Dorwin Teague, Raymond Loewy, Harley Earl and others, Bel Geddes, as well as designing cars and products, also produced a lifting-body BWB-type design proposal in the 1930s. Bel Geddes was a true 'renaissance man' and the benefits of the all-wing appealed to him both in pure engineering and design and styling terms.

However, stepping back to circa 1910–1925, there *were* previous all-wing, flying-wing and lifting-body type patent applications to Burnelli, and not just that of Hugo Junkers. In essence these were the first BWBs, so clearly, the Boeing/NASA 2007 BWB iteration cannot, as *Time* Magazine stated, really be framed as an 'invention'. Junkers also created a ten-engined, all-wing giant airframe in 1930 and made a German patent application. Of note, B.S. Shenstone, who was studying with Junkers at Dessau from late 1929, worked on this prototype design. That may be where and when his all-wing interest began. Junkers had built a Ju G.38 transport all-wing in 1927 and it visited airports all over Europe. This machine too, was surely a BWB in all but marketing name.

The designer of the Ford Trimotor, W. Stout, also had suggested a low-aspect ratio all-wing design in 1919. Other flying wing or early BWB designers of the 1920s and 1930s included little-known names such as W. Lamgguth, J. Charpentier, A. Soldenhoff and C. Snyder. The well-known Frenchman, Charles Fauvel, also suggested what can only be termed as all-wing BWBS ideas in the late 1920s. The Paris-based designer Jacques Gerin, a contemporary of Gabriel Voisin, André Lefebvre and André Citroën, also designed a large all-wing tailless airliner proposal in 1936. Intriguingly, also in Paris, the Romanian, F. Mihail, who trained formally in aeronautical maintenance, suggested his *Stabiloplan* flying wing – with a tail – in the 1930s, after a decade spent exploring such concepts. His first patent for a self-stabilising wing type monoplane was submitted in France in 1922.

Many of the above could qualify as precursors to the BWB *if* the BWB is to be cited as a distinct species that is separate from the all-wing, but that is an argument unlikely to be settled easily. Either way, we still look to a German, Hugo Junkers, as the true father of the all-wing that was also a BWB device.

It seems that, as in the 1930s, when the falsehood that benefits of the monoplane over the biplane were claimed to suddenly have been researched and realised (completely ignoring the early pre-1910 monoplanes), we are now in an era of education and research that will soon announce that it has solved the issues of the all-wing based BWB and that modern high fidelity computational fluid dynamics and recent in-flight testing, have 'solved' the age-old problems. It feels as if another feint of a historical narrative to reinforce the now and ignore the knowledge of the past has been preordained in the BWB story for public consumption and national ego.

Chapter Thirteen

Drag Wake

T he all-wing machine, the nurflügel technology, was indeed another worldly experience. Its efficiencies were legendary, yet its actual flight characteristics were beyond even that. This *was* a different world. And it was one that could have taken man so far, way back in the past. Instead, a deliberate denial took place. Such was the secret of the all-wing and its flight, post-war science, decided to take another route – or so it wanted you to believe. From media stories in the late-1940s, saying that the future was an all-wing world, to the ordered destruction of the entire USAF fleet of Northrop all-wing machines, was less than a decade. In that time a bright all-wing technology future was killed. Even an all-wing design for the world's first jet airliner had been drawn up, only to be replaced by the moderately swept-wing equipped, conventional configuration of the DH Comet.

Now, of course, things are different and the all-wing is all the rage.

How could they, the powers of perceived wisdom, deny this for so long? But then of course they did not, for those powers simply 'stole' or 'borrowed' the idea and its refinements and sat upon the concept for five or six decades, only then to announce that they had finally 'refined' the old all-wing concept, which they said had been a failure and which was now the future – after an interlude of over half a century, a deliberate interlude, a time in which the all-wing truth was, shall we say, obscured.

B.S. Shenstone had, in his 1963 presidential year at the Royal Aeronautical Society, awarded Walter Horten the RAeS Bronze Medal, but it would be 1993 before Walter's brother Reimar received the RAeS Gold Medal for his all-wing tailless works. These were the same Hortens who had been dismissed by the establishment, the Royal Aircraft Establishment and its Wilkinson Report in 1946. By the 1990s, minds once wrapped in the conceits of power had begun to open – purely by application and modern research development, of course.

After all, 'aerodynamics' and its modern advances were really invented in the 1970s – according to some of today's soothsayers of certainties within aerospace. The facts are that early aviation, circa 1850–1910, had been populated by all-wing or flying wing planforms, yet soon nice, straight, tapered planks of wings - biplane wings - were deemed to be the fashion. It was a fashion where the conceit of consensus overwhelmed the actuality of opposing evidence – a not unusual situation in the human condition. Thus, the monoplane was delayed by years, the all-wing delayed by decades. Society, especially learned society, dismissed the all-wing planform and configuration that early aviators had promoted, instead to focus on canvas, wires, woodwork, bracing struts and drag-inducing, speed and range-sapping, horrible excrescences called tails and fuselages and cabins.

Yet secretly, in the following decades behind the public facade, the 'experts' and their governments would pour millions of their nations' (taxpayers') currencies into developing the very thoughts of the new, the eccentric, the elliptic, the all-wing, the related circular disc-wing, and put such ideas to military use, in secret. It is a strange tale of human ego, denial and discovery and of the all-wing men who were brave enough to endure, to persevere, only in some cases, to be arrested, carted off and made to design the future for the new forces of imperial foreign policy on *both* sides of the Iron Curtain.

How apt that exploration of space by the United States should have resulted from the Soviet leap into space based on the very same science that America had seized from Germany – which the Americans had failed, due to political and military in-fighting, to develop as quickly as the Russians. How funny that the desperate Americans should (not least by the comments of J. Foster Dulles) have to verbally attack the Russians for having made their leap ahead using others (German) science, which, the Americans noted, had been stolen off the wicked Nazis and was of little innovation.

What massive hypocrisy! Having caught up – using the *same* stolen science – America would launch Apollo rockets utterly based on von Braun's weapons of mass destruction and then launch re-usable re-entry 'Space Shuttle' vehicles stemming from the hand of Hans Multhopp.

1945–1975: Missed Opportunities and 'Project Cancelled'[1]

To evidence the enduring 'attitude' of the British and their learned men, and their need to deny the past or the new in a straightjacket of mental constraint, we can look at the 1970s writings of Derek Wood, a man who had the temerity to think different thoughts.

As editor-in-chief of Jane's *Defence Weekly* and numerous other distinguished portals of aviation writing, Wood was accepted in his field. In 1975, Wood published his book *Project Cancelled: The Disaster of Britain's Abandoned Aircraft Projects*. This text laid bare the effects of the fiddlings, by politicians, upon British aviation research, design and production, circa 1945–1970. It also framed the manner in which German advances had been wasted by a British establishment that wanted to deny them. The book caused great controversy – after all, this story was not public knowledge; whatever would the funder – the taxpayer – think?

Derek Wood's further, devastatingly accurate conclusions were framed in an article that was to be published after the book's first edition (views eventually incorporated into the book's 1986 second edition). Before that happened, Wood's 1976 views were deemed too controversial for publication and he was effectively leaned on by the government, the 'establishment', and the Ministry of Defence and made to tone down his findings. In fact, the whole print run of the *Royal Air Force Yearbook 1976*, which contained Wood's article, was pulped. Wood had suggested that a more enlightened, more intelligent post-war policy would have prevented the great waste of design and money that was British post-war aerospace reality. These views were only published in their original form in the 1986 reprint of the book – having been redacted in the 1976 original – when nearly four decades on from the Second World War, the British Government *still* did not want the story of the German science and its denial, and its stealing, admitted to, or aired in public. It was a conspiracy theorist's dream.

Critically for the then, the now, and the future as discussed in this book, Wood made it clear in a suggested 'Alternative Scenario' that an advanced post-war aerospace design crucible, using *Anglo-German* technology, could have secured Britain a glittering future if only it had been accepted and developed rather than denied. So here was an expert's opinion that the German technology *was* crucial – yet the lid was kept on this story and Wood had to wait until the 1980s to see his truths in print.

The ultimate paradox, now obvious, was that Wood may not have fully stated to what extent the West (principally the Americans, Russians, and the British) had indeed studied and used the German and Nazi research. For the truth was only beginning to be let loose in the form of the NASA Space programme, and then in the first decade of the twenty-first century in the form of the 'Stealth' fighter and bomber that were the F-117A and B-2 respectively – both being all-wing and one being tailless. Throw in the *Aurora* project, BAE's *Demon* idea, various drones, and an imminent rash of all-wing and tailless aircraft across the military and civil arena, and the machines that Derek Wood did not live to see, would finally manifest in a future for so long deliberately withheld. It was a bizarre and incredible scenario, but it was created by the rational – the establishment – so it seemed plausible and sensible in the face of all the silly stories other people made up about UFOs, anti-gravity, discs, and Nazi occultists. Yet the delusion was borne of the establishment and the deluded were the taxpayers who funded it all.

Aviation history owes Derek Wood a huge gratitude for being strong enough to see beyond the veneer of the corporate men, the learned men and, in particular, the less than learned politicians (specifically ministers), in whose often cretinously and ego-driven 'here today, gone tomorrow' hands, the entire fate of British aircraft design and manufacturing was held within – to such nationally devastating and final effects in the 1950s and 1960s that Sir George Edwards and the Rt Hon Tony Benn MP, as men from differing worlds, agreed that retaining a British engineering base might be a good idea.

Despite their pleas, ultimately at the hands of Labour and Conservative policies, so ended British aviation and its world-beating potential. So ended many jobs and many billions of pounds of fiscal income that were denied to the exchequer and the nation in a post-war austerity era of great poverty and debt. So America grabbed the spoils of war, Concorde's success notwithstanding.

One of Derek Wood's key points was to highlight how, if Britain had not wasted (or ignored) what it captured from Germany in 1945, then British aircraft design – notably supersonic aircraft design and its cancellation – might not have lost or wasted the years and the money that it did.

In refusing to accept or admit German advanced design in 1945, the British and their arrogant attitude cost themselves advances that, for example, the American space research bodies did not. The British handed supersonics to the Americans. Furthermore, the British, via the cancellation of the Vickers V-1000 and BAC TSR-2, and the ruination of the Trident and the 'air-bus' type design debate debacle, etc., would (paraphrasing Sir George Edwards at the time), hand the entire world market for civil, and then military aircraft, to the United States of America, and who knows, maybe that was the plan?

Add in the wasted military projects and the significance of post-war British ministerial ignorance, and the blinkers of the British attitude become very obvious – as do the costs to Britain. Derek Wood's views, circa 1976, did of course concur with those made by Sir Roy Fedden in the summer of 1945, when he was in Germany actually staring the advanced science and scientists in the face, and imploring the British Government to seize the opportunity, which as history records, it failed to do.

So the evidence to support the claims made herein, is out there, and the German science has become its own anonymous epitaph. The names of the men who built it and from whom its provenance was denied by the burglars, are just another forgotten riddle in the history of the politicisation of science.

The legacy of German (of the earlier regional and later greater German constitutions) science, pre-1933 and then also Nazi-funded science post-1933, has touched not just the aerospace revolution, but also the lives of people using everyday goods and devices across the world. But it is the rocket science and wing technology that has touched man's flight and aerospace thinking, now to manifest as the future of civil airliners and military uplift that will be the 'blended wing', that new corporate-speak euphemism for the true all-wing future that has, finally, arrived. That it was 'developed' by American, British and other experts, is true, and all credit to them, but like so many developments in aerodynamics from 1950 to date, no matter how clever the design, the roots of such brilliance appear to lie in the German discoveries of aerodynamic science. Even Whitcomb's winglet design of the 1970s has a German research antecedent. Of Dieter Kuchemann and his work on wings for Vickers and for Concorde, few even know. And if a forward swept-wing airframe – perhaps with swivelling oblique wing – ever does get beyond a prototype airframe of the type like the NASA AD-1, then we will all know where to look for the true origins of that design – that being in Richard Vogt's forward sweep design with roots in the 1940s Blohm and Voss PV209 and in his oblique wing studies.

Perhaps the most poignant irony is seen when we consider the fact that during the Korean and Vietnam wars respectively, some of Germany's advanced 'wonder weapons' were actually tested in combat – by the airframes that the Americans, and the Russian-supplied Chinese and Vietnamese, had built using that very Germany technology. They then deployed it in Asia against each other. So the secrets of the German swept-wing revolution that came too late to affect the Second World War did see action and achieve proof of concept; but in the hands of America and Russia, just as occurred with German missile and rocket technology. The engines that powered these machines were based on German jet engine developments and the Rolls-Royce jet engine that the British Government had naively given to the Soviet Union in 1945. What a remarkable outcome.

There has to be the further irony that the origin of our all-wing future lies partly in the science of war and the stolen secrets of the uncredited scientific genius of its originators, and in an early aviation history prior to 1910 when the all-wing monoplane was yet to be dethroned by the backwards technology of the biplane and all its drag.

Therein lies the legend and the lesson of man's aerial brilliance and his self-limiting assumptions of so-called perceived wisdom. The all-wing, the monoplane, the swept-wing, all have had many fathers and for a time the all-wing monoplane was an aerodynamic orphan, but now it has achieved its deliberately delayed maturity. Aerodynamics might finally have grown up. Across the years 1850 to date, across two centuries and beyond, the amazing all-wing and tailless story can be found. If only the biplane had not been forced upon us, if only the evil of Nazism had not punctuated the all-wing and its development, for then our all-wing present and future, would have been with us long ago.

As it is, the present and the future of aerodynamics and aerospace, of flight itself, have been framed by the denial of early advance, and the stolen science of the more recent past. There may be more 'secrets' to come.

Notes

Chapter 1

1. Vollprecht, B.E. & Reason, S.J., 'Lechfeld Airfield.' Report CIOS ER 39: PB 105 (1–61) May 1945, and also as by Ziegler, M., *Raketenjager Me 163*. Transl A. Vanags, London, MacDonald 1963.

2. Lasby, G., *Project Paperclip, German Scientists and the Cold War*. Atheneum, New York 1971.

3. Beyerchen, A., 'German Scientists and Research Institutions in Allied Occupation Policy', *History of Education Quarterly*, Vol 22, No.3. Education Reform and Policy in Germany. Autumn 1982, pp: 289–299.

4. BIOS: Final Report No. 447, Item No. 30, Interrogation of Dr Otto Roelen of Ruhrchemie A.G., November 1945 in London.

5. Wills, C., Communications and personal interview at Wings, Ewelme, Oxfordshire, UK, 2011.

6. CIOS Report: *The Horten Brothers/Interrogation Notes*. PB 19711–14 (1–1362): 18th–22nd–31st May 1945. London.

7. Beyerchen, A., 'German Scientists and Research Institutions in Allied Occupation Policy', *History of Education Quarterly*, Vol 22, No.3. Education Reform and Policy in Germany. Autumn 1982, pp: 289–299.

8. Fedden, R., 'Inquest on Chaos', *Flight*, 29 November 1945.

9. Murrow, Edward R., CBS radio broadcast from London, 12 November 1944.

10. Walker, C. Lester., 'Secrets by the Thousands', *Harpers* Magazine, October 1946.

11. Hardesty, Von, & Eisman, G., *Epic Rivalry; the inside story of the Soviet and American Space Race*. National Geographic Society, Washington D.C. 2007, pp: 11–30.

12. Foster Dulles, J., *Foster Dulles Papers*, located at the Eisenhower Library.

13. Cole, L.F., 'Blended Wings?' Research Letter, *Flight International*, 20 July 2004.

14. Myhra, D., *The Horten Brothers and Their All-Wing Aircraft*, Schiffer Military History. Atglen, PA., 1998, pp: 245 – 246.

15. Cole, L.F., *Secrets of the Spitfire: the Story of Beverley Shenstone, the Man Who Perfected the Elliptical Wing*, Pen and Sword Books Ltd., Barnsley, 2012.

16. Ackroyd, J.D., 'The Spitfire Wing Planform, a Suggestion'. *RAES Journal*. Vol 2, 2013, RAeS, London.

17. Schilperood, P, *The Extraordinary Life of Josef Ganz*, RVP, New York, 2012.

18. Shenstone, B.S.S., 1940 Statement and unpublished notes.

19. *Flight* Editorial Headline, 9 January 1947.

Chapter 2

1. Voisin, G., My 1000 Cars, English Transl Ref edition, Winstone, D.R.A. Faustroll Publ, 2012.

2. Cole, L.F., *Secrets of the Spitfire: the Story of Beverley Shenstone, the Man Who Perfected the Elliptical Wing*, Pen and Sword Books Ltd., Barnsley, 2012.

3. Gibbs-Smith, C.H., Aviation: a Historical Survey, Science Museum/HMSO London 1970/2nd Ed.1985.
4. Gibbs-Smith, C.H., Early Flying Machines 1799–1909. Publ Science Museum/HMSO London 1975.
5. Mondey, D, et al., The International Encyclopaedia of Aviation, Octopus Books, London, 1977.
6. Gibbs-Smith, C.H., Aviation: a An Historical Survey, Science Museum/HMSO London 1970/2nd Ed.1985.
7. Shenstone, B.S.S., Unpublished notes.
8. Gibbs-Smith, C.H., Aviation: a Historical Survey, Science Museum/HMSO London 1970/2nd Ed.1985.
9. L'Art de voler a la Maniere des Oiseaux.
10. Gibbs-Smith, C.H., Aviation: a Historical Survey, Science Museum/HMSO London 1970/2nd Ed.1985.
11. Mechanics Magazine London, 25 September 1852.
12. Goupil, M.A., La Locomotion Aerienne.
13. Penaud, A., 'Aeroplane Automoteur: Equilibre Automatique', L'Aeronaute, January 1872.
14. Gibbs-Smith, C.H., Aviation: a Historical Survey, Science Museum/HMSO London 1970/2nd Ed.1985.
15. The Hargreves Papers: RAeS NAL, Farnborough, UK.
16. Winstone, G.R.A., Gerin. Faustroll Publishing, 2014.
17. Lanchester, F.W., Aerodonetics, 1908.
18. Gibbs-Smith, C.H., Early Flying Machines 1799–1909, Publ Science Museum/HMSO London 1975.

Chapter 3

1. *Luft-Wissen*, 943, Vol. 10, No5, pp: 154–155.
2. Schenk, H., 'Finanzierung u Organissation d Luftverkehers', 1930.
3. Gruberg, V.L., 'It Must Not Happen Again', *Flight*, 16 August 1945.
4. Shenstone, B.S.S., & Scott-Hall, S. 'Glider Development in Germany. A Technical Survey'. NACA Technical Memorandum No. 780, 1936.
5. Diekmann, B, & Krieg, M., 'The Influence of August Kupper and Robert Kronfeld on British Gliding and Aviation', *Vintage Glider Club News*, Vol 142, Winter, 2014.
6. Muttray, H., 'Die Aerodynamishe Zusammenfugung von Tragelflugel und Rumpf' (The Aerodynamic Aspect of Wing Fuselage Fillets) *Luftfahrtforschung*, 1934, 11(5).
7. Kármán, T. von, *The Wind and the Beyond*, Little Brown, Boston, 1967.
8. Lippisch, A.M., Statement to Press, Berlin Tempelhof, 1931.
9. Lippisch, A.M., *The Tailless Aeroplane*, Lecture, Rhon-Rossiten Gesellschaft Deutsche W.G.L.
10. Shenstone, B.S., Unpublished notes.

Chapter 4

1. Myhra, D., *The Horten Brothers and Their All-Wing Aircraft*, Schiffer Military History, Atglen, PA, 1998.
2. Horten, R., 'Nurflugelflugzeng Horten IV': *Flugsport*, 18 February 1942.

3. Dabrowski, H.P., *The Horten Flying Wing in World War II: The History & Development of the Ho 229*, Transl David Johnson. Schiffer Military History, Vol. 47, Schiffer Military History, Atglen, PA, 1999.

4. Horten, R., 'Problem of the All-Wing Aircraft', *Flugsport*, 10 June 1936.

5. Wills, C., Personal communications, Wings, Ewlme, Oxfordshire, UK, 2011.

6. Horten, R., 'Planeadores Alas Volantes', *Revista Nacional de Aeronautica*, October 1953, No: 139, pp: 46–47, Buenos Aires, Argentina; 'Veleritos 'Sin Cola', *Revista Nacional de Aeronautica*, October 1949, No: 10, pp: 17–18, Buenos Aires, Argentina; 'Ala Volante Caza 'Horten IX', *Revista Nacional de Aeronautica*, May 1950, No:5, pp: 19–20, Buenos Aires, Argentina; 'Desarrollo de Aviones Rapidos Sin Cola', September 1952, No:126, pp: 20–21, Buenos Aires, Argentina. Note journal now *Aeroespacio/Revista Nacional Aeronautica y Espacial*.
   Horten, R. & Selinger, P. F., *Nurflügel: Die Geschichte der Horten-Flugzeugbau 1933–1960*: Weishaupt Verlag, Graz, 1983.

7. Bowers, A.H., & Lednicer, D.A., 'A Retrospective: Flying Wing Design Issues': NASA Dryden Flight Research Center, Edwards, CA, and Analytic Methods, Inc., Redmond, WA.

8. Bullard, D., www.Nurflugel.com. Horten research papers incl Bowers, A., et al.

9. Wills, C., Personal communications, Wings, Ewlme, Oxfordshire, UK, 2011.

10. CIOS Report: *The Horten Brothers/Interrogation Notes*. PB 19711–14 (1–1362).

11. Royal Aircraft Establishment, Farnborough, Hants, UK. Report: 'The Horten Tailless Aircraft; Author: Wilkinson, K.G., B.Sc., D.I.C. Technical Note. Aero 1703, October 1945. Class number 629.13.014.48 (43) Horten RAE Report No. P.A. 259/1 US Tech Note No. Aero 1703, October 1945.
    CIOS Report: *The Horten Brothers/Interrogation Notes*. PB 19711–14 (1–1362).

12. Royal Aircraft Establishment, Farnborough, Hants, UK. Report: 'The Horten Tailless Aircraft'. Author: Wilkinson, K.G., B.Sc., D.I.C. Technical Note. Aero 1703, October 1945. Class number 629.13.014.48 (43) Horten RAE Report No. P.A. 259/1 US Tech Note No. Aero 1703, October 1945.

13. Ibid 4.

14. Ibid Wills, C., Personal Communications, Wings, Ewlme, Oxfordshire, UK, 2011. .

15. Myhra, D., *The Horten Brothers and Their All-Wing Aircraft*, Schiffer Military History, Atglen, PA., 1998.

16. CIOS: T-2 Report: *German Flying Wings Designed by Horten Brothers*. Wright-Patterson AFB, 1946.

17. Jacobsen, A., *AREA 51*, Little, Brown and Company, New York, 2011.

18. CIC Regional Files I01006. Operation Harass, 6 January 1948. Declassified 6 July 1994.

19. Myhra, D., *The Horten Brothers and Their All-Wing Aircraft*, Schiffer Military History, Atglen, PA., 1998, pp: 248–249.

Chapter 5

1. Junkers, H., Patent Application 1910.

2. Shenstone, B.S.S., Archive Notes.

3. Myhra, D., *Secret Aircraft Designs of the Third Reich*, Schiffer Military History, Atglen, PA., 1998. p. 249.

4. Lippisch, A.M., Archives, University of Iowa.

5. Ziegler, M., *Raketenjager Me 163*, Transl: A. Vanags, London, MacDonald, 1963. Motorbuch Verlag, Stuttgart, 1978.
6. Wills, C., Personal communications, Wings, Ewlme, Oxfordshire, UK, 2011.
7. Myhra, D., *Secret Aircraft Designs of the Third Reich*, Schiffer Military History, Atglen, PA. 1998. pp 120–125.
8. 'Athodyds for Aircraft' (citing Hooker, S.G. & Relf, E.F.). *Flight*, 15 August 1946.
9. Am. Phys Soc., *Nexus* Magazine, Oct 2014.
10. Smith, J., 'The Nazi Bell', *Nexus* Magazine, Oct 2014.
11. Shenstone, B.S.S., 'Sucking off the Boundary layer: Original efforts for Boundary Layer Control'. *Aeronautical Engineering*, 27 January 1939.
12. Cole, L.F., *Secrets of the Spitfire: the Story of Beverley Shenstone, the Man Who Perfected the Elliptical Wing*, Pen and Sword Books Ltd., Barnsley, 2012.
13. Shenstone, B.S.S., Personal letters.
14. Campagna, P., 'Nazi UFO? Released Documents Increase Speculation that Nazis did Research Disc Technology'. *UFO Magazine*, 2000, United Kingdom, pp: 74–75.
15. Swanborough, G. & Gunston, W., *Soviet X Planes*, Midland Publishing, 2000.

Chapter 6
1. Jet-Propelled Flying Wings, *Flight*, 9 January 1947.
2. Taylor, J.W.R., 'Flying Wing Design', *Flight*, 19 April 1947.
3. 'All-Wing Aircraft' (J.K. Northrop, Wilbur Wright Memorial Lecture), *Flight*, 5 June 1947.
4. Lippisch, A.M., *The Tailless Aeroplane* Lecture, Rhon-Rossiten Gesellschaft, Deutsche W.G.L., December 1932.
5. Horten, R., Nurflugelflugzeng Horten IV: *Flugsport*, 18 February 1942.

Chapter 7
1. Myhra, D., *Secret Aircraft Designs of the Third Reich*, Schiffer Military History, Atglen, PA., 1998.
2. Ewans, J.R., 'Aerodynamics of the Delta', *Flight*, 10 August 1951.
3. Smelt, M.A., High Speed Airflow, *Flight*, 17 & 24 October 1946.
4. BIOS: Final Report No. 447, Item No: 30, Bayerische Motoren Werke (BMW).
5. Smith, C.G., 'German Jet Aircraft', *Flight*, 14 June 1945.
6. 'Athodyds for Aircraft' (citing Hooker, S.G. & Relf, E.F.), *Flight*, 15 August 1946.
7. Smith, C.G., 'German jet Aircraft', *Flight*, 14 June 1945.

Chapter 8
1. 'Facing the Heat Barrier. A History of Hypersonics', First Steps in Hypersonic Research, NASA.
2. Brzezinski, M., *Red Moon Rising*. Bloomsbury, London, 2007.
3. Taylor, J.W.R. & Munson, K., *History of Aviation*, New English Library, 1972.
4. Cole, L.F., 'Sason's Secret Fighter', *Aeroplane Monthly*, August, 1998.
5. 'Facing the Heat Barrier. A History of Hypersonics', First Steps in Hypersonic Research, NASA.
6. Heppenheimer, T.A., Facing the Heat Barrier: A History of Hypersonics, NASA History Series (NASA SP-2007-4232).
7. Tokaev, G.A., 'Russia's Jet Progress', *Flight*, 25 August 1949.

8. Lippisch, A.M., *Results for the Deutsche Forschungsanstalt fur Segelflug Smoke Tunnel*, Unrevised Proof, RAeS, 15 December 1938.
9. Wood, D., *Project Cancelled: The Disaster of Britain's Abandoned Aircraft Projects*, Janes, 1976.
10. Myhra, D., *Secret Aircraft Designs of the Third Reich*, Schiffer Military History, Atglen, PA., 1998.

Chapter 9
1. Lasby, G., *Project Paperclip, German Scientists and the Cold War*, Atheneum, New York, 1971.
2. Wisnewski, G., *Drahtzieher der Macht*, Taschenbuch, Munich, 2010, (Transl) Publ Clairview Books, 2014.
3. Bernhard, of the Netherlands (House of Orange), Prince, Personal communications with the author at Schiphol Airport and in-flight, Koninklijke Luchtvaart Maatschappij, AMS-LHR, 1994.
4. Lasby, G., *Project Paperclip, German Scientists and the Cold War*, Atheneum, New York, 1971.
5. CIOS Reports: Library of Congress, Washington D.C.
6. Walker, C. Lester, 'Secrets by the Thousands' *Harpers* Magazine, October, 1946.
7. Hardesty, Von, & Eisman, G., *Epic Rivalry; the inside story of the Soviet and American Space Race*, National Geographic Society, Washington D.C., 2007.
8. Fedden, R., 'Inquest on Chaos', *Flight*, 29 November 1945.
9. Dorril, S., *Fifty Years of the Special Operations Executive*, Fourth Estate, London, 2008.
10. Fedden, R., 'Inquest on Chaos', *Flight*, 29 November 1945.
11. Wood, D., *Project Cancelled: The Disaster of Britain's Abandoned Aircraft Projects*, Janes, London, 1976.
12. Fedden, R., 'Inquest on Chaos', *Flight*, 29 November 1945.
13. Bower, T., *The Paperclip Conspiracy*, Michael Joseph, London, 1987.
14. Myhra, D., *Secret Aircraft Designs of the Third Reich*, Schiffer Military History, Atglen, PA., 1998, p: 181
15. Cook, N., *The Hunt For Point Zero: One Man's Journey To Discover the Biggest Secret Since the Invention of the Atom Bomb*. Century Random House, London 2001. Also cited in: *Hitler's Geheimwaffenchef*. ZDF TV. 19 June 2014.

Chapter 10
1. Cole, L.F., *Secrets of the Spitfire: the Story of Beverley Shenstone, the Man Who Perfected the Elliptical Wing*, Pen and Sword Books Ltd., Barnsley, 2012.
2. Ackroyd, J.A.D., 'The Spitfire Wing Planform, a Suggestion'. *Journal of Aeronautical History*, Vol 2, 2013, pp: 121–134, RAeS, London.
3. Agnew, K., 'The Spitfire: Legend or History? An Argument for a New Research Culture in Design.' *Journal of Design History*, Vol 6, No.2 1993, pp: 121–130.
4. Hoerner, S.F., *Fluid Dynamic Drag*, Brick Town, 1958.
5. Cole, L.F., *Secrets of the Spitfire: the Story of Beverley Shenstone, the Man Who Perfected the Elliptical Wing*, Pen and Sword Books Ltd., Barnsley, 2012; and cited from: Ackroyd, J.A.D. & Lamont, P.J., 'A comparison of Turning Radi for Four Battle of Britain Fighter Aircraft', *Aeronautical Journal*, February 2000.Vol 104, (1032), pp: 53–58.

6. Shenstone, B.S.S., Archives. Letter from R. Pierson, Vickers, 1939.

7. Cole, L.F., *Secrets of the Spitfire: the Story of Beverley Shenstone, the Man Who Perfected the Elliptical Wing,* Pen and Sword Books Ltd., Barnsley, 2012.

8. Ackroyd, J.A.D., 'The Spitfire Wing Planform, a Suggestion'. *Journal of Aeronautical History*, Vol 2, 2013, pp: 121–134, RAeS, London.

9. CIOS Report: *The Arado 234: Performance, aerodynamic problems and history of development.* PB19713 (I-1362) ARCO 184, June 1945.

10. Myhra, D., *Secret Aircraft Designs of the Third Reich,* Schiffer Military History, Atglen, PA., 1998, pp:159

11. CIOS Report: *The Arado 234: Performance, aerodynamic problems and history of development.* PB19713 (I-1362) ARCO 184, June 1945.

12. Lee, G.H., 'Aerodynamic and Aeroelastic Characteristics of the Crescent Wing'. RAeS Lecture, *Flight,* 27 April 1954 & *Flight,* 14 May 1954.

13. 'The Shape of Wings to Come'. A Summary of D. Keith-Lucas Lecture. *Flight,* 26 September 1952.

14. Myhra, D., *Secret Aircraft Designs of the Third Reich,* Schiffer Military History, Atglen, PA, 1998.

Chapter 11

1. Gibbs-Smith, C.H., *Aviation: a Historical Survey,* Science Museum/HMSO, London, 1970, 2nd Ed. 1985.

2. 'John Dunne', *Flight,* 18 February 1911.

3. Poulsen, C.M., 'Tailless Trials'. Dunne Tribute, *Flight,* 27 May 1943.

4. King, H.F., 'Family of Faireys', Forty Year Retrospective, *Flight,* 22 July 1955.

5. Miles, F.G., 'Getting Down To It', Editorial Comment, *Flight,* 5 May 1938.

6. 'The Shape of Wings to Come'. A Summary of D. Keith-Lucas Lecture, *Flight,* 26 September 1952.

7. Ibid p 408.

8. Wills, C., Personal communications, Wings, Ewlme, Oxfordshire, UK, 2011.

Chapter 12

1. Liebeck, R.H., 'Design of the blended-wing-body subsonic transport', AIAA Aerospace Sciences Meeting and Exhibit, 40th, Reno, Nevada, USA, 14th – 17th January 2002.

2. Warwick, G., 'Boeing Works With Airlines on Commercial Blended Wing Body Freighter', *Flight International,* 21 May 2007.

3. Krauss, S., 'Pre-Burnelli Lifting-Body, All-Wing and BWB Origins', TWITT: http://www.twitt.org/PreBurnelliPatents.

Chapter 13

1. Wood, D., *Project Cancelled: The Disaster of Britain's Abandoned Aircraft Projects.* Janes, London, 1976.

Sources and Bibliography

The following reference titles are published and unpublished works. They are sourced from: Author's collection; Private archives; Private communications; RAeS; RAeS National Aerospace Library; National Archives, Washington D.C.; US Library of Congress Archive Service; FIAT/CIOS/BIOS/ BIGS documents; National Research Council Canada; Parkin Archives; Lippisch Archive University of Iowa; The Christopher Wills Collection; Shenstone Archives; British Gliding Association; Vintage Glider Club; Rhon Wasserkuppe Archives; *Flight* and *Flight* Global Archive; *Aeroplane* magazine archives; Nurflügel.com (D. Bullard); The Wing is The Thing (TWITT).

Ackroyd, J.A.D., 'The Spitfire Wing Planform, a Suggestion', *Journal of Aeronautical History*, Vol 2, 2013. pp: 121–134. RAeS, London.

Ackroyd, J.A.D. & Lamont, P.J., 'A comparison of Turning Radii for Four Battle of Britain Fighter Aircraft', *Aeronautical Journal*, February, 2000, Vol 104, (1032), pp: 53–58.

Ahlborn, F. Prof., *Uber die Stabilitat der Drachenflieger*, 1897.

Anderson, J.D., *A History of Aerodynamics*, Cambridge University Press, 1997.

Appleyard, D.C. & Biot, M.A., 'Horten Tailless Aircraft', CIOS Report: 25/157. PB 260, 1945.

Bader, D. Sir., Grp Capt., Personal communications at Marlston, Newbury, Berkshire, UK, 1981.

Bernhard, of the Netherlands (House of Orange), Prince, Personal communications with author, Schiphol Airport and in-flight Koninklijke Luchtvaart Maatschappij, AMS-LHR, 1994.

Betz, Prof Dr, Notes via B.S. Shenstone.

Beyerchen, A., 'German Scientists and Research Institutions in Allied Occupation Policy', *History of Education Quarterly*, Vol 22, No.3. Education Reform and Policy in Germany, Autumn 1982, pp: 289–299.

Biechteler, C., 'Versuch zur Beseitgung von Leitwerkschutteln', *Zeitschrift fur Flugtechnik und Motorluftschiffartvol*, Vol 24, No.1: 14 January 1933.

BIOS: Report 254: German Aircraft Industry report of visit by representatives of SHORT Bros. (Rochester & Bedford) LTD., on 24th – 29th September 1945: Reported by: Mr W. Swallow, Chief Production Engineer – Short Bros. and Mr D. Keith-Lucas, Chief Aerodynamics Assistant – Short Bros.

Bowers, A.H., & Lednicer, D.A., 'A Retrospective: Flying Wing Design Issues', NASA Dryden Flight Research Center, Edwards, CA and Analytic Methods, Inc., Redmond, WA. Presented to the members of The Wing Is The Thing (TWITT) on 20 September 1997, Gillespie Field, El Cajon, CA. USA.

Bower, T., *The Paperclip Conspiracy*, Michael Joseph, London, 1987.

Brooklands Museum, Vickers archives.

Brzezinski, M., *Red Moon Rising*, Bloomsbury, London, 2007.

Burrows, W.E., *This New Ocean: The Story of the First Space Race*, New York Modern Library, 1999.

Campagna, P., Nazi UFO? 'Released Documents Increase Speculation that Nazis did Research Disc Technology', *UFO Magazine* 2000, UK, pp: 74–75.

Chance Vought Aircraft Stratford, Connecticut: Engineering Dept: 7/18/46 C.G.D; Excerpt from LGB-164/Advance Report, 'Ten Years Development of the Flying Wing High-Speed Fighter'; Paper presented by the Horten Brothers, Bonn. Flying Wing Seminar, 14 April 1943.

CIOS Reports: Library of Congress, Washington D.C.

CIOS Report: *The Horten Brothers/Interrogation Notes*. PB 19711–14 (1–1362), 18th – 22nd – 31st May 1945. London.

CIOS/RAE Report: Royal Aircraft Establishment, Farnborough, Hants, UK. *The Horten Tailless Aircraft*, Author: Wilkinson, K.G., B.Sc., D.I.C.; Technical Note: Aero 1703, October 1945, Class number 629.13.014.48 (43): Horten RAE Report No. P.A. 259/1: US Tech Note No. Aero 1703, October 1945.

CIOS Report: The Interrogation of Franz Protzen at 6, Hall Road, St Johns Wood, London on 14 June 1945, PB138 (I-68).

CIOS Report: *The Arado 234: Performance, aerodynamic problems and history of development*, PB19713 (I-1362) ARCO 184: June 1945.

CIOS Report: XXVIII-47: 'High Speed Tunnel and other Research in Germany', Reported by: A. Thom, RAE, M.A.P.G.P. Douglas, RAE, M.A.P. CIOS Target Nos. 25/71 & 25/82.

Cobain, I., 'The Secrets of the London Cage'. *The Guardian*, 12 November 2005.

Cole, L.F., 'Blended Wings?', Research Letter, *Flight International*, 20 July 2004.

Cole, L.F., 'SAAB's Secret Fighter'. *Aeroplane Monthly*.

Cole, L.F., *Secrets of the Spitfire: the Story of Beverley Shenstone, the Man Who Perfected the Elliptical Wing*, Pen and Sword Books Ltd., Barnsley, 2012.

Cole, L.F., *Vickers VC10*, The Crowood Press, Ramsbury, 2000.

Cole, L.F., PhD/B.Sc. Research and test data.

Cook, N., *The Hunt For Zero Point: One Man's Journey To Discover the Biggest Secret Since the Invention of the Atom Bomb*, Random House, London.

Chertok, B.E., *Rakety I Lyundi* (Rockets and People), Transl, NASA/History Series, 2005.

Cunliffe-Owen, Publicity material.

Cunningham, J.C., (de Havilland) Personal Communications, Buckinghamshire, UK, 1999.

Dabrowski, H.P., *The Horten Flying Wing in World War II: The History & Development of the Ho 229*, (Transl David Johnson), Schiffer Military History, Vol. 47, Schiffer Military History, Atglen, PA.

Diekmann, B, & Krieg, M., 'The Influence of August Kupper and Robert Kronfeld on British Gliding and Aviation', *Vintage Glider Club News*, Vol 142: Winter 2014.

Dittmar, H., Family of – Personal Communications, October 2008.

Dorril, S., *Fifty Years of the Special Operations Executive*, Fourth Estate, London, 2008.

DVL, *Report on the Testing of the Flying Characteristics of the Horten IX V-1*. Berlin-Adlershof, 7 July 1944.

Eells, R., 'Aeronautical Science. German Documents'. *Quarterly Journal of Current Acquisitions* 3 (4) Library of Congress, August 1946.

Elmhirst, T., AVM, Sir, Asst. Chief Air Staff/Intelligence, 'The Luftwaffe and its Failure', *Flight*, 31 October 1946.

Evans, J.R., 'Aerodynamics of the Delta', *Flight*, 10 August 1951.

Evans, S.H., 'American Notebook', *Flight*, 17 November 1949.

Evans, S.H., Private technical correspondence to B.S. Shenstone.

Farquharson, J., 'Governed or Exploited? The British Acquisition of German Technology 1945–1948', *Journal of Contemporary History*, Vol 32, No1 (Jan 1997).

Fedden, R., 'Inquest on Chaos', *Flight*, 29 November 1945.

Flight/ Flight International/ International/ Flight Global: selected editorial articles from archives 1910–1960.

Flight, John Dunne, 18 February 1911.

Flight, 'The Tailless Aeroplane', 8 December 1932.

Flight, All-wing Comments, 21 April and 5 May 1938.

Flight, 'Unorthodox Transport', 22 December 1938.

Flight, 'The Horten Flying Wing', 5 August 1943.

Flight, 'German Jet Aircraft', 14 June 1945.

Flight, ''The Armstrong-Whitworth Flying Wing', 9 May 1946.

Flight, 'Rocket Fighters', 23 May 1946.

Flight, 'Recent Aerodynamic Developments', 13 June 1946.

Flight, 'Athodyds for Aircraft' (citing Hooker, S.G. and Relf, E.F.), 15 August 1946.

Flight, 'The Luftwaffe and its Failure', 31 October 1946.

Flight, 'Jet Propelled flying Wings', 9 January 1947.

Flight, 'All-Wing Aircraft', Wright Memorial Lecture by J. K. Northrop, 5 June 1947.

Flight, 'The Shape of Wings to Come', A Summary of D. Keith-Lucas' Lecture, 26 September 1952.

Foster Dulles, J., *Foster Dulles Papers* located at the Eisenhower library.

Gibbs-Smith, C.H., *Early Flying Machines 1799–1909*, Publ Science Museum/HMSO London, 1975.

Gibbs-Smith, C.H., *Aviation: a Historical Survey*, Science Museum/HMSO, London, 1970. 2nd Ed. 1985.

Gimbel, J:, *Science Technology and Reparations: Exploitation and Plunder in Post-war Germany*, Stanford University Press, 1990.

Gimbel, J., 'US Policy and German Scientists: The Early Cold War'. *Political Science Quarterly*, Vol 101, No 3 (1986).

Good. L., *Quarterly Journal of the National Archives*, Vol 27, No1: 1995.

Goodhart, H.C.N., Rr Adml, RN., Personal Communications, Inkpen, Berkshire; and Devon, UK.

Goupil, M.A., *La Locomotion Aerienne*.

Green, W., *Warplanes of the Third Reich*, MacDonald, London, 1974.

Griehl, J., *Luftwaffe Over America*, Greenhill Books, London, 2004.

Journal of Aeronautical Sciences, July 1947.

Gruberg, V.L., 'It Must Not Happen Again', *Flight*, 16 August 1945.

Gyorgyfalvy, D., 'Performance Analysis of the Horten IV Flying Wing', Congress of OSTIV, Cologne, Germany, June 1960.

Hall, C., 'The Eisenhower Administration and the Cold War; Framing Astronautics to Serve National Need'.

Hardesty, Von, & Eisman, G., *Epic Rivalry; the inside story of the Soviet and American Space Race*, National Geographic Society, Washington D.C., 2007.

Heinkel, E., *Stutmisches Leben*, Preetz, Mundus Verlag, 1963.

Hoerner, S.F., *Fluid Dynamic Drag*, Brick Town, 1958.

Horten, R., 'Flugzengkonstruktion, Gericht uber die Sitzung Nurflugel flugzeng'. Berlin (Lilienthal Gesellschaft fur Luftfaburtforschung).

Horten, R., 'Problem of the All-Wing Aircraft', *Flugsport*, 10 June 1936.

Horten, R., 'Nurflugelflugzeng Horten IV', *Flugsport*, 18 February 1942.

Horten, R., 'Horten IV Konstruktions ein Zelheiton' (sp), *Flugsport*, 31 March 1943.

Horten, R., 'Plastic All-wing Aircraft', *Flugsport* 35/16, 1943, pp: 172–173.

Horten, R., 'Better performance with Tailless Sailplanes', *InterAvia*, Vol IV, February 1949, pp: 249–251.

Horten, R., 'Planeadores 'Alas Volantes', *Revista Nacional de Aeronautica*, October 1953, No: 139, pp: 46–47; Buenos Aires, Argentina.

Horten, R., 'Veleritos 'Sin Cola', *Revista Nacional de Aeronautica, Aeroespacio, (Revista Nacional Aeronautica y Espacial)*, October 1949, No: 10, pp: 17–18; Buenos Aires, Argentina.

Horten, R., 'Ala volante Caza 'Horten IX', *Revista Nacional de Aeronautica, (Aeroespacio, Revista Nacional Aeronautica y Espacial)*, May 1950, No: 5, pp: 19–20; Buenos Aires, Argentina.

Horten, R., 'Desarrollo de aviones rapidos sin cola,' *Revista Nacional de Aeronautica (Aeroespacio, Revista Nacional Aeronautica y Espacial)*, September 1952, No: 126, pp: 20–21, Buenos Aires, Argentina.

Horten, R. and Selinger, P. F, *Nurflügel: Die Geschichte der Horten-Flugzeugbau 1933–1960:* Weishaupt Verlag, Graz. 1983.

Howland, R.C.K., & Shenstone, B.S.S., 'The Inverse Method for Tapered and Twisted Wings', *The Philosophical Magazine*, Vol XXII, July 1936.

Junkers Flugzeug und Motoren Werke A-G. Archive materials.

Klein, A.L., 'Effects of Fillets on Wing-Fuselage Interference', CalTech: American Society of Mechanical Engineers, *Transactions*, January 1934.

Knight, M.R., 'Models: Tail-less Experiments,' *Flight*, 6 January 1938.

Lanchester, F.W., *Aerodynamics*. Constable, London, 1907.

Lanchester, F.W., *Aerodonetics*. Constable, London, 1908.

L'Art de voler a la Maniere des Oiseaux.

Lasby, G., *Project Paperclip, German Scientists and the Cold War,* Atheneum, New York, 1971.

Lee, G.H., 'Aerodynamic and Aeroelastic Characteristics of the Crescent Wing', RAeS Lecture, *Flight*, 27 April 1954 & *Flight*, 14 May 1954.

Lee, R.E., Only the Wing, Smithsonian's Institute Scholarly Press; Washington D.C., USA, 2011.

Lilienthal, O., *Der Vogelflug als Grundlage der Fliegekunst.*

Lippisch, A.M., *The Delta Wing: History and Development*. Iowa State University Press, Ames, 1981.

Lippisch Archives at the University of Iowa.

Lippisch, A.M., 'Results for the Deutsche Forschungsanstalt fur Segelflug Smoke Tunnel', Unrevised Proof, RAeS, 15 December 1938.

Lippisch, A.M., 'The Tailless Aeroplane' Lecture Rhon-Rossiten Gesellschaft Deutsche W.G.L., December 1932. Reported in *Flight*, 8 December 1932.

Lippisch, A.M., Personal correspondence to B.S. Shenstone, 1931–1939.

Mechanics Magazine, 25 September 1852.

Miles, F.G., Getting Down to It, *Flight*, 5 May 1938.

Multhopp, H., 'Die Berechnung der Auftriebsverteilung von Tragflügeln', 1938.

Muttray, H., 'die aerodynamische Zusammenfugung von tragelflugel und Rumpf, *Luftfahrtforschung*, 1934, 11. (5), pp: 131–139 and as NACA Tech. Mem. No. 764, 1935.

Muttray, H., Investigation of the Effect of the Fuselage on Wing of a Low-Wing Monoplane, *Luftfahrtforschung*, 11 June 1933. Research data 1928–1933.

McGovern, James, *Operation Crossbow and Overcast*, William Morrow & Company Inc., 1964.

Modern Mechanics' Museum, Register, Journal, and Gazette, 25 September 1852.

Mondey, D, et al. *The International Encyclopaedia of Aviation*, Octopus Books, London, 1977.

Myhra, D., *The Horten Brothers and Their All-Wing Aircraft*, Schiffer Military History, Atglen, PA., 1998.

Myhra, D., *Secret Aircraft Designs of the Third Reich*, Schiffer Military History, Atglen, PA., 1998.

NASA: 'Facing the Heat Barrier: A History of Hypersonics'.

National Aerospace Library/RAeS archives.

National Research Council Canada, 'Tailless', *Flight*, 7 October 1943.

Nickel, K., & Wohlfarht; (Transl Brown, E.) 'Tailless Aircraft in Theory and Practice', AIAA New York, NY. 1994.

Nurflügel.com (D. Bullard): www.nurflügel.com

Office of Technical Services, Classified List of Reports, 1,800 reports of German science: Complied by Hollweg, O.W., & Oliver, B., Issued October 1947.

Oliver, H., (Ed.), *Camp 020: MI5 and the Nazi Spies*, Publ. Public Records Office, London.

Operation Epsilon, *The Farm Hall Transcripts*, Bristol, Philadelphia, and Los Angeles, Institute of Physics Publishing/University of California Press, November 1993.

Ordway, F. III, & Sharpe, M.R., *The Rocket Team (25 Years Ahead)*, Apogee Books, Canada, 2003.

OSTIV. Congress Reports (various) via Shenstone B.S.S.

Parkin, J.H., 'Aeronautical research in Canada: the Organisation of the Aeronautical Laboratories under the National Research Council and Some of the Special Problems Under Investigation', *Aircraft Engineering and Aerospace Technology*, Vol 21, 1949.

Parkin, J.H., 'Aeronautical Research in Canada 1917–1957', Memoirs of J.H. Parkin, Vols 1 & 2, National Research Council of Canada, Ottawa.

Penaud, A., 'Aeroplane Automoteur: Equilibre automatique', *L'Aeronaute*, January 1872.

Poulsen, C.M., 'Tailless Trails'. *Flight*, 27 May 1943.

Prandtl, L., Tragflugeltheorie; I Mittelungen, Nach, der Kgl. Gesselschaft der Wiss; zu Gottingen, Math-Phys. Klasse, 1918, pp: 451–477.

Royal Aircraft Establishment (RAE), *The Horten Tailless Aircraft*, Report: K.G. Wilkinson, RAE Report, October 1945: No P.A. 259/1; U.S Tech Note No. Aero 1703/Air Docs Div (TSRPR-5) Classification No: 629.13.014.48 (43) Horten.

Rust, K.C., & Hess, W.N., The German Jets and the USAF, *Journal of the American Aviation Historical Society*, Vol 8, No 3, 1963.

Schenk, H., *Finanzierung u Organisation d Luftverkehers*, 1930.

Schmid, F., 'Vorläufige Baubeschreibung Des Nurflügel 229', (Foreword Description of the Construction of Flying Wing 229'; USAAF Transl Patek, R.); No. 526 F-TS526-RE, 21 Feb 1946.

Shenstone, B.S.S., Private papers and family personal communications.

Shenstone, B.S.S., 'A method of Determining the Twist Required on a Tapered Wing in Order to Attain Any Desired Lateral Stability at High angles of Attack', *The Aeronautical Journal*, RAeS 1932.

Shenstone, B.S.S., & Scott-Hall, S., 'Glider Development in Germany. A Technical Survey', NACA Technical Memorandum No. 780 1936.

Shenstone, B.S.S., 'Sucking Off the Boundary layer: Original efforts for Boundary Layer Control', *Aeronautical Engineering*, 27 January 1939.

Simpson, C., *Blowback: America's Recruitment of Nazis and its Effects in the Cold War*, Weidenfeld and Nicholson, New York, 1988.

Smelt, M.A., 'High Speed Airflow', *Flight*, 17 & 24 October 1946.

Smith, G.G., 'Turbines and the Flying Wing', *Flight*, 13 May 1943.

Smith, G.G., 'In Germany Today', *Flight*, 27 September 1945.

Smith, J., 'The Nazi Bell', *Nexus Magazine*, Oct 2014.

Smith, J.R., & Kay, A., *German Aircraft of the Second World War*, Putnam, London, 1972.

Steiger-Kirchofer, C., *Vogelflug und Flugmaschine*, 1891.

Stephenson, B., Edit VGC News: Vintage Glider Club (UK), Personal communications 2011–2014.

Swanborough, G., & Gunston, W., *Soviet X Planes*, Midland Publishing, 2000.

Taylor, J.W.R., 'Flying-Wing Development'. *Flight*, 17 April 1947.

Taylor J.W.R., & Munson, K., *History of Aviation*, New English Library, 1972.

The Rocket and the Reich; Peenemünde and the Coming of the Ballistic Missile Era (Cambridge, Mass: Harvard University Press, 1996).

Tokaev, G.A., 'Russia's Jet Progress', *Flight*, 25 August 1949.

Trubshaw, B., Personal communications Fairford, Gloucestershire, UK, 1999–2002.

Tyndale, W., *The Geneva Bible*, Edition Tomson & Junius: Christopher Baker, London, 1599.

T-2 Report: *German Flying Wings Designed by Horten Brothers*, Wright-Patterson AFB, 1946.

US Army Report on Horten Brothers (Flying Saucers), Deputy Director of Intelligence European

Command, Frankfurt, APO 757, US Army, 16 December 1947. Author: Pretty, H.H., Lt Col, GSC US Army.

US National Archives and Records Administration; Joint Intelligence Objectives Agency/Data.

US Naval Technical Mission in Europe, Report TI 58618/TR 7645/ELC 2763B, declassified 23 March 1950, Central Air Documents Office Intelligence Department, Wright Patterson AFB, 1950. Horten Tailless Aircraft, Authors: Biot, M.A., & Jayne, J.M., Technical report 76–45 AD-A 800–146.

US Technical Translation No 516: 14 February 1946, 'Tailless Aeroplane Theories' (Theorein Am Schwanzlosen Flugzeug), USAAF. (Transl. Charlins, A.)

Vollprecht, B.E., & Reason, S.J., Lechfeld Airfield, Report CIOS ER 39: PB 105 (1–61) May 1945.

von Kármán, T., *The Wind and the Beyond*, Little Brown & Co, Boston, 1967.

von Reitzenstein, Family information and personal communications.

Walker, C. Lester., 'Secrets by the Thousands', *Harpers Magazine*, October 1946.

Weishaupt, H., & Horten R., *Nurflügel: Die Geschichte der Horten-Flugzeuge 1933–1960*, 1983.

Weyl, A.R., 'Tailless Aircraft and Flying Wings', *Aircraft Engineering*, December 1944, January 1945, February 1945.

Weyl, A.R., 'Stability of Tailless Aeroplanes', *Aircraft Engineering*, March 1945 and April 1945.

Weyl, A.R., 'Tailless Aeroplane Control Systems', *Aircraft Engineering*, May 1945 and August 1945.

Weyl, A.R., 'Wingtips for Tailless Aeroplanes', *Aircraft Engineering*, September 1945.

Weyl, A.R., 'Stalling Phenomena and the Tailless Aeroplane', *The Aeroplane*, 25 April 1947, 9 May 1947, 27 June & 11 July 1947, 1 August 1947, 8 December 1947.

Weyl, A.R., 'The Biology of the Flying Saucer': The Story of Low Aspect Ratio Aircraft', *The Aeroplane*, 13 February 1948, 5 March 1948, 2 April 1948.

Wills, C., Personal communications/family information. Interviews at Wings, Ewlme, Oxfordshire, 2010–2011.

Wisnewski, G., *Drahtzieher der Macht,* Taschenbuch, Munich, 2010. (Transl) Publ, Clairview Books, 2014.

Wood, D., *Project Cancelled: The Disaster of Britain's Abandoned Aircraft Projects,* Janes, 1976.

Worley, B., (Pseud. for B.S. Shenstone.) *Aeronautical Sidelights,* William Pearson, London, 1941.

Young, R.L., Operation Lusty: Harold Watson's "Whizzers" Went Hunting for German Jets and Came Back With Several Jewels, *Air Force Magazine*: 88: pp: 62–67.

Zeitschrift fur Flugtechnik und Motorluftschiffart (Z.F.M.) Archives.

Ziegler, M., *Hitler's Jet Plane: The Me 262 Story,* Greenhill Books, translated from *Turbinejager*.

Ziegler, M., *Raketenjager Me 163,* Transl A. Vanags, London, MacDonald, 1963. Motorbuch Verlag Stuttgart, 1978.

Ziemke, E.F., *The US Army in the Occupation of Germany 1944–1946*, Center of Military History, United States Army, Washington D.C., 1990.

Appendix I

Glossary of Terms /Acronyms

ACUE:	American Committee for a United Europe
AG:	Aktiengesellschaft (Company Group)
Akaflieg:	Academic Flight
AVA/AVG:	Aerodynamishce Versuchsanstalt Gottingen (Aerodynamic Experimental Establishment Gottingen)
Bf:	Bayerischen Flugzeugbau (merged with Messerschmitt hence Me Bf)
BIGS:	British Interrogation of German Scientists
BIOS:	British Intelligence Objectives Committee
BMS:	Bayerischen Motoren Werke
C_D:	Coefficient of Drag
C_{Di}:	Coefficient of Induced Drag
C_{DL}:	Coefficient of Lift
C_{DO}:	Coefficient of Drag at Zero Lift
CFD:	Computational Fluid Dynamics
CIA:	Central Intelligence Agency (USA)
CIOS:	Combined Intelligence Objectives Sub-Committee U.S/U.K.
CSDIC:	Combined Services Detailed Interrogation Centre
DFS:	Deutsche Forschunginstitut fur Segelflug (German Research Institute for Glider Flight at Gottingen)
DLSV:	Deutsche Luftsportverband (German Aviation Sport League)
DVL:	Deutsche Versuchsanstalt fur Luftahrtforschung (German Research Institute for Flight)
FIAT:	Field Intelligence Agencies/Technical (USA)
Flugzeugbau:	Flight Design Bureau /Workshop
Fw:	Focke-Wulf
Go:	Gothaer
He:	Heinkel
Ho:	Horten
JIOA:	Joint Intelligence Objectives Agency (USA)
Ju:	Junkers
KWI:	Kaiser Wilhelm Institut
LFA:	Luftfahrtforschungsanstalt Hermann Göring Volkenrode (Flight Research Institute Hermann Göring at Volkenrode)
LFS:	Luftfahrtforschungsanstalt (Flight Research Institute)
Lp:	Lippisch

Me:	Messerschmitt
NACA:	National Advisory Committee for Aeronautics (USA)
NASA:	National Aeronautics and Space Administration (USA)
NPL:	Nation Physical Laboratory (U.K.)
NSDAP:	Nationalsozialistiche Deutsche Arbeitpartei (National Socialist Workers Party-NAZI)
OSS:	Office of Strategic Studies (USA)
OSTIV:	Organisation Scientifique et Technique du Vol à Voile
OTS:	Office of Technical Services (USA)
RAE:	Royal Aircraft Establishment (U.K.)
RAeS:	Royal Aeronautical Society (U.K.)
RRG:	Rhon Rossitten Gesellschaft (Rhon Rossitten Works) Wasserkuppe, merged with DFS 1933
RLM:	ReichsLuftfahrtministrium (Reich/German Air Ministry)
Ta:	Focke-Wulf design bureau under Kurt Tank
TIOC:	Technical Industrial Intelligence Committee (USA)
TTIB:	Technical Industrial Intelligence Branch (USA)
USAAF Air Tech/Intel:	US Army Air Force Technical Intelligence Service
VFR:	Verein fur Raumschiffarte (Society for Space Travel/Exploration)

Appendix II

List of German and Austrian aeronautical scientists, as of 2 January 1947, cited under Operation Paperclip as known to/ interrogated by Allied Forces.
Source: Joint Intelligence Objectives Agency archives.

Note: Some names cited are prior to relocation to various locations within the USA and UK, including: Wright Field, Dayton, Ohio; Fort Bliss, Texas; White Sands, New Mexico; Point Mugu, California; Navy Yard, Washington D.C.; RAE Farnborough.
Note: Titles as Prof, Dr, Dr-Ing, Dipl-Ing, to be assumed respectively.

*No responsibility, nor liability, can be accepted or implied for any errors or mistakes contained in this information.

Name & Subject Specialisation

Amann, R.M. – Jet Engines

Ambros, O. – Jet Engines

Angele, W. – Guided Missiles

Antmann, H. – Aircraft Engineer

Baumker, A. – Aerodynamic research facilities

Bee, H. – Jet Engines

Betz, A. – Aerodynamics

Boccius, W.G. – Flight Testing

Bock, O.H. – Supersonics

Borkman – Aerodynamics Mathematician

Braun, R. – Aerodynamics

Braun, von, M. – Guided Missiles

Braun, von, W. – Guided Missiles – Rockets

Brede, H. – Jet Propulsion

Daniels, K. – Aircraft Designer

Dauhm, W. – Rockets

Daus – Rockets

De Beek, G.W. – Guided Missiles

Debus, K. – Guided Missiles

Decher, S. – Jet Engines

Decker – Aerodynamics

Dehlinger, U. – Metals Research

Dellmeir, G. – Wind Tunnels

Dirksen, B. – Structures & Materials

Dittmar, H. – Test Pilot

Doblehoff, F. – Jet Propelled Helicopter Design

Dornberger, W. – Rocket Production

Eber, G. – Supersonics

Eckert, B. – Aerodynamics

Eckert, E.R. – Aerodynamics

Eckert, H.E. – Wind Tunnels

Eckert, O. – Aerodynamics

Ehrhardt, H.P. – Rockets

Erfurth, K. – Designer

Erle, G. – Jet Engines

Fichs, W.H. – Supersonics

Fiedler, W. – Rockets/Missiles

Fischer, H. – Aerodynamics

Fornoff, H. – Jet Engines

Franz, A. – Jet engines

Friedrich, E.O.H. – Rockets – Missiles

Georgii, W. – Aerodynamics

Gothert, B.A. – Aerodynamics

Gothert, R. – Aerodynamicist

Graulich, L. – Jet Propulsion

Groth, P.E. – Aerodynamics

Gruenwald, K.H. – Aerodynamics
Guderlein, H. – Guided Missiles
Guderley, G. – High Speed Aerodynamics
Guendel, H.S. – Guided Missiles
Günter, S. – Aerodynamics
Hartenstein, W. – Jet Engines
Hein, R. – Jet engines
Heinemann, W. – Aerodynamics
Hell, W.H. – Rockets
Herbert, A. – Rockets
Herman, R. – Supersonics
Hickert, M. – Jet Propulsion
Hirth, W. – Aerodynamics
Hoerner, S.G. – Engineer – Aerodynamics
Hohe, S. – Wind Tunnels
Hohenemser, K. – Aerodynamics
Hohenner, W. – Rockets
Hohmann, B. – Guided Missiles
Hoke, H. – Flight Test Research
Hollmann, H.E. – Rockets
Horten, R. – Aerodynamics
Horten, W. – Aerodynamics
Huber, F. – Aerodynamics
Hubert, J. – Aerodynamics
Hurmann, G. – Aerodynamics
Jansen, H. – Aerodynamics
Jennerich – Aerodynamics
Kaufmann, W. – Aerodynamics
Kinner, W. – Aerodynamics
Klingeman, P.G. – Aerodynamics
Klinger, W. – Guided Missiles
Klingler, G. – Aerodynamics
Knackstedt, W.F.H. – Supersonic Flow
Knemeyer, S. – Aeronautics
Kohlma, E. – Aerodynamics
Kolb, A. – Aerodynamics
Kollert, W. – Rockets
Krauter, J. – Aerodynamics
Kretschmer, W. – Aerodynamics
Kuchemann, D. – Aerodynamics
Kuckert, J. – Supersonics
Kutzsche, E.W. – Rockets
Lahde, R.N. – Rockets – Missiles
Lehnert, R. – Supersonics
Leibach – Jet Engines
Leist – Jet Engines
Lippisch, A.M. – Aerodynamics – Supersonics

Lucht, R. – Airframe design
Ludweig, H. – Aerodynamics
Lusser, R. – Rockets – Missiles
Lutz, O. – Aerodynamics
Maetzke, H. – Rocket Development
Melkus, G. – Supersonics
Messerschmitt, W. – Aerodynamics – Airframes
Meyer, H. – Jet Engines
Meyer, J. – Jet Engines
Mirus, F. – Aerodynamics
Muenzbert, H.G. – Jet Engines
Muenzer – Diesel Engines
Muller, H. – Jet Engines
Multhopp, H. – Aerodynamics
Neubert, W. – Guided Missiles
Neugebauer, F.J. – Aerodynamics
Orosinski, W.K. – Guided Missiles
Pohlhausen, K. – Aerodynamics
Prandtl, L. – Aerodynamics
Pretsch, J. – Aerodynamics
Preyer, H.D. – Guided Missiles
Prym, W. – Jet Propulsion
Quick, A.W. – Aeronautics
Radinger, von – Guided Missiles
Raentsch, K. – Instrument Design
Raffel, M. – Aerodynamics
Raimann, A. – Aircraft and Rockets
Rau, H. – Aerodynamics
Reinhardt, H. – Gas Turbines
Richter, G. – Aerodynamics
Richter, H. – Jet Engines
Ringleb, F.O.A. – Aerodynamics
Rister, H.J. – Aerodynamics
Rock, E. – Aerodynamics
Rosin, H. – Aerodynamics – Jet Engines
Roskopf, H. – Jet Engines
Ruden, P. – Aeronautics
Rudolph, A. – Guided Missiles
Rueff, F. – Naval Research
Ruehlemann, E. – Guided Missiles
Ruf, F. – Aircraft Design
Ruhnke, M. – Jet Engines
Sachs, H. – Resistors
Sack, M. – Jet Engines
Sallwey, H. – Rocket Turbopumps
Sammeck, A. – Design – Rockets

Index

Stedman, AVM, E., 116, 169
Steiger-Kirchofer, C., 23, 45–6, 121
Stern, W.J., 161
Stout, W., 210
Stringfellow, J., 17, 38
Stuhlinger, E., 14
Sukhoi, 190
Supermarine Company, x, 19, 24, 32, 42, 65,
    111, 115, 129, 197, 210
  design of Spitfire, 73–9, 98, 129, 133,
    167–75
  Schneider Trophy, 32, 41, 168–69, 175
Swallow, W.S., 161
Swept-wing research, xi, xv, 1, 16, 25, 40,
    61–74, 96, 98, 100–105, 123, 128–32,
    140–45, 147–52, 162, 171–76, 178–83,
    191–99
  de Havilland swept wing , 183
  Horten, 75–94
  Saunders-Roe swept wings, 184

Tailless Advisory Committee, 24, 90, 148, 197
Tank, K., 7, 31, 76, 93, 99, 105–106, 124,
    140, 146, 162
Tatin, V., 49–51
Teague, W.D., 210
Technical Industrial Intelligence Branch
    (TIIB), 3, 157
Technical Industrial Intelligence Committee
    (TIIC), 11, 157
Temple, du, de la Croix, F., 46
Time Magazine, 210
Toftoy, Colonel, H.N., 163
Treaty of Versailles, 15, 31, 37, 41, 58–62, 70,
    95, 100, 127, 145
Treaty of Yalta, 160
Trent Park, 7
Trichel, Colonel, G., 163
Trubshaw, B., xiv
Truman, President, H., 22, 156, 159
Tsiolkovsky, K.E., 143

Udet, General, E., 75, 109
Unidentified Flying Object (UFO), ix, x, xi,
    18, 22, 107–10, 112, 214
Uranium, 166
  uranium researchers detention in London,
    7, 158
Ursinus, O., 72
US Army Air Force Technical Intelligence
    Service (USAAF Air Tech/Intel), 2, 7,
    163

US Military Government of Germany, 8
US Navy, xii, 2, 69, 139, 163

Vampyr, 58–9, 66
Verein für Raumschiffahrt (VfR), 142
Vergeltungswaffen weapons, 7
  V-1, 7, 138
  V2, xii, 7, 22, 132, 143, 148, 155, 159, 160,
    165
Verne, J., 18, 46, 50, 143
Vickers Company, xvii, 19, 41, 102, 114, 138,
    152, 169, 216
  design of Valiant, 6, 178
  S.508, 189
  V1000, 151, 180, 215
Voepel, H., 175
Vogt, R., 7, 24, 95, 104, 106, 128–30, 162,
    199, 216
Voigt, W., 2, 4, 95–6, 104, 106, 129, 162,
    179–80
Voisin, G., 29, 36, 41, 48–52, 122, 211
Voith Company, 5
Volkenrode, 134, 161, 164, 199
Volkswagen, 9
  design of Beetle car and J. Ganz, 27
von Braun, *see* Braun
von Kármán, *see* Kármán
von Ohain, *see* Ohain
von Reichenbach, *see* Reichenbach
von Reitzenstein, *see* Reitzenstein
Vuai, T., 53
Vulcan, see Avro

Walker, T., 43–4, 49
Wallis, Sir, B., 152, 171, 179
Warsitz, E., 136
Washimi, Dr, 118
Wasserkuppe, 41, 58–74, 77–8, 90, 116, 148,
    169, 174, 201
Watson, Colonel, H.E., 2, 90, 141, 159, 164
Wegemeyer, 174
Weihe, 66, 203
Weiss, J., 55, 180
Weissinger, Dr, 79
Westland, 64, 195
  all-wing work with Geoffrey Hill, 195
  Pterodactyl, 196
White Oak, ML, 3, 163
White Sands, NM, 13, 15
Whittle, Sir, F., 26, 98, 135–37
Wilbur Wright Memorial Lecture, 121
Wilkinson, K.G., 25, 81, 89–94, 186, 201